The Middle East Riddle

The Middle East Riddle

A Study of the Middle East Peace Process
and Israeli-Arab Relations
in Changing Times

LUIS FLEISCHMAN, Ph.D.
Author of *Latin America in the Post-Chávez Era*

Washington, DC

Library of Congress Control Number: 2020922086
ISBN 978-1-7333980-8-4 paperback (alk. paper)

New Academia Publishing, 4401-A Connecticut Ave. NW, #236,
Washington, DC 20008
info@newacademia.com - www.newacademia.com

For Laura, Maia, and Julian

Contents

Preface   ix
Acknowledgements   xiii

Introduction   1
Chapter 1 The Demise of Oslo: What Went Wrong?   13
Chapter 2 The Permanent Palestinian Revolution   53
Chapter 3 The Arab World and The Peace Process   83
Chapter 4 The Impact of the Arab Spring   119
Chapter 5: Thinking About Solutions   155

Notes   179
Bibliography   215
Index   239

Preface

The idea to write this book emerged from my repeated observations of the Israeli- Palestinian dynamic after the collapse of the Camp David Summit in the summer of 2000. One of the facts that most surprised me was that Israel continued to be the target of accusations despite the concessions it made both at the Summit and afterward. For example, the French government of President Jacques Chirac blamed the collapse of the talks on then-Likud leader Ariel Sharon, claiming that his visit to the Temple Mount in late September 2000 caused the violence that ultimately led the European Commission to adopt a resolution condemning Israel's use of force against the Palestinians. At a non-governmental organization (NGO) Forum that took place in conjunction with the 2001 World Conference against Racism in Durban, South Africa, a resolution was adopted declaring Israel a racist and apartheid state. This resolution was also supported by large numbers of NGOs, including the prestigious Human Rights Watch.

The consequences of this adverse view of Israel, extended to the Boycott, Divestment and Sanctions (BDS) movement, a nihilistic, anti-Zionist campaign aimed at delegitimizing the very existence of the State of Israel. Followers of BDS consider the State of Israel illegitimate and support the one-state solution, which aims to recover an Arab majority in Israel and erase the identity of the country as a Jewish state.

On the other hand, criticism of the Palestinians came mostly from Israel or from supporters of Israel in the world. The argument focused on the Palestinian narrative, on their demands such as the right of return, and on their responsibility for the failure of multiple negotiations attempts.

It seemed that this process of blaming and counter-blaming may be missing the point, hence obscuring other possible resolutions to this impasse. The purpose of this book is to explore alternatives by reevaluating the Oslo peace process as well as assessing options to respond to this ongoing crisis.

As somebody who worked in the organized American Jewish community in the field of public diplomacy, and who is also a political sociologist by training, I tried to make sense of the situation. If Israel offered peace and concrete concessions three times only to be rejected or ignored by the Palestinian side, including by moderates such as Mahmoud Abbas, there must be an explanation that requires analysis. If multiple diplomatic efforts have failed, there must be a reason why they failed. If there is an explanation for this failure, perhaps we can begin to think with a fresh mind about new solutions rather than resort to blame or insist on doing the same things all over again, only to obtain the same failed results.

I viewed the Oslo peace process between the Palestinian Liberation Organization (PLO) and Israel as a sign of hope. I was devastated by the murder of Israeli Prime Minister Yitzhak Rabin, the man who signed the Oslo agreements with PLO leader Yasser Arafat. I even scheduled a trip to Israel in May 1996 to make use of my right as an Israeli citizen to vote for the Labor candidate for prime minister, Shimon Peres, a Rabin ally who ended up losing by a small margin to Benjamin Netanyahu. I was deeply worried about the continuity of the peace process as I observed Netanyahu's lack of enthusiasm for the Oslo agreements and Hamas' sabotage of the peace process. Then, I celebrated the return of the Israeli Labor Party to power in 1999 under the leadership of Ehud Barak, only to be disappointed by the failure of the Camp David Summit, the outbreak of the Second Intifada and the collapse of subsequent peace negotiations. More than anything, I was shocked by the level of profound hostility displayed by Palestinian armed groups and some sectors of the Palestinian population toward Israel. It was hard to forget scenes such as the lynching in Ramallah of two Israeli soldiers at the hands of a Palestinian mob assisted by Palestinian police, including the individual who proudly waived his bloodstained hands after the brutal murder.

It was with the outbreak of the Second Intifada and the intensification of anti-Zionist rhetoric among the Palestinians when I began to suspect that Palestinian animosity towards Israel was so ingrained that it would be very difficult to reverse. After Israel's withdrawal from Gaza, Hamas's parliamentary victory, and its violent snatching of the Gaza Strip from Fatah, I began to view the conflict with more pessimism. I began to realize that the Palestinians are facing a problem that diplomacy and peace negotiations would not be able to solve. There was no Palestinian power capable of enforcing order.

During the second Netanyahu government that began in 2009, the prime minister began to look at the possibility of reaching a separate peace with the Arab world. He began to approach Arab leaders based on common enmity towards Iran.

This led me to explore whether Arab countries have changed some of their attitudes towards Israel in the wake of such cooperation and to what extent this can contribute to peace.

I have been very skeptical about the Arab states and their leaders' past approaches to peace and normalization with Israel. A peace agreement between Egypt and Israel was signed in 1979. However, there has been also a parallel Egyptian resentment and coldness towards Israel. Likewise, early in the Oslo peace process, Arab countries, under the guidance of Egypt, withdrew from the multilateral talks aimed at guaranteeing the Israeli-Palestinian peace on a regional basis. At the end of the Camp David Summit, the same Arab countries refused to respond to US President Bill Clinton when he called on them to intervene to save the Oslo peace process.

However, lately we are seeing some cooperation between Israel and some Arab Sunni states based on common interests, mainly a common enmity with Iran and terrorist groups. The recent peace and normalization agreement between Israel and two Arab countries, the United Arab Emirates and Bahrain, proves that progress with the Arab world is possible. Despite this, I wondered whether cooperation on this basis between Israel and some Sunni Arab states constituted a sufficient condition to bring peace between Israel and the Arab world or between Israel and the Palestinians.

But there was another element that left a profound impression on me and this is the eruption of the Arab Spring. My academic interest in the issue of democracy — an issue I broadly discussed in my doctoral dissertation *State and Civil Society in Argentina*, my book *Latin America in the Post Chavez Era*, as well as in several articles and opinion pieces — has led me to focus on the Arab Spring as a new opportunity for finding a constructive resolution. I was fascinated by the Arab Spring and the courage displayed by Arab subjects against their oppressors. I saw the Arab Spring as an important event in the Arab world, where finally the voices that have been silenced by dictatorship could be heard. I was curious to see whether the lifting of the veil in the Arab world and the weakening of authoritarian regimes could bring about a significant change that could ultimately enhance the chances of peace between the Arab World and Israel.

Could a new way of thinking emerge in the Arab world in the living rooms of Arab households, the cafes, the informal conversations among citizens or within the political parties? Is radical Islam or Islamism the only alternative to authoritarianism, or is there a new critical third way? If there is, could this third way give birth to some sort of Arab liberalism and eventually change Arab attitudes towards Israel? Finally, can the Arab Spring contribute to a final peace between Israel and the entire Arab world, including the Palestinians?

Acknowledgements

I am grateful to Dr. Anna Lawton, Publisher of New Academia Publishers, for the opportunity to put together these ideas by publishing this book. I also wish to thank her staff for their hard work.

I am deeply indebted to Dr. Josef Olmert from the University of South Carolina, Dr. Miriam Elman from Syracuse University, Dr. Robert Rabil from Florida Atlantic University and two anonymous readers for providing me with very valuable comments and feedback. Likewise, I am very appreciative of Shalom Cohen, Israel's former Ambassador to Egypt, for his input and useful comments. I also wish to express my deep gratitude to Dr. Alma Keshavarz, Julian Fleischman, Dr. Rosanna Gatens and Dr. Laura Kalmanowiecki - Fleischman for editing and revising the manuscript and providing me with useful suggestions. Their input made this book better.

Many thanks to Joan and Martin Baron, as well as Judy Ellman, for supporting this project and helping me complete this book, and to Dr. Kenneth Stein, from Emory University, for providing me with useful information and literature. I also want to extend my gratitude to Dr. Abdullah Swalha from the Center for Israel Studies in Amman, Jordan; to Dr. Nadim Shehadi, director of the program on the regional dimension of the Palestinian refugee issue in the Middle East Peace Process at Chatham House; Khaldoon Bakhail, a young intellectual and peace activist from Yemen; and Professor Chhaibi Abderrhaim, from King Mohamed V University of Rabat, for allowing me to interview them and gather important information about the post-Arab Spring mood.

Finally, I want to thank Dr. Stephen Sussman, co-president of the Palm Beach Center for Democracy and Policy Research, and to Dr. David Dalin for their friendship and intellectual partnership.

Luis Fleischman, Jupiter, Florida, September 2020

Introduction

The main objective of this book is to analyze the continuing failure of the Israeli-Palestinian peace process and to reflect on alternative solutions to its current format and assumptions. This study seeks to understand how and why the Oslo process failed. After studying this question, we will analyze the consequences of such failures and ask if, under the current circumstances, we can continue to pursue the bilateral Israeli-Palestinian negotiations with the same goals and strategies as we have been following.

This study will analyze both the shortcomings of the peace process as well as opportunities for advancement. At the same time, we will examine current changes in the region and explore how these changes could impact peace between Israelis and Palestinians and between Israelis and the Arab world. The book will advance conclusions and proceed to analyze the new ingredients that could lead to alternative solutions to the bilateral negotiations. The goal of this examination is to learn lessons from the past, examine current circumstances and new developments, and consider different solutions.

Launched in 1993, the Oslo peace negotiations provided hope for an agreement between the Israelis and Palestinians. Almost a quarter century later, and despite multiple efforts, peace has not been achieved; instead, stagnation has dominated the last decade. The book aims for new visions, theories and solutions to this prolonged conflict, while considering new political and geo-political developments in the region.

Negotiations to reach a final agreement failed at the 2000 Camp David Summit. Israeli Prime Minister Ehud Barak offered a peace agreement at the summit and even accepted parameters for a peace agreement proposed by U.S President Bill Clinton in December 2000 that went further than Barak's own proposals at Camp David. The proposals went as far as Israel's offer to withdraw from most of the West Bank through land swaps to compensate the Palestinians for West Bank land taken from them. The proposals also included the division of Jerusalem and the creation of a Palestinian state in more than 90% of the West Bank and the entire Gaza Strip. At Camp David, the Palestinian leadership rejected Barak's proposals by demanding the right of return of millions of Palestinians and their descendants to what were their homes before Israel's independence in 1948. Palestinians also demanded control over the holy sites in Jerusalem, including the Western Wall. This proposal was rejected because it would mean that the Western Wall, an important landmark to the Jewish people, would fall under Palestinian control.

Negotiations continued against the backdrop of uncontrolled Palestinian violence (known as the Second Intifada) perpetrated by organized Palestinian groups. Negotiations failed again after Clinton offered his own proposal, the "Clinton Parameters," which were discussed in Taba, Egypt, early in 2001. The Clinton parameters proposed further Israeli withdrawal from the West Bank than the Barak proposal did and co-Administration of the Holy sites by the Palestinians, the Jordanians, the Saudis and the Israelis. Whereas the Israelis accepted the Clinton proposal, the Palestinians rejected it. Later, in 2005, Israel unilaterally withdrew from Gaza and dismantled all settlements in Gaza and several in the West Bank.

An additional offer was made by Israeli Prime Minister Ehud Olmert in 2008. The Olmert proposal kept previous proposals in play and offered joint control of the holy sites, among other compromises. In each of these cases, the Palestinians either failed to respond to the offer, as was the case with the Olmert proposal, or placed the "right of return" as a key demand, despite Israel's categorical rejection of it.

On the Israeli side, expansion of the settlements in the West Bank continued. Israel argued that the issue would be resolved in the final status discussions, where issues of borders, Jerusalem, the case of Palestinian refugees, security and water supply issues would be decided and a comprehensive final agreement would be signed after five years of confidence-building, as stipulated at the beginning of the Oslo process. However, many both in and outside Israel (including in the United States) believed that settlement expansion contributed to a crisis of confidence between both sides, the opposite of the Oslo process's intent.

As chances of an agreement diminished and the Israeli right gained strength, Jewish settlements expanded even further. Moreover, Palestinian terrorist attacks perpetrated during the Second Intifada (2000-2005) triggered the tightening of Israel's control over the Palestinian population, including the establishment of checkpoints and other restrictions on movement. Israel also prohibited the selling and construction of new Palestinian houses in areas next to Jewish settlements (the so-called Area C), further intensifying the crisis. Even the dividing fence built between Israel and the West Bank to prevent terrorist attacks, raised Palestinian concerns of Israeli intrusion into their property and everyday life. Although these Israeli policies were reasonably aimed at protecting Israeli citizens, they also weakened the confidence the Oslo process was designed to build.

Nevertheless, despite the turmoil of the Second Intifada, negotiations continued. Then President George W. Bush followed through with his "Road Map for Peace" and the Annapolis Conference; however, both failed. In 2009, Israelis elected Benjamin Netanyahu, a hawkish leader who offered the security and protection that the Israelis badly felt they needed. Netanyahu was less concerned about reaching a peace agreement, expressing the prevailing attitude among many Israelis that there was no partner for peace. Although U.S President Barack Obama tried to revive the peace process by tirelessly pursuing bilateral negotiations, his efforts, did not generate even the slightest hint of potential progress.

In this book, we reject the idea that Israel alone was responsible for the failure of the peace process. We will also challenge the arguments made by those who claim that the Oslo process was a Palestinian sham or a mere stage toward the larger goal of restoring the entirety of Israeli land to Palestinian hands.

According to Israeli scholar Asher Susser, Israelis pursued negotiations with the Palestinians within the framework of United Nations Security Council Resolution 242, adopted in the aftermath of the 1967 Six-Day War. According to this framework, negotiations with the Palestinians would be based on exchanging land conquered in 1967 for a lasting peace agreement. According to Susser, the Israelis did not understand that, "from the Palestinian point of view, to retrieve all of the West Bank was to retrieve only 22 percent of historical Palestine. Israelis already had 78 percent."[1] For the Palestinians, the problem was not 1967 but 1948, when the war that led to the creation of the State of Israel turned them into refugees. While the Palestinians have demanded the "right of return" and Israeli citizenship for Palestinian refugees and their descendants, the Israelis have demanded Palestinian recognition of Israel as the nation-state of the Jewish people. However, Susser claims, "the Palestinians will not recognize Israel as the nation-state of the Jewish people, for to do so would be asking the Palestinians to recognize that Palestine is Jewish, and they won't. So, when it comes to these 1948 questions, there has been no progress between Israel and Palestine."

Israeli scholar Benny Morris claims that Palestinian Liberation Organization (PLO) Chairman Yasser Arafat's commitment to recognizing Israel and the two-state solution was doubtful given his public pronouncements and incitement against Israel, his failure to curb terrorism, and his constant public remarks denying Jewish history and its connection to the land.[2] For Morris, Arafat's anti-Zionism remained alive despite the Oslo peace process. Morris suggests that Oslo could have been the result of a strategy developed by Arafat deputy and a PLO leader, Salah Khalaf (also known as Abu Iyad). Khalaf proposed a gradual takeover of all historic Palestine (i.e. Israel, the West Bank, and Gaza) by accepting a two-state solution first, and later trying to take over the entire Israeli territory.[3] Indeed, the fact that Palestinians demanded the "right of return" during the negotiations over the final status in Camp David and afterwards seems to be consistent with Khalaf's strategy.

Morris' view is reinforced by former Knesset member Einat Wilf, and Israeli journalist Adi Schwartz, as well as by historian Ephraim Karsh. After thoroughly analyzing Palestinian rhetoric and documentation, Wilf and Schwartz conclude that, peace has not yet been achieved because the Palestinians have yet to renounce their demand for an exclusive Arab Palestine "from the River to the

Sea" – a demand most evident in their continued refusal to agree to any language, any formulation, and certainly any agreement that would undermine and foreclose the Palestinian demand for return to the sovereign state of Israel. A true Palestinian reckoning with the notion that the Jewish people, as a people and as a nation, possess a right, no less than them, to self-determination in the land that both peoples call home, is yet to take place.[4]

Karsh argues that Arafat's objective had been clear since 1968, the year in which the Palestinian National Charter called for the destruction of Israel. Arafat's idea was to transfer all Palestinian resistance to the West Bank and Gaza. From there, a popular armed revolution would emerge and allow the undermining of Israel from within, by terrorizing the population, thereby inflicting damage on Israel's economy, encouraging emigration and discouraging immigration, and creating an atmosphere of insecurity that would make life inhospitable for the Israelis.

Thus, Karsh argues that the Second Intifada was a war of terror deliberately launched by Arafat in which he succeeded in bringing "the Palestinian war from Israel's borders into Israel proper by the politics of stealth. [Arafat] has every reason to hope that the work he began will be continued by the next generation of Palestinian leaders. That work is nothing short of the dismantlement of Israel."[5] Karsh believes that Arafat and his team, through the Second Intifada, wanted to bring about a situation as close as possible to the one experienced in 1948, where the Jewish population was at war with forces operating in the midst of Jewish civilians.[6]

Columnist Yossi Alpher argues that sensitive issues, such as the status of the Holy Sites and the refugee question, generated a gap between the parties and ruled out partial progress under the never-abandoned mantra of "nothing is agreed until everything is agreed." In this way, the Oslo process was held hostage to unbridgeable narratives. In addition, Alpher attributes the failure of the peace process to the emergence of extremism on both sides: on the one hand, Hamas, and on the other hand, the increasing power of Jewish orthodox groups who believe in a messianic mission in the expansion of settlements.

Alpher also points out that there are no leaders like Anwar Sadat, Menachem Begin or Yitzhak Rabin, who are able to take courageous steps toward peace with the enemy. Alpher rightly points out that Mahmoud Abbas, Chairman of the Palestine Liberation Organization (PLO) and President of the Palestinian Authority (PA), lacked the courage to take far-reaching steps to pragmatically overcome Palestinian dogmas and chimeras such as the "right of return." This, in Alpher's view, brought about Abbas' rejection of the Olmert offer and led to an irreversible path away from peace.[7]

Seth Aniska, author of *Preventing Palestine*, offers a historicist explanation for the failure of the peace process. He argues that the failure of Oslo has roots in the Egyptian/Israeli peace agreements reached in the late 1970's.[8] According to Anziska, a Palestinian state could have been already established during the Egyptian/Israeli peace negotiations. Instead, the 1979 Camp David agreement between Egypt and Israel gave birth to the autonomy plan, which proposed limited self-rule to the Palestinians. Anziska believes that the autonomy plan was an idea proposed by then-Israeli Prime Minister Menachem Begin, who rejected a Palestinian state. Egyptian president Anwar Sadat and U.S. President Jimmy Carter went along with Begin because Sadat wanted the Sinai back and Carter wanted a successful peace agreement in the end. The Autonomy Plan not only prevented a Palestinian state but also allowed the expansion of Israeli settlements in what Begin and his Likud party considered the historical and biblical land of Israel.

Aniska ignores two important points, however. First, during that time the PLO was a terrorist organization and an enemy of Israel; secondly, even if, in the Egyptian/Israeli Camp David Accords, a plan for Palestinian autonomy was conceived, this does not mean that Oslo had to necessarily follow that exact blueprint. The fact is that a Palestinian state, in addition to other concessions, was offered by Israeli negotiators at different junctures that were more generous than the idea of Palestinian autonomy conceived in the late 1970's.

Yossi Beilin, a former advisor to then Foreign Minister Shimon Peres and a key player in the Oslo negotiations, points out that the Oslo peace process took place between two asymmetric partners. According to Beilin, Israel managed to convince the Palestinians not to insist on a settlement freeze, but Israel continued to build settlements after the process began. In return, the Palestinians violated parts of the Accords, such as refusing to extradite to Israel Palestinian citizens who committed acts of terror. Benjamin Netanyahu, who was elected Prime Minister for the first time in 1996, delayed Israeli withdrawals from the West Bank as agreed to under the Accords. The election of Netanyahu confirmed Palestinian fears that a change of government in Israel could reverse the prospects of peace.[9] Beilin implies that this provoked a violent reaction from the Palestinians.

Beilin, like his superior Peres, believed that mutual recognition and economic prosperity in the region was a sufficient foundation for a political solution to be reached. However, no political solution between the Israelis and Palestinians has been accomplished thus far, despite the multiple opportunities to rectify those miscalculations.

Along these lines there is another explanation offered by the scholar Jonathan Rhynold. Rhynold argues that since Israelis viewed the peace process as an issue of Israeli security (a divorce between Israelis and Palestinians that would end the occupation and stop security threats from the Palestinian territories) and not as an issue of Palestinian rights, they continued to build settlements without being sensitive enough to Palestinian concerns. The Palestinians, on the other hand, continued demanding the "right of return" since they viewed peace without the "right of return" as capitulation.[10]

There is no question that the Oslo agreements were ill conceived. They did not place limits on settlements, nor did they prescribe specific regulations and requirements. The Oslo agreements deferred the final status of borders and Palestinian statehood to future negotiations without establishing clear boundaries of permissible and impermissible actions while negotiations were taking place. The Declaration of Principles (DOP), which set the framework of the Oslo Process was vague, and there is no question that this vagueness distorted the meaning that each side gave to the nature of the negotiation. Oslo intended to do what Kenneth Stein and Samuel Lewis have described as the benefit of narrowing the topics of discussions to less contentious issues, while postponing the insoluble issues for later, presumably to maintain momentum toward a final bilateral negotiation.[11] In other words, both sides held fundamentally irreconcilable narratives that exploded during the negotiations. However, this is only part of the problem and does not tell the whole story. In order to deepen our understanding of the problem and seek out alternative solutions to the Israeli-Palestinian problem, this book offers a comprehensive sociological explanation of what went wrong. The focus of analysis will be the PA's inability to establish governance and real legitimate authority, thus preventing the Palestinian leadership from assuming administrative and political responsibility for a Palestinian state.

Fatah, the PA's ruling party, was defeated in the 2006 parliamentary elections by the radical Islamist and anti-peace Hamas. The defeat was widely interpreted as the Palestinian population's reaction to what it perceived as a corrupt Fatah government. The PA's deficit of legitimacy was aggravated by its crisis of governance and authority. Indeed, in the Palestinian territories, there is a problem of factionalism and competing sovereignties that threatens the monopoly of violence of the central authority. This factionalism is multi-dimensional. It exists both within Fatah and between Fatah and other factions. Within Fatah, there is a conflict between the old guard of the PLO, which came from exile in Tunis, and the young generation, which actively participated in the First Intifada. Hamas undermined the peace process by conducting acts of terror in the aftermath of Oslo. Hamas terror challenged the authority of Fatah through violence aimed at the Israeli population, with the goal of sabotaging the peace process. However, as will be discussed, terror against Israel turned into an instrument of competition for popularity between Fatah's young generation and Hamas. The attitude of Fatah's young generation suggests that the PA was having problems to impose law and order and manage sovereignty. Thus, there is a crisis of legitimacy of the Palestinian government before a Palestinian state has even been officially created.

This book will argue that Palestinians suffer from factionalism, anarchy and a crisis of popular legitimacy that prevents them from exercising governance. This leaves them incapable of making risky decisions like signing a peace agreement or establishing an independent state. This book systematically argues that the PA is currently incapable of implementing a peace agreement and is also unable to sustain the stability of an independent state without facing the risk of a coup d'état, like the one Hamas carried out in Gaza in 2007. As such, the Palestinian leadership is presently unwilling to install a Palestinian state, in order to avoid a direct challenge to the integrity of the old Fatah leadership.

Furthermore, in order to placate the very forces that have challenged Fatah rule and, in an effort to regain popular legitimacy, the PA has resorted to anti-Israel propaganda, an element that has had serious negative consequences not only for the peace process but also for the prospect of peace in the generations to come.

We will argue that the Palestinians themselves are victims of such policies, because a permanent mobilization and war footing prevents the possibility of a normal life. The status quo may be convenient for the weak ruling Fatah, but it does not resolve the situation of Palestinians themselves who give up private goals by living constantly mobilized against disparate and imaginary collective goals that never materialize, such as the elimination of Israel, the re-conquering of the entire historical Palestine, and the return to their former homes.

We thus conclude that, given the political and social inability of the Palestinians to reach an agreement with Israel, the old formulas that advocated for a bilateral Israeli-Palestinian negotiation need to be challenged. This book moves in the direction of exploring the potential factors that could lead to a solution outside the bilateral framework.

This book turns to the Arab world, which has the potential to guarantee and secure an Israeli-Palestinian peace treaty. However, when such opportunities have arisen in the past, they have left the weak Palestinians to decide alone and with the feeling that any compromise (particularly on Jerusalem) may face disapproval in the Arab and Muslim world. The Arabs have historically shied away from supporting a genuine peace agreement and instead contributed to reinforcing the most intransigent Palestinian positions. It is here that the book attempts to find a way to restore a positive role for the Arab world given changes in their geo-political interest and in the domestic dynamics of the Arab states, particularly after the Arab Spring.

Israel and Sunni Arab countries have a common cause in defense against the threat of Iran and violent, radical Islamist groups. Furthermore, the Arab Spring has given slow birth to a more domestically oriented Arab civil society that is less inclined to zealotry on the Israeli-Palestinian conflict, and more likely to encourage discussion of political and public affairs and even challenge the Arab traditional understanding of Israel and the conflict.

Each of the chapters that follow will examine the political failure of Oslo, the complex responsibility for its demise, the role of parallel and competing narratives about the contested land, and whether it is possible to move the Israeli-Palestinian conflict into a place that can benefit both peoples. Chapter 1 will develop the idea of the crisis of the Palestinian Authority in more detail. It analyzes the Oslo negotiations from their inception to the present. The chapter examines events throughout the negotiations, including what Palestinians and Israelis argued, offered, and rejected, and how the parties justified their positions. Likewise, it will compare the negotiating experiences of both Palestinian leaders, Yasser Arafat and Mahmoud Abbas, as well as the differences between both personalities, including their ideas and attitudes. The chapter concludes that the Palestinian hesitancy and rejectionism during negotiations was linked not to a specific point of view but rather to a situation of structural decomposition and instability that paralyzed the Palestinian leadership. Thus, it will be argued that independence is not a national aspiration of the Palestinian leadership at the moment. This chapter will argue that such a situation has consequences that are detrimental in the long run to the entire peace process. The crisis of the PA not only delays the peace but in fact aggravates the crisis. The Palestinian leadership feels the need to appease Hamas, other radical groups, and Palestinian dissidents. As a result, the Palestinian leadership embarks on a fierce systematic anti-Israeli propaganda campaign with potentially devastating consequences for the mindset of younger Palestinian generations and for future chances of peace.

Chapter 2 explains the Palestinians move away from the peace process. The chapter explores in detail the connection between the weakness of the PA and the war of propaganda against Israel that ensued. The propaganda is systematic and has toxic consequences for younger generations. It not only discourages reconciliation with Israel, but also perpetuates the Palestinian mindset of permanent revolution, which prevents the Palestinians from conducting normal lives based on free will and individual choice. The propaganda is not limited to criticism of the Israeli government's policies or manipulation to maximize gains in the negotiations; rather, it categorically denies the connection between the Jewish people and the land of Israel.[12] Through school curricula and mass media, it conveys a message of complete rejection of the State of Israel and indirectly promotes violence against it even though Abbas has publicly rejected violence.

The chapter examines this phenomenon not only as it affects the current generation of Palestinians, but also as it may affect generations to come. As Palestinian feelings of hostility and anger towards Israel intensify, the possibility of a solution based on bilateral engagement decreases. Consequently, the book moves in the direction of solving the Israeli-Palestinian conflict outside the bilateral track. It is in this sense that the book turns to the Arab world as we view Arab states and societies as an important force potentially capable of either having an influence on the Palestinians or of securing and enforcing a lasting peace agreement.

Chapter 3 analyses the role that the Arab world as a whole could play in achieving a sustainable peace between Israelis and Palestinians outside the track of bilateralism. This chapter acknowledges that the Arab world has not played an effective or active role in the Israeli-Palestinian peace process in the past. At Camp David when President Clinton requested several Arab countries to persuade Arafat to accept a compromise agreement with Israel, only Jordan and Tunisia answered the call.[13] Arab countries rejected any compromise on Jerusalem that would have left the Muslim Holy Sites under Israeli sovereignty. Egypt, the only country in the Arab world to sign an agreement with Israel, walked away from such responsibility. Indeed, many Arab leaders withdrew from the multilateral talks which were supposed to facilitate and guarantee the Israeli-Palestinian peace process. The chapter will analyze the complex sociological, psychological and political components that have motivated the Arabs to adopt such detached and sometimes even hostile attitude towards the peace process.

However, this book also identifies crucial changes in the Middle East that may be potentially important in the future of peace between Israel and the Palestinians and of course between Israel and the Arab world in general. The Arab world is undergoing a major transformation that involves two crucial elements. One is geopolitical and relates to the emergence of an aggressive competition between the Islamic Republic of Iran and Sunni Arab states. Israel has turned at least temporarily into an ally of Sunni Arab states. The big question asked and explored in the chapter is if this marriage of convenience between Israel and the Arab world can be expanded into a force capable of bringing about a solution to the conflict between Palestinians and Israelis. Under the current circumstances, the rise of Iran as a threatening force in the Middle East and the rise of Sunni extremism in the form of the Islamic State (ISIS, also known as ISIL) have become serious challenges for these regimes. Nevertheless, they have also generated opportunities for cooperation with Israel. Thus, I will attempt to assess how transformational this new cooperation might be and to what extent it can generate a momentum that could open the door to improved Arab-Israeli relations and a more peaceful future.

The Arab Spring is another equally important element of change that will be analyzed in Chapter 4. The Arab Spring's most important consequence seems to be the unprecedented gradual entrance of civil society into the Arab polity and a more vigorous Arab public sphere. I will argue that this phenomenon is likely to change the social contract between the Arab states and civil society by giving a greater voice to the Arab grassroots that will impact the priorities of Arab states' national agendas. Chapter 4 explores the extent to which these changes could affect Arab attitudes towards Israel and the Israeli-Palestinian and Arab conflict.

Finally, Chapter 5 will suggest various solutions to the Israeli-Palestinian conflict. It will recommend different alternatives to the Oslo peace process while considering the factors analyzed above: the current state of the Palestinians; the state of the Arab countries; the new geopolitical map in the region; and the Arab Spring.

CHAPTER 1

THE DEMISE OF OSLO –
WHAT WENT WRONG?

The Oslo Accords were intended to launch a process that would eventually end the conflict between Israelis and Palestinians. The final result was to be a peace agreement with no further claims on either side. It was assumed that the end of the Israeli-Palestinian conflict would also be the end of the Israeli-Arab conflict, as the former represented the heart of the Israeli-Arab conflict. As Cyrus Vance, Secretary of State in the Carter Administration, pointed out in the late 1970's "No peace agreement will be either just or secure if it does not resolve the problem of the Palestinians in the broadest sense."[1] Vance believed that as long as the Palestinian problem remained unresolved, the conflict would continue, even if Israel reached separate agreements with Arab states as it did with Egypt. Indeed, as part of the 1979 Camp David Accords, the Carter Administration actively encouraged and pushed for the agreement to hold talks on Palestinian self-rule or autonomy. The Oslo Accords represented a continuation of this proposal from the Egyptian/Israeli agreement of 1979.

Oslo indeed was seen as a window of opportunity to end not only the Israeli-Palestinian conflict but also the Arab/Israeli conflict altogether. This chapter will examine the Oslo peace process and the circumstances that have brought about its virtual death.

The Oslo Process

In order to develop an educated estimate of the future of the peace process, it is important to first understand the history of the peace process so that we may better grasp the realities on the ground and the internal dynamics of each side.

The First Intifada (1987-1993), a Palestinian uprising, created a social movement against Israeli control of the West Bank and Gaza. This led the Israelis to conclude that the occupation of Palestinian territory and control over its people were no longer possible.

Left-wing Israelis always feared that annexation of the West Bank and Gaza could endanger the Jewish character of Israel because it risked losing Israel's Jewish majority. However, the First Intifada forced the right-wing Israeli government to deal with the Palestinian problem. Thus, in early 1989, Israel proposed a peace initiative, followed by the Madrid Conference (1991) where Israel held a dialogue with representatives of the West Bank and Gaza. These representatives had ties to the Palestine Liberation Organization (PLO). Eventually a backchannel between Israel and the PLO was created that led to the Oslo Accords. The First Intifada also sensitized the Israeli public to the future of the West Bank and Gaza and their inhabitants.[2] This helped propel the successful election in 1992 of Yitzhak Rabin, the leader of the Labor Party, which ran on a platform that pledged to work towards peace with the Palestinians.[3]

On the Palestinian side, the PLO feared that the Intifada might have robbed them of their historical leadership over their people. Because the PLO leadership was in exile in Tunisia, the Intifada took place without PLO leadership. The First Intifada was a spontaneous social movement that involved the Palestinian grassroots, and various sectors of Palestinian civil society. It received no instructions or orders from the PLO. As Zeev Schiff and Ehud Yaari have pointed out, it was a rebellion of the poor, of the forgotten. It was a leaderless uprising.[4]

Equally important, it was during the First Intifada that Hamas, an offshoot of the Muslim Brotherhood, was officially born. A leader of the Democratic Front for the Liberation of Palestine, one of the organizations of the PLO, expressed fear that the PLO could lose popular power among Palestinians if the uprising were viewed in history as a social uprising and not as a nationally motivated movement [5] According to scholar James Gelvin, the Oslo process offered the PLO a way to shore up its leadership in light of its fear that an alternative Palestinian leadership could replace them.[6] The social movement born out of the Intifada, and the powerful uprising launched outside the authority of the PLO, led Chairman Yasser

Arafat to adopt steps aimed at quickly securing control of Palestinian territories.

Although the 1968 Palestinian National Charter, which we will discuss in detail in Chapter Two, called for the entire liberation of all historical Palestine through armed struggle - including Israel, the West Bank and Gaza- the idea of securing control over the West Bank and Gaza first resulted from PLO resolutions adopted in the 1970's.

In one instance in 1974, the PLO adopted a proposal to establish a mini-state in the West Bank and the Gaza Strip. However, the PLO insisted that such a state would be temporary until all of Palestine (including Israel) could be "liberated."[7] Negotiations or compromises with Israel were rejected outright.

During the Oslo meetings, however, PLO and Israeli interests converged insofar as the former was afraid of losing power to new groups that emerged during the First Intifada, while the latter was looking for a way out of the West Bank and Gaza.

The Oslo Accords, signed in September 1993, were intended to build trust and confidence between the parties by proposing gradual steps over time. The goal was to follow the Oslo process by signing a final status agreement after five years on all the remaining issues, including the borders of Israel and Palestine, the Israeli settlements, the status of Jerusalem, Israel's military presence and the issue of Palestinian refugees.

According to the terms of the agreements, Israel first withdrew its administration from Gaza and Jericho, a city in the West Bank. Israel evacuated military bases and other fixed installations and handed them over to the Palestinian Police. Israel continued to be responsible for the external and internal security of the settlements and the Israelis living in the Gaza and Jericho areas. Israel proceeded to redeploy its military forces to the settlements.[8] In less than a year after signing the agreements, a full Palestinian administration was functioning in Gaza and Jericho while PLO leader Yasser Arafat moved to Gaza. Two years later, in September 1995, Oslo II was signed. This agreement established the extension of Palestinian self-rule to the West Bank. It was agreed that the Palestinian territories would be divided into three areas: A, B, and C. Area A comprised most of the urban centers and municipalities and Area B included about 450 villages. Area C, the largest area, constituting about 61% of the West Bank, included most of the Jewish settlements as well as a large unpopulated territory. [9]

In Area A, there was to be a full withdrawal of Israeli troops and a transfer of authority to the Palestinians. In Area B, administrative authority would be conferred to the Palestinians, while security control would remain in Israeli hands. Finally, Area C would be under complete Israeli control, both administratively and militarily. Israel was to continue its withdrawals in three further redeployments. [10]

The goal was to gradually consolidate Area B into Area A, while Area C, which included Jewish settlements established in the territories taken by Israel in 1967, would be subject to a final status agreement. Other issues to be discussed in the final status agreement included the future of Jerusalem, water rights, and the problem of Palestinian refugees who fled or left their homes during the 1948 Arab-Israeli War. Palestinian self-rule was to be established in the West Bank, and negotiations on a final peace agreement were expected to begin at the end of the second year. Most of the Palestinian population fell into Areas A and B, while Area C included the Jewish settlements and smaller Arab communities. However, scattered Jewish settlements prevented Palestinian contiguity in Area B, leaving it a kind of "land archipelago."

Implementation of the Oslo Accords soon faced obstacles that diminished the initial optimism and enthusiasm it generated. Palestinian terrorism increased, generating panic in Israel and second thoughts about the Oslo agreements. At the same time, Israeli settlements increased, particularly in area C. There was a reason for the vagueness in the Oslo agreements regarding what was and was not permissible before a final status agreement was reached. As former Israeli Foreign Minister Shlomo Ben Ami perceptively observed, the First Intifada created an urgency for Arafat and the PLO to restore their control over Palestinian territories in the West Bank and Gaza. The Israelis on the other hand, were comfortable avoiding public commitments with respect to the vision of a permanent agreement, partly because of fear of negative public reactions. On the Israeli side, Rabin, the Israeli Prime Minister who signed the Oslo agreement with Arafat, neglected to mention the idea of a Palestinian state in order to appease those Israelis who were still afraid of an Israeli withdrawal.[11] Whatever the reasons were, the result was that the lack of clarity in those agreements allowed both sides to act without clear limitations, and often irresponsibly.[12]

The Israeli-Palestinian Dynamics

Under the Oslo Accords, trust between the Israelis and Palestinians was to develop mutually. Palestinians were expected to contain terrorism, while Israelis were to implement gradual withdrawals. Coexistence was to be tested on the ground. The idea was to eventually create a situation of divorce, or separation between the two communities, ending with two different states. However, that trust was not successfully built. It suffered a severe blow when right wing Jewish extremist Baruch Goldstein massacred 29 Muslim worshippers at the Cave of the Patriarchs in the West Bank city of Hebron. The Israeli government reacted robustly, criminalizing the extremist right-wing Kach movement and imposing limitations on Israeli settlers. The situation was more complicated on the Palestinian side. A series of Palestinian terrorist attacks perpetrated by Hamas took place. The perception was that Arafat and the newly created Palestinian Authority (PA) did very little, if anything, to prevent it. Between 1993 and 1996, nearly 300 Israelis were killed by terrorist attacks. By comparison, during the six years of the First Intifada, 172 Israelis were killed. The terrorism that prevailed in the years following the signing of the Oslo Accords made Israelis feel very insecure.[13]

Arafat's aggressive rhetoric evoking jihad, as well as references to the agreements with Israel as temporary, increased Israelis' anxiety.[14] As terrorist attacks by Hamas intensified, the atmosphere in Israel worsened. In 1995, Prime Minister Rabin was assassinated by an Israeli right-wing militant. Although the overwhelming majority of Israelis condemned the assassination, many began to lose faith in the efficacy of the Oslo agreements and demanded more security. Israelis also doubted Arafat's sincerity and his ability and will to control terrorism.[15] Yet, at this time Yossi Beilin, a key advisor to Foreign Minister Shimon Peres, reached an informal agreement with Mahmud Abbas (also known as Abu Mazen), a high-ranking

PA leader who later succeeded Arafat as President. The unofficial accord became known as the Beilin-Abu Mazen Agreement and was reached shortly before Rabin's assassination. The proposal sought to create a Palestinian state and expand the boundaries of municipal Jerusalem by including the village of Abu Dis, which would become the capital of the Palestinian state. Questions related to the Temple Mount and Islamic Holy Sites would be deferred to later negotiations. Jewish and Muslim denominations would be granted special status and access to the Old City. Israel would retain a limited military presence in the West Bank for a period of twelve years. There would also be a territorial accommodation in which Israel would be allowed to retain settlement blocs, but with land compensation (land swaps) to Palestinians. The question of Palestinian refugees would also be deferred to a later time.[16]

The Beilin-Abu Mazen accord, though not embraced by the Israeli and Palestinian leadership, established the idea that peace was possible. Likewise, it established a blueprint for future drafts, including the Barak concessions at Camp David, and later the Geneva Initiative, which aimed to revive hopes for a resolution amidst the Second Intifada (or Al-Aqsa Intifada).

The First Netanyahu Administration

Against the backdrop of terrorism and Israeli panic, the more hawkish and conservative Likud party, headed by Benjamin Netanyahu, was narrowly elected into office in 1996. Although some members of his own coalition were opposed to Oslo, Netanyahu did not run on an anti-Oslo platform because he viewed the Accords as binding. His administration's policy was to toughen Israel's position by demanding from Arafat a fulfillment of his commitments to control terrorism and adjust the Palestinian charter calling for the destruction of Israel. Additionally, he demanded a stop to the incitement and hostile anti-Israel propaganda promoted by the Palestinian Authority (PA) [17] Netanyahu also expressed his commitment to an entirely Israel-controlled Jerusalem and moved to close the PA and PLO institutions in the city, [18] even though the fate of Jerusalem was to be addressed in the final status negotiations. He also allowed the continued building of settlements on Palestinian territory through "market forces." The government would only release "public lands, transportation lands and allow natural growth."[19]

The Netanyahu administration also delayed redeployments and treated Arafat with great distrust.

In 1997, Netanyahu signed the Hebron Agreements, which included redeployment of Israeli forces from 80% of the Hebron area. This action left the area under Palestinian control while leaving 450 settlers in the heart of the city and maintaining control of the Tomb of the Patriarchs. [20] Furthermore, in 1998, Netanyahu signed the Wye River Agreement aimed at continuing implementation of the Oslo II accord. The Wye agreement specified that Israel would withdraw from an additional 13 percent of the West Bank within a time frame of three months. Meanwhile, the PA made a commitment to revise the Palestinian National Charter, to fight terror, strengthen security cooperation, and to cease anti-Israel propaganda and rhetoric.[21] The agreement was supported by an overwhelming majority in the Knesset, the Israeli parliament, and by 80 percent of the Israeli population at large.[22] Interestingly enough, however, the atmosphere of bitterness and distrust between the two parties intensified during this period. Indeed, Netanyahu carried out a redeployment from Hebron. Under pressure from his right-wing partners, he quickly moved to build settlements in Har Homa, an area between Jerusalem and Bethlehem that would effectively cut contiguity between the two cities.[23] Likewise, delays in redeployment, coupled with the Har Homa settlement, prompted Arafat to suspend negotiations and refused to control terrorist activity. Divisions also continued over the number of illegal weapons the PA was harboring. Tensions between the parties were beginning to contaminate the atmosphere.

Yet, despite signing the Wye River Agreement, Netanyahu did not approve of gradual redeployment. In his view, such gradualism further poisoned the character of peace negotiations. Instead, he proposed a Camp David-style conference similar to the one conducted between Israel and Egypt under U.S auspices 20 years earlier. Here, all issues would be resolved at once, since in Netanyahu's view, the gradual approach proposed in Oslo was not building confidence, but rather the opposite.

This point is crucial. Netanyahu was elected by a small margin in 1996, following a wave of terrorist attacks that swept Israel. His anger at the attacks and his demands for changes in Arafat's behavior caused the peace process to lose momentum. Netanyahu's style and the pressure he was subjected to from his right-wing coalition created distrust on the part of the Palestinians. Likewise, the Wye Memorandum was not properly implemented, further aggravating the situation. However, Netanyahu's positions did succeed in bringing about improvements in the security situation, effectively reducing the number of terrorist attacks.

The redeployments carried out by Israel after the Wye River Agreement created a crisis in the Netanyahu government. Despite Netanyahu's attempts to appease his coalition, the Likud Party split. A new party, called the National Movement, was formed and included former Prime Minister Yitzhak Shamir and Benny Begin, son of Likud founder Menachem Begin.

Ironically, as the Netanyahu administration delayed implementation of the Wye agreements, the Israeli population began to trust the peace process again, particularly because the security situation improved. In 1999, as faith in the peace process was reviving among Israelis, Netanyahu began to face challenges in the government coalition and within his own Likud party. As a result of opposition to the Hebron and Wye agreements from Netanyahu's own base, the Prime Minister sabotaged the Wye agreement. He delayed implementation of the agreed withdrawals. As Netanyahu's coalition began to collapse, he appealed to the Labor Party to join his government. Labor refused despite having supported the Wye Agreements. Faced with lack of political support, Netanyahu called for early elections, which were scheduled for May 1999. [24]

Ehud Barak, leader of the Labor Party alliance, the One Israel party, was elected Prime Minister with a sound majority.

The Government of Ehud Barak and the Camp David Conference

Barak was elected Prime Minister with a mandate, independent of parliamentary support. A 1996 law allowed the electorate to vote separately for their Prime Minister and a party of their choice. Before this law was passed, a Prime Minister could not form a government if he did not have majority support in the Knesset and the Knesset could remove the Prime Minister with a vote of non-confidence. Nevertheless, the result of the new law was that, although Barak's executive mandate was strong enough to act as Prime Minister, his support in parliament was not as solid. Parliament's support was needed to pass any legislation or to approve a peace agreement.

Barak was elected with 56 percent of the vote, but with a very loose coalition in parliament which took only 62 out of 120 Knesset seats. Furthermore, that coalition was composed of disparate parties whose ideologies and platforms were poles apart on domestic and foreign policy. It was clear shortly after the election that an independent executive mandate was not enough to provide the PM with the strength he needed to secure political support for a peace agreement. However, the personal mandate Barak received seemed to reflect the Israeli public's support for the continuation of the legacy of peace established by Rabin. This led to the Camp David Conference in the summer of 2000 where Israelis and Palestinians came face to face to sign a final status agreement that would resolve all the outstanding issues including borders, a Palestinian state, Jerusalem, the settlements, security arrangements and the refugees.

Barak's negotiating style was deliberative, and he was extremely cautious before making any decisions. Many Palestinians felt neglected when he initially focused his efforts on a peace agreement with Syria. He infuriated Arafat when he rebuffed his demands for the withdrawals from three Arab villages near Jerusalem. However, Barak eventually became fixated on the Palestinian track and like Netanyahu before him; he preferred to enter into a final status agreement without temporary redeployments because he was afraid that partial withdrawals could raise serious opposition that could undermine his peace efforts. Indeed, as soon as Barak considered the withdrawal from the three Arab villages near Jerusalem—as it was stipulated in the Sharem Ha Sheikh memorandum he signed and in which he made commitments to partial withdrawals—[25] opposition within Barak's coalition began to crystallize. The possibility of giving up the village of Abu Dis became a real threat to Barak's government. Still, he opted to delay the decision while simultaneously making conditional the return of Abu Dis once a final agreement was achieved. As President Bill Clinton observed about Barak, "Barak believed that if he could present a comprehensive peace plan to Israeli citizens, [the Knesset] would vote for it as long as Israel's fundamental interests were met: security, the protection of its religious cultural sites on the Temple Mount, an end of the Palestinian claim to an unlimited right of return to Israel and a declaration that the conflict was over". [26]

This made sense. After all, the majority of Israelis did approve of the first Camp David agreement two decades earlier, in which the Sinai Peninsula was returned to the Egyptians in exchange for peace. Indeed, when Egyptian president Anwar Sadat visited Jerusalem in 1977 and announced his intention to make peace with the Israelis, even hawkish leaders such as then-Defense Minister Ezer Weitzman, understood that Sadat's step presented a unique opportunity to end the state of war with their most powerful Arab neighbor. Weitzman's attitude, to a certain extent, reflected what former United States Ambassador to Israel and peace negotiator, Martin Indyk, pointed out about Israeli psychology: "a battered and insecure people whose collective Jewish psyche had hungered for acceptance after centuries of harsh oppression, would respond positively to visible indications of peaceful intentions."[27] Weitzman embraced Sadat's peace initiative almost immediately, a gesture that transcended the ideology of the party to which he belonged. Weitzman had been the chair of the Likud campaign that comfortably won the elections merely six months before Sadat's initiative. His attitude represents this very "collective Jewish psyche" Indyk describes. The election of pro-peace candidates Rabin in 1992 and Barak in 1999 epitomizes such attitudes.

According to Ambassador Dennis Ross, former United States envoy to the Middle East, the Palestinians failed to see that Barak was taking courageous steps to move the peace process forward and was maneuvering through a difficult political situation.[28]

In the summer of 2000, the parties gathered at Camp David for a conference sponsored by President Bill Clinton. Prime Minister Barak arrived at the conference in the midst of a serious political crisis that followed the loss of his coalition's parliamentary majority. Still, he decided not to postpone the meeting, let alone cancel it. He was convinced that he could appeal to the Israeli people to support an agreement with the Palestinians, even without a majority coalition. Barak took a big risk to his own political future but went to the conference with, to paraphrase Max Weber, an ethic of conviction and responsibility.

Using a basic negotiating tactic, Barak initially offered the Palestinians only sixty-six percent of the territory in question. An additional twenty-two percent would become Palestinian territory in a five to ten-year period. Israel would annex twelve percent of the territories in the settlement blocs.[29] The Palestinians would not have a border with Jordan, as the Israelis proposed to leave a military presence in the Jordan Valley for security reasons. The proposal certainly had some flaws, including the fact that Israeli settlements would block the territorial contiguity of the Palestinian state. Furthermore, Barak proposed to organize Palestinian territory into cantons rather than a state, a proposal that the Palestinians rejected.[30]

Yet, as negotiations evolved, the Israeli team offered more concessions until finally Barak made a more reasonable and generous offer. The offer included a Palestinian state with ninety percent of the West Bank and an eastern border with the Jordan River. Israel would hand over some of its own territory in exchange for the annexation of the settlement blocs. On Jerusalem, Barak offered the Palestinians sovereignty over East Jerusalem and "custodianship" over its Holy Site Haram Al Sharif, known to Jews as the Temple Mount. That offer was far-reaching and unprecedented. Israel broke the dogma of a unified Jerusalem under Israeli control, a gesture President Clinton fully acknowledged and admired. Barak agreed to concede territories in East Jerusalem, in the Old City and the Temple Mount. Barak even offered to relinquish a permanent presence in the Jordan Valley and install some kind of an international force there.[31]

However, the Palestinian reaction was cold. Palestinians did not respond to the territorial concessions. Instead, they demanded monetary compensation for the years of occupation of the Palestinian territories.[32] Furthermore, Arafat tried to downplay Barak's offer by pointing out inaccurately that Rabin offered him ninety percent of the West Bank years ago. According to Indyk's account, Rabin, who over the years became the symbol of peace, never seriously considered giving up more than eighty percent of the West Bank. Then, to make matters worse Arafat brought up a very curious issue that was invoked again in the summer of 2015 by his successor, Abbas: "the Jews are trying to undermine Muslim control of Haram Al Sharif by demanding to pray at the Temple Mount."[33] In both of these cases, this provocative statement incited turmoil and Palestinian violence, and threw a wrench into the peace negotiations.

President Clinton and the American team put pressure on Arafat, who feared that if he accepted the Israeli offers, there would be a revolution against him.[34] Arafat demanded Palestinian sovereignty over all of East Jerusalem, including the Holy Sites. An advisor to Arafat years later explained that the chairman saw himself as the defender of the holy city and the vanguard fighter, not only for Palestinians, but for the entire Arab and Muslim world.[35] Furthermore, in order to defend his position on Jerusalem, Arafat astonishingly asserted that the ruins of the old Jewish Temple did not lie under the Haram al Sharif, but rather in the West Bank city of Nablus.[36]

The question as to why Arafat would negotiate without the support of other Arab and Islamic nations is a curious one, and will be discussed in depth in Chapter 3. If Arafat was negotiating about Jerusalem as an envoy of the Muslim world rather than of the Palestinians, then why not let the Muslim world reach a separate agreement with Israel or involve them directly in the negotiation process? Would it not be easier for Arafat if the Muslim world shared responsibility for the outcome of the negotiations? If Arafat truly believed he was the defender of the Muslim holy city, the conflict was not only with the Palestinians; the conflict was with the larger Arab-Muslim world and, as such, Palestinian leadership lacked the strength and authority required to reach such an agreement.

Arafat's intransigence on Jerusalem surprised President Clinton, who was frustrated and disappointed that Arafat was willing to sacrifice a Palestinian state for the sake of complete control over Jerusalem's holy sites.[37] Arafat's negotiation tactics did not fit the common-sense rule of negotiations, namely, that negotiations must include reasonable concessions. It was clear that Israel could not accept all of the demands that Arafat wanted, such as the "right of return," which entailed granting an estimated three million Palestinians citizenship and the right to live in Israel proper. Such an arrangement would eliminate the Jewish character of the State of

Israel, the reason d'être of Israel's creation. It would also lead to a demographically binational state in which a bloody and vicious civil war between Palestinian and Jewish Israelis would inevitably be unleashed. In other words, the insistence on the "right of return" was a formula for war, not for peace.

That demand remained intact well after the 2000 Camp David summit. Shortly after Camp David, another Palestinian intifada erupted in which 1,100 Israeli lives were lost to terrorist attacks between 2000 and 2005.[38] The groups that participated included the most intransigent Islamist groups, Hamas, Islamic Jihad, and the Tanzim, an armed group linked to Arafat's Fatah faction.

Despite the violence, efforts by the United States to revive the peace process brought about a new initiative in December 2000, weeks before President Clinton's departure from the White House. Clinton presented a new set of parameters for peace after meeting extensively with and listening to the demands and concerns of representatives from the Israelis and the Palestinians. Clinton presented an ultimatum to both sides based on those parameters, urging them to accept and move toward a final peace agreement. The Clinton Parameters went even further than Barak's offer at Camp David, primarily on territorial issues. They called for the establishment of an independent Palestinian state in all of Gaza and at least ninety-five percent of the West Bank, and offered one to three percent territorial compensation to Palestinians. The Palestinian state capital would be in East Jerusalem, which included the Arab suburbs and the Arab quarters of the Old City. Palestinian refugees would have the "right of return" to the newly created Palestinian state, but not to Israel proper. Palestinians would also have sovereignty over Haram Al Sharif.[39]

The Clinton Parameters also suggested keeping seventy percent of the Jewish settlers in five percent of the West Bank, while withdrawing from the rest of the settlements or dismantling them entirely. Israel was asked to relinquish Jewish sovereignty over the entire Temple Mount with the exception of the Western Wall, and the Palestinians were asked to abandon the "right of return" to Israel. In other words, the Clinton Parameters were a reasonable solution to the conflict, and Israel accepted the proposal. However, Arafat responded once again by insisting on the "right of return" and by demanding control over the entire Temple Mount, including the Western Wall.[40] In other words, he demanded control over all the Muslim, Jewish, and Christian holy sites, including the Western Wall, the holiest site for the Jewish people. The reality is that such an attitude of insisting on control over Jerusalem's holy sites, and demanding the "right of return" seven years after Oslo, was not a reasonable negotiating strategy. It is true that negotiations often begin with unreasonable and often absurd demands but when such unreasonable demands continue to be at the forefront of negotiations so late in the process, it does not fit the logic of conventional, realistic negotiations in which the involved parties seek a successful outcome.

The negotiations on the Clinton Parameters in Taba, ultimately failed. Some argue that both sides were very close to an agreement. Others claimed that the American influence was weak as the Clinton presidency was coming to an end, and the administration of George W. Bush was transitioning in.[41] The Palestinians argued that Ehud Barak was likely to lose the election and that he had no power to make a deal. However, the dovish Shlomo Ben Ami, then Israeli Foreign Minister gives a different account of the Taba negotiations. He believed that the Palestinians were not interested in a deal. In Ben Ami's words,

> Taba did not allow an agreement, not because of the fact that the Israelis' qualitative political time was a desperately diminishing asset, but because the Palestinians treated the [Clinton] Parameters as non-committal and insisted on changing and challenging them on each point. For us [the Israelis], the parameters represented the outer limits of our capacity for compromise ...for the Palestinians it was a non-binding platform, 'a prison', as [Palestinian negotiator and later Prime Minister] Abu Ala put it to me. [42]

According to Indyk, Arafat was listening to advisors who were telling him that he could get a better offer from incoming president, George W. Bush.[43] Arafat may have relied on the position adopted by Bush's father, former president George H.W. Bush, who was less sympathetic towards Israel. However, that notion would later be proven wrong, as Bush would go on to demand serious reforms from the PA, including Arafat's removal from leadership roles. Still, Arafat's assumptions about Bush made sense given his father's tense relationship with the Israeli government. Nevertheless, it was unlikely that Sharon would be easier to deal with than Barak.

Making Sense of the Palestinian Attitude

If we assume that the Palestinian leadership was indeed seeking the conclusion of a peace agreement, simple logic cannot explain Arafat's maximalist, uncompromising approach.

Many theses and theories have developed to explain why the peace process failed. Some, including former President Clinton and his advisors, blamed Arafat and the Palestinians for the failures. Others blamed Israel and the United States in general. In the aftermath of the Camp David Summit, the Palestinian leadership argued in its defense, that the United States was not a fair broker, and that it sided with Israel. The Palestinians also argued that they felt pressured to make binding decisions at the Camp David Conference instead of letting the summit function as one phase in an ongoing negotiation. They expressed anger towards Barak for refusing to implement partial withdrawals as was stipulated in Oslo, and instead wanted to go straight to a final status agreement. They blamed Clinton as well, accusing him of rushing an agreement in order to achieve one final victory in the Middle East before leaving office.[44] This position was also held by Robert Malley, an advisor to Clinton on Arab affairs, and Hussein Agha, a PA advisor, who recognized that Barak wanted to achieve peace and a final agreement, but faulted him for refusing to make gradual concessions and for allowing the expansion of settlements in the areas around Jerusalem. Malley and Agha also argue that Barak applied enormous pressure on Arafat to accept the deal, which intimidated the Palestinian leader. They also argue that Barak's early focus on trying to reach an agreement with Syria added to distrust among the Palestinians who felt neglected by the Israeli leader.[45] However, even if we accept those arguments, it is still difficult to explain subsequent Palestinian rejections of peace proposals.

Aaron David Miller, a Middle East scholar and former American negotiator, provides another interpretation. He focuses on the role played by U.S mediation, criticizing the Clinton Administration for its lack of assertiveness and creativity. He believes that the Americans were far too passive, had no negotiation strategy, and were unable to establish clear guidelines for achieving peace. In Miller's view, the United States never understood what it took to close the deal. He blames the Clinton team for not being tough enough on both Israelis and Palestinians, for having chaotic meetings without direction, and for lacking a timetable or any kind of attainable, intermediate objectives.[46]

Miller's analysis does not seem sufficient to explain the failure of the negotiations. The "Clinton Parameters" offered clear guidelines and a framework for a final peace agreement. The failure of Camp David and the Clinton Parameters initiative can only be tested by the events that occurred afterwards. The fact is that subsequent U.S mediations in successive administrations also failed to achieve results despite American diplomats' active involvement, which also included proposals for solutions.

James Gelvin provides another interpretation of Oslo's demise.[47] His book, *The Israeli-Palestine Conflict: One Hundred Years of War* explains the stalemate in the peace process only in terms of political will. Gelvin treats the peace negotiations as a "give and take" process. He blames Prime Minister Barak for undermining the peace process by initially ignoring the Palestinians in favor of an arrangement with Syria, despite the fact that Barak abandoned the Syrian track in the end and offered the Palestinians various concessions, including a state of their own. Gelvin also attributes the causes of the Second Intifada to a one-time incident, the visit by Israel's opposition leader Ariel Sharon to the Temple Mount. According to this argument, the visit of an Israeli leader to the Temple Mount constituted a sort of casus belli. However, a single incident is insufficient to explain the destruction of the entire peace process. As noted earlier, the Second Palestinian Intifada was deliberately commenced. It was led not by a spontaneous manifestation of Palestinian civil society, but by dissenting armed groups, including Hamas, Islamic Jihad, and, most importantly, groups associated with the ruling Fatah party. The fact that the Second Intifada was perpetrated by organized groups and not by spontaneous forces attests that a single incident could not have been the cause of a violence that lasted five years, with all the fury and hatred that came with it. Gelvin believes that had the two sides reached mutual trust, peace could have been achieved.

Palestinian-American historian Rashid Khalidi analyzes the peace process and its failure as a process in which the Palestinians gradually lost any chance of creating their own state.[48] In Khalidi's view, the Palestinians lost the opportunity to build their own state on a contiguous territory because of Israeli settlements, which he views as creating irreversible facts on the ground. Khalidi does acknowledge Palestinian mistakes and shortcomings, including corruption, use of unnecessary violence, disconnection from the grassroots, and inability to build a solid infrastructure. However, he still portrays the Palestinians as helpless and historically abandoned by the world. Khalidi does not analyze the Israeli-Palestinian negotiations, nor what was offered and rejected or why. He calls the Israeli offers unacceptable without explanation and describes the United States and Israel as forming a biased, anti-Palestinian alliance. He does provide some useful insights in his criticism of Palestinians and Arabs, including the Palestinian responsibility for failing to accommodate peace and continuing to maintain a public rhetoric hostile towards Israel. However, he fails to reach conclusions, either theoretical or practical, beyond stressing the victimization of the Palestinians and the disproportionate political and military superiority of the Israelis.

As we have pointed out, hardly two months after the collapse of negotiations at the second Camp David summit, a wave of Palestinian violence erupted. Many have blamed Arafat for intentionally initiating the violence. However, the situation seems to be more complex, although Arafat himself was certainly not blameless. Indeed, Arafat's Minister of Communications, Emad El Faluji, stated in a speech delivered a few months after the violence erupted, that Arafat planned the violence immediately after he returned from Camp David.[49] El Faluji suggested that this was a way to send the United States a message that Arafat would not surrender to American pressure. Years later, Arafat's widow, Suha Arafat, also pointed out that her late husband planned the intifada to send a message to the world that he had not abandoned the Palestinian cause.[50]

Nevertheless, Arafat shook hands with an Israeli Prime Minister and publicly negotiated with the State of Israel, the country Palestinians considered the source of their catastrophe. In fact, Arafat gained multiple critics over Oslo, including radical Islamist groups such as Hamas, who seek Israel's destruction, and other Palestinians such as Edward Said. The latter defined Oslo as a "set up" as well as a "capitulation." Arafat was called a traitor and Hamas reinforced this characterization of him. Furthermore, the PA continued to negotiate after Camp David and during the Second Intifada, until January 2001, when a new round of negotiations in Taba ended inconclusively. The commission led by former Senator George Mitchell to investigate the events leading up to the Second Intifada concluded that Arafat did not orchestrate the violence.[51]

Curiously enough, as we will see further in this chapter, Mahmoud Abbas also refused subsequent peace offers that were even more generous than the ones given to Arafat. Abbas's history is one of moderation. He is a man, who in the 1970s was involved in secret meetings with members of the Israeli Zionist Left. He even reached an agreement in principle with former Israeli General Matti Peled, in which both agreed on both the recognition of Israel as a "Zionist state" and the creation of a Palestinian state.[52] Abbas was a fervent supporter of compromise with the Israelis and, as we noted earlier, he presented a plan for a permanent solution along with Yossi Beilin, then the Israeli Minister of Economy and Planning. Thus, we can ask whether Palestinian avoidance of a peace agreement is the result of an ingrained dogma that refuses to recognize the existence of Israel, or whether there are other external factors that prevent the PA from reaching a peace agreement with Israel based on a two-state solution.

Should reaching a compromise between the Israelis and Palestinians be so difficult to accomplish? As former American diplomat and scholar Dan Kurtzer has pointed out, the basic guidelines for the solution are there.[53] If that is the case, then why is reaching an agreement such a difficult goal to achieve? Shlomo Ben-Ami claims that before the 2000 Camp David Summit, Arafat claimed that Israel's pullout from Lebanon in the summer of 2000 under guerilla and military pressure from Hezbollah "had exposed him to domestic criticism for not following in the footsteps of his old disciples," namely Hezbollah.[54] This suggests that Arafat already felt the internal pressure to resort to violence in order to extract more concessions from the Israelis. Whether Arafat believed that the "Lebanonization" of the Palestinian conflict was a real option, as the dovish Ben-Ami suggests, is not clear. He may have. What is clearer, however, is the fact that the all-powerful, authoritarian Arafat was paying attention to domestic criticism, suggesting that he felt his authority was not strong enough to resist internal opposition.

The scholar Jeremy Pressman underscores the issue of factionalism and internal conflict in the PA. Pressman correctly describes a divided Palestinian political apparatus: first, he claims, there is a serious confrontation between Fatah and Hamas, which has already been mentioned; secondly, within the dominant Fatah group itself there is a confrontation between the old guard of the PLO, who came to the Palestinian territories from exile in Tunis in 1994, and the young generation who actively participated in the First Intifada. The latter, under the leadership of Marwan Barghouti, dominated the security organizations (Tanzim) and a large number of local elected officials. They also claimed to fight for freedom, against corruption, and for inclusion in Fatah's decision-making process. They also believed in violence and the use of force as a means to achieve political goals.[55] This generation aspired to gain as much power as possible within the Fatah organization, and thus it played a key role in the Second Intifada, joining Hamas as the main source of violence.

In addition, it is important to point out that Arafat's rule became extremely authoritarian. The factions that represented the PLO lost representation after the PA was established. The Palestinian Legislative Council, the PA's unicameral legislature, lost power as Arafat increased his executive powers by expanding the bureaucracy. The bureaucracy became the largest provider of jobs, and used these jobs to reward loyalty and punish critics. Likewise, Arafat created multiple security agencies and a large police force[56]. These steps further alienated other Palestinian groups. The Popular Front for the Liberation of Palestine (PFLP) was probably the most disaffected faction within the PLO and later adopted the Hamas method of suicide bombings against Israelis. Hamas was the most organized and deadly dissident group. Terrorist attacks indeed served to undermine, sabotage and spoil the peace process, as Hamas contends that Israel is illegitimately built on Muslim land. As scholar Wendy Pearlman explains, the peace process threatened the existence of the group itself, and, therefore, terrorist attacks were also aimed at reaffirming its place in Palestinian society.

In other words, Hamas was struggling for relevance among the Palestinians.[57] But there is another element here, and that is the perception that terrorist attacks increase the popularity of those groups that perpetrated them. As Canadian author Mia Bloom has pointed out, Palestinian factions use violence to gain prestige among the Palestinians. Therefore, different Palestinian organizations, including factions within Fatah, itself, engage in terrorist attacks in order to "outbid" each other. [58] Terror becomes a means to compete for popularity. This competition among factions is enabled by what Pearlman has called "lack of organizational cohesion." Pearlman describes the Palestinian situation as one of fragmentation, which she rightly defines as pluralism without rules, incapable of producing cooperative behavior, and lacking a structure capable of exercising authority or the proper mechanisms to resolve differences. This makes infighting inevitable.[59]

Pearlman provides an analysis of how Palestinian organizations have historically used terror to undermine and sabotage initiatives by the leadership of the PLO in order to compete with them.[60] The Second Intifada indeed had the involvement of Hamas, but this time there was an active participation of the Tanzim and the Al Aqsa Brigades, both armed groups associated with Fatah.

Tanzim emerged in the First Intifada as an armed group but was later co-opted by Fatah in the aftermath of the Oslo Process in order to counteract the activities of Hamas and other Islamic groups. Thus, Tanzim recruits were used to populate Palestinian security forces and Arafat's personal Force 17. This was also part of Arafat's strategy to exercise power by keeping the PA's security apparatus divided and thus secure personal loyalty.[61]

In total, Arafat had about 13-armed militias. However, many of these armed groups acted against Israel on their own, particularly during the Second Intifada. Groups associated with the secular Fatah began to adopt Islamist and anti-Semitic rhetoric. They also participated in more than three hundred terrorist attacks against Israelis, some of them in cooperation with their rival, Hamas. It may be surmised that in order to maintain the upper hand, Arafat had to persuade the public that he initiated the violence and needed to somehow prove it, for example, by releasing terrorists from prison and allowing them to operate from within jails.[62] This challenge, which prompted Arafat to maintain his authority by pleasing his competitors, marks the beginning of an era in which the Fatah-ruled PA began to lose its authority and its ability to exercise leadership. At this point, the situation became more turbulent as it evolved, leading to a series of events that reduced the chances of reaching a peace agreement.

The following exchange between Palestinian Interior Minister Nasr Yussuf and Israel Defense Forces (IDF) Lieutenant General Amnon Lipkin Schahak sheds light on the dilemma. The dialogue begins with Yussuf's request for arms:

> The security structure is the key. The street has a lot of weapons. In Gaza we have two battalions, each with 400 men. Each of the battalions has 70 Kalashnikovs. In every family, they have more arms. The soldiers have little income and they sell their weapons... We have no security institutions today and, in our backyard, we have gangs...We will need financing and can build all structures of cooperation [between the Palestinians and Israelis].[63]

Schahak replies as follows:

> Israel has an interest in strengthening Fatah. At the same time, those who have betrayed us have been Fatah, not Hamas. We gave to your people 30,000 weapons and you used them to shoot at us.[64]

This shows the serious state of anarchy in which the PA found itself. Besides competition between the factions, where the peace process became the main casualty, the ability of Fatah to reverse the state of anarchy was minimal, to say the least. Weapons were sold by the soldiers and dispersed throughout the Palestinian territories, while the PA lacked the monopoly on the means of violence. Yussuf begged the Israelis for more weapons precisely in order to restore that monopoly, but Schahak, himself a political dove, claimed that Israelis did not trust the Palestinians' ability to deliver. This led to the idea of a unilateral Israeli withdrawal, which will be discussed in the next section.

The Second Intifada erupted at a time when the Palestinians were very close to achieving a state of their own, and where ninety percent of the Palestinians were already under Palestinian civilian and political control (although not security control). Furthermore, travel between the West Bank and Gaza was possible, as was travel overseas. After a peace treaty was signed with Jordan in 1994, the Palestinians gained economic opportunities and other types of access to Jordan, while tens of thousands of Palestinians continued to travel to Israel to work. Following the terror and violence of the Palestinian Second Intifada, Palestinians had to face an increasing military presence, curfews, checkpoints, and the construction of a security fence that took 8.6 percent of the West Bank, with the latter declared not to be a final border.[65] None of this was a favorable outcome for Palestinians.

The Presidency of George W. Bush and the Government of Ariel Sharon

A year and a half after taking office, President George W. Bush declared his support for a Palestinian state but urged changes in Palestinian leadership. Arafat's exit was necessary because he was more of an obstacle than a positive element in the equation. The continuation of terrorist attacks against Israel involved groups associated with Fatah. Likewise, in 2002 Israeli forces intercepted the *Karine A*, a Palestinian ship illegally carrying more than fifty tons of arms from Iran to the PA. According to the Oslo agreements, the PA was forbidden from procuring weapons.

The operation involved cooperation between Fatah and the pro-Iran group Hezbollah, considered by Israel and the United States to be a terrorist group.[66] Thus, Arafat as president of the Palestinian Authority, head of the PLO and Fatah was seen as part of the problem and not interested in promoting a solution. The interception of

Karine A came as the U.S was already deeply involved in the global war against terrorism, a war launched in the aftermath of the Al Qaeda attacks in New York and Washington on September 11, 2001. Thus, the *Karine A* episode diminished Arafat's credibility in Bush's eyes. [67]

Terrorist activities continued to force Israel to enter the Palestinian territories in order to destroy the sources of terrorism. During Operation "Defensive Shield" (April 2002), the IDF temporarily seized parts of the West Bank that belonged to Area A. President Bush then urged, in a historic speech on 24 June 2002, the democratization and reform of the Palestinian Authority. He also reaffirmed his support for a Palestinian state. This was to be implemented by the establishment of a new plan whose formal title was "A Performance-Based Roadmap to a Permanent Two-State Solution to the Israeli-Palestinian Conflict," also known as "The Roadmap."[68]

The Roadmap was to be implemented in three phases. Phase I compelled the PA to end all terrorist activity and violence. Israel would also be obliged to freeze all settlement activity and remove settlement outposts erected after March 2001. Phase I also required subordinating the Palestinian Security Forces into three services reporting to a new Interior Minister rather than to Arafat. Likewise, funds given to the PA would be kept out of Arafat's hands, and a Prime Minister with empowered executive authority was to be appointed to carry out the functions of government, including Palestinian institutional reform.

Phase II would include a large international conference between the parties, including Arab countries and restoration of some Arab ties with Israel.

Phase III would include a second international conference that would lead to a final status agreement between the Israelis and the Palestinians, and add any finishing touches to issues such as borders, Jerusalem, refugees, and settlements. It would also include a comprehensive agreement to normalize relations between Israel and other Arab countries.[69] No new phase would start without completion of the previous one, and they would occur in chronological order.

Arafat agreed under pressure to appoint Mahmoud Abbas as Prime Minister in March 2003. Abbas was seen by Israeli Prime

Minister Ariel Sharon and Bush as the man who could bring peace and democracy to the Palestinians. His record as a moderate and architect of the Beilin-Abu Mazen accord seem to have offered more hope. Nevertheless, Abbas and Arafat had a tense relationship. Although Abbas was undermined by Arafat and ultimately forced to resign, Arafat's death in 2004 catapulted Abbas into the presidency of the PA, a position he continues to hold.

Unfortunately, it was too late to reverse the existing situation and its dynamics. On the Palestinian side, terror continued without end. Israelis were terrified and were forced to manage the situation on their own since the PA was not capable of controlling it. Internal divisions, the constant threat of Hamas, and other elements paralyzed the PA government. Abbas attempted to achieve reconciliation with Hamas through a series of truces, but bloody fights erupted between the two groups. The PA's weakness was evident during the civil war that erupted in the aftermath of the Israeli withdrawal from Gaza in 2005. The quarrel climaxed with the coup d'état that Hamas perpetrated against Fatah in the summer of 2007 and which put an end to PA sovereignty over Gaza. The coup was ruthless; Fatah loyalists were murdered mercilessly, including being thrown from buildings to their deaths.

On the Israeli side, a new election gave Sharon a fresh victory in January 2003 after a coalition crisis. Sharon's cabinet approved "The Roadmap" shortly afterwards in May 2003. Furthermore, a day after the cabinet decision, Sharon delivered an unprecedented speech before a Likud Party meeting in Haifa where he spoke of the unsustainability of the occupation. Sharon stated:

> You may not like the word, but what is happening is an occupation—to hold 3.5 million Palestinians under occupation. I believe that is a terrible thing for Israel and for the Palestinians... [The occupation] can't continue endlessly... Do you want to stay forever in Jenin, in Nablus, in Ramallah, in Bethlehem? I don't think that's right.[70]

That speech reflected the conclusion reached by Rabin and a large sector of the Israeli public that the occupation was no longer viable, and that there must be some sort of divorce from the Palestinians in the West Bank and Gaza. The speech was public, before a hawkish audience. It made the Israeli Prime Minister accountable and also put him at risk of losing many supporters in his own party. In a speech at the White House Sharon reiterated this view:

> It is in Israel's interest not to govern the Palestinians but for the Palestinians to govern themselves in their own state. A democratic Palestinian State fully at peace with Israel will promote the long-term security and well-being of Israel as a Jewish state.[71]

As previously mentioned, Sharon did not display any confidence in Arafat and firmly believed Arafat was the same terrorist he had always been. However, he believed that Abbas was different from Arafat and a man of good intentions. Abbas appeared to confirm that view, which was also shared by Washington. When on the same day Sharon delivered his speech to the White House, Abbas delivered his own:

> A new opportunity for peace exists, an opportunity based upon President Bush's vision and the quarter's road map, which we have accepted without any reservations. Our goal is two states, Israel and Palestine, living side by side in peace and security. The process is one of direct negotiations to end the Israeli-Palestinian conflict and to resolve all permanent status issues and end the occupation that began in 1967 under which Palestinians suffered so much. At the same time, we do not ignore the suffering of the Jews throughout history. It is time to bring all this suffering to an end.[72]

Yet, Abbas was unable to stop terrorism, regardless of his good intentions. Arafat continued to control the security forces and constantly undermined him, as terrorism ceaselessly continued.[73] Thus, Sharon introduced an initiative to unilaterally disengage from the Palestinians in 2003.

Despite the setbacks and disappointments on the Palestinian side, surprising developments took place. The hawkish Sharon had already accepted the idea that holding the Palestinian territories was not in the long-term interest of Israel due to the demographic threat they could represent to the Jewish majority. Sharon proposed a unilateral withdrawal from Gaza and dismantlement of the settlements in the Strip and the northern West Bank. These ideas split the right-wing Likud Party. It was then that Sharon decided to leave Likud to found a new party called Kadima. Many in the Palestinian camp received the Gaza disengagement proposal with cynicism. The argument was mainly that the disengagement plan was a cynical attempt to build settlements in the West Bank and annex Greater Israel. [74] Yet, nothing seemed to confirm those suspicions. Sharon's own Likud party turned down the proposal to put such withdrawal to a referendum and later also rejected Sharon's initiative to bring the Labor Party into the governing coalition in order to create a majority for disengagement. Furthermore, many in the Likud party joined the opposition in repudiating Sharon's address to the nation at the beginning of the winter term of Israel's parliament.[75] Sharon finally won a parliamentary majority thanks to the support of the Left.

Why would Sharon break with his traditional political alliances and make common cause with the Left if his intention in withdrawing from the Gaza Strip was to take over the West Bank? Part of this Palestinian cynicism was the result of the letter President Bush sent Sharon in April 2004. In that letter Bush points out the following:

> As part of a final peace settlement, Israel must have secure and recognized borders, which should emerge from negotiations between the parties in accordance with UNSC Resolutions 242 and 338. In light of new realities on the ground, including already existing major Israeli populations centers, it is unrealistic to expect that the outcome of final status negotiations will be a full and complete return to the armistice lines of 1949, and all previous efforts to negotiate a two-state solution have reached the same conclusion. It is realistic to expect that any final status agreement will only be achieved on the basis of mutually agreed changes that reflect these realities.[76]

This part was widely interpreted as an American green light to build settlements in the West Bank. However, the Bush letter accepted the fact that certain population centers already established in the West Bank would remain part of Israel under a final peace agreement. The letter is careful enough to stress the fact that any final status would require the consent of the Palestinian negotiating partner. Furthermore, the letter makes clear that Israel cannot set the final borders or establish a political status quo unilaterally:

> ...certain responsibilities face the State of Israel. Among these, your government has stated that the barrier being erected by Israel should be a security rather than a political barrier, should be temporary rather than permanent, and therefore not prejudice any final status issues including final borders, and its route should take into account, consistent with security needs, its impact on Palestinians not engaged in terrorist activities...As you know, the United States supports the establishment of a Palestinian state that is viable, contiguous, sovereign, and independent, so that the Palestinian people can build their own future in accordance with my vision set forth in June 2002 and with the path set forth in the roadmap.[77]

It is indeed a Palestinian state that Bush had in mind and not the Israeli annexation of Area C. Sharon's incessant fight with the Likud, his recruitment of support from the Left, and his ultimate departure from the Likud to form a new party reflected the significance of Sharon's beliefs.

Sharon pointed out that the occupation of 3.5 million Palestinians would affect the Jewish character of the State of Israel. It would be logical to assume that Sharon also thought that annexation of the West Bank (with the possible exception of the "settlement blocs") would not be less dangerous to a Jewish majority than the annexation of Gaza.

After the withdrawal from Gaza, southern towns in Israel became vulnerable to Hamas rocket attacks, raising concerns among the Israelis about the wisdom of the withdrawal. Likewise, the situation showed the risks involved in the disengagement, which was opposed by several Israeli military officers precisely because they believed it would leave Israel vulnerable to attacks from Gaza.[78] These arguments were unfortunately proven to be correct. In less than 10 years after the withdrawal from Gaza, Israel was forced to fight two major wars in Gaza and one limited incursion. All this without counting the continuing surgical strikes against militants and their operations.

However, the withdrawal from Gaza was due to the desperate need of Israel to separate from the Palestinians, which in practical terms meant ending the occupation. It was thought to be a trial run before a significant withdrawal from the West Bank. The peace process was totally frozen before the disengagement primarily because of the inability of the PA to exercise control over terrorism. This was further aggravated by the collapse of the PA in Gaza at the hands of Hamas in June 2007. This event was the final chapter of a violent tension that existed between Fatah and Hamas after the latter won a parliamentary victory. During that period, hundreds of Palestinian men, women, and children were killed by Hamas militants who attacked, not only individuals but also PA institutions, including its security services and officials.[79]

Ironically, the Hamas putsch came even as a Saudi-mediated reconciliation agreement between Hamas and Fatah had concluded a few months earlier in the city of Mecca, Saudi Arabia. Israel's disengagement may have facilitated the Hamas takeover of Gaza, but the PA was already undergoing a legitimacy crisis because Palestinians perceived it as a corrupt entity. The 2006 Palestinian parliamentary elections won by Hamas were proof of this legitimacy crisis. But during the Hamas takeover of Gaza, there were some Fatah members who cooperated with Hamas or deserted to Hamas' side. Many Fatah officers fled despite having a better equipped fighting unit than Hamas.[80]

This episode further reflects the PA's crisis. Already in the year 2005, the Palestinian chief negotiator Saeb Erekat acknowledged that the PA did not have "bullets to fight [Hamas and the Islamic Jihad] for even 10 minutes."[81] Furthermore, he acknowledged that Hamas had the power of a parallel authority.[82]

Thus, not surprisingly, in the aftermath of Hamas's coup d'état in Gaza, the Americans and Israelis rushed to save the PA by increasing security cooperation. Furthermore, the U.S and Israel tried to boost the economic development of the PA. Abbas appointed Salam Fayyad as Prime Minister of the newly created Palestinian Emergency Government. Created in the aftermath of the Hamas takeover of Gaza, the Palestinian Emergency Government was comprised of twelve ministers, most of them technocrats associated with Fatah. However, the government also included representation from diverse sectors of the West Bank including Christians, women, representatives from East Jerusalem, from refugee camps and even from the Gaza Strip. The idea was to show Palestinian unity. Abbas stated that the government would bear full responsibility not only for the West Bank but for the Gaza Strip as well. He also added that his government represented "one police force, one law and one legitimate gun for the entire homeland".[83] Fayyad, a pragmatic economist who received his doctorate in the United States and served previously as the PA's Minister of Finance, pointed out that the new government's top priority would be to put an end to anarchy and restore order and the rule of law. [84] In fact, however, a situation of multiple sovereignty with one Fatah-led government in the West Bank and a Hamas-led government in Gaza was to remain the reality of the Palestinians until this very day despite repeated Israeli military operations against Hamas in Gaza.

Although there were improvements in economic and security cooperation between the Palestinian Authority and Israel, the situation was already beyond repair. Western fear of Hamas had made Abbas immune to international criticism despite the fact that corruption in the PA was rampant, persecution of political enemies was routine, human rights were consistently violated and peace with Israel was not achieved. Likewise, younger generations, who demanded reform and transparency in the PA, were excluded from any important decision-making roles.[85]

Yet, the PA's authoritarian methods did not suffice to counteract the threat of Hamas that continued to claim power over the entire PA. Such an unstable condition of dual power provided limited hope for a peace deal. Abbas' international immunity also increased the pressure on Israel to deliver peace despite the serious governability and legitimacy problems the PA faced. These conditions made it impossible for him to sign a credible peace agreement. Yet Abbas became the only hope for achieving peace with Israel. Securing his political survival was crucial with the prospect of no other alternative. He took good advantage of the situation, but, unfortunately, only to secure his own survival.

The Peace Offer of Israeli Prime Minister Ehud Olmert

Sharon's successor, Ehud Olmert, was elected Prime Minister by an Israeli public emotionally fatigued by the Second Intifada and eager to solve the Palestinian question with or without negotiations. Olmert moved to implement a unilateral withdrawal from Gaza.

U.S Secretary of State Condoleezza Rice began to apply heavy pressure on Olmert to reach a final status agreement. But the question remained: Why would the Israelis take the risk of signing a peace agreement with an entity that was so unstable?

Nothing could assure the Israelis that the PA had full control of the situation, despite the progress made by Prime Minister Salam Fayyad's government since his appointment in 2007.[86]

Some in Israel assessed that there had been no progress made on security.[87] Still, despite these objections Olmert took the chance and made an offer to the Palestinians. Olmert was in a very delicate position as well, although not nearly as delicate as Abbas. His popularity as Prime Minister was at a record low. His poor management of the 2006 military operation against Hezbollah in Lebanon and accusations of corruption significantly weakened Olmert and eventually led to his resignation.

Even under these circumstances, Olmert made an offer to Abbas. According to Olmert and later confirmed by others, including senior Palestinian advisor Saeb Erekat, the offer included a little under ninety-four percent of the West Bank with land swaps to make up for the 6.3 percent taken from the West Bank. These land swaps would include 5.8 percent from Israeli lands and 0.5 percent for a projected link between Gaza and the West Bank. The Palestinians would claim East Jerusalem as their capital, while Israel, the Palestinians, Jordan and the United States would jointly govern the Old City, including the holy sites. The Saudis would also be included, provided that they recognize the State of Israel. The Arab neighborhoods would be part of the Palestinian state and the Jewish neighborhoods part of Israel. An international force would be posted in the Jordan Valley to protect the Palestinian-Jordanian border. There would be no "right of return" for five years, with the exception of between three and four thousand Palestinian refugees per year.[88]

Abbas, however, accepted no less than the June 1967 borders "without detracting one single inch and without detracting a single stone from Jerusalem, or from the holy Christian and Muslim places."[89] This was not the first time Palestinians made this demand. During the negotiations with Israel in early 2000, then Palestinian Prime Minister Abu Ala claimed that the borders of the Palestinian state have been determined by resolution 242, and that these borders are the pre-Six-Day War line. Therefore, as Indyk observed from the Palestinian viewpoint:

> ...all historical Palestine was rightfully theirs and had been taken away from them by force. In accepting Resolution 242 they had explicitly recognized Israel's right to control 78 percent of the territories of the Palestinian mandate. Now they argued it was unfair to be expected to bargain over 22 percent that encompassed the West Bank and Gaza. Arafat and Abu Ala would be judged by his people according to one standard alone: how much of that 22 percent he gave away.[90]

In Arafat's view, he had already conceded recognition of Israel in the 1988 Algiers Declaration.[91] He did not need to give further concessions. Now, it was the responsibility solely of the other side to do its part.[92]

If this is the case, the Palestinians never felt they needed to concede anything to Israel or recognize its needs. However, the reality is that the PA was too weak to accept any offer or compromise with Israel, believing that it would leave them vulnerable to attacks domestically and from the greater Arab world. There are those who try to make sense of the Palestinian attitude or justify its claims such as the Geneva Initiative group- a group of high profile moderate Palestinian and Israelis who presented a peace plan in the middle of the Israeli-Palestinian violence. In the group's own words:

Barak and Olmert offered the Palestinians realistic proposals only when they were already on their way out of office. It is true that Ehud Barak's proposal in Camp David did go further than any previous Israeli proposal, but it was far from anything the Palestinians could viably accept. Olmert's proposal was submitted at the end of his term when it was clear his resignation as Prime Minister would occur in a matter of days.[93]

These arguments ignore the fact that Barak's offers took place well before he called for new elections in the Knesset. Secondly, if an agreement were to be achieved while both prime ministers were in charge, and the Israeli Knesset approved them, the agreements would be binding. Both prime ministers believed they could get support from the Knesset and the public once the agreement was signed.

The exposure of the documents known as the *Palestine Papers* published by *Al Jazeera* in 2011, painted the Palestinian leadership as traitors. These documents revealed that the Palestinians had considered compromises during secret negotiations with the Olmert government. The documents created shock waves across the Arab world and were strongly condemned by Hamas and even by sectors within the PLO. [94]The fact that the Qatar-based *Al Jazeera* published it with the intention of denouncing the PA, serves as a reminder of the fact that when the Palestinians negotiate, they are not alone in negotiating a mere solution to the Palestinian problem; there is a larger constituency behind them with tacit veto power. Abbas vehemently and angrily denied the veracity of the *Palestine Papers*,[95] confirming that his room for maneuver was limited when it came to compromises in the negotiations.

It is reasonable to assume that Abbas had the Arab and Muslim worlds opinion in mind, as Arafat did when he claimed that Jerusalem transcended the Palestinian issue. The same applies to the "right of return," a demand expressed by Arab states, Hamas and other dissident Palestinian groups. Most importantly, the Palestinian leadership suffered from a tremendous deficit of legitimacy at home and felt its authority was threatened. That problem was further intensified a few years later when the Arab Spring broke out in a number of countries in the Middle East.

The Arab Spring effectively challenged the old secular authoritarian states that had ruled the Arab world for decades. This posed a challenge to the PA as well. Indeed, the PA was facing opposition that it often met with repression, including the arrest of PA critics, crackdowns on the media, and repression of labor strikes and union leaders. Most notably, the PA responded to a teachers' strike in 2016 by outlawing unions, arresting labor leaders and replacing them with PA proxies, even targeting union members with violence. The PA also established checkpoints in the West Bank to deter people from attending the protests. According to Abbas biographers Grant Rumley and Amir Tibon, the PA's crackdown against the press in the West Bank was even worse than Hamas' repressive treatment of the media in Gaza.[96]

Anti-Abbas sentiments have spread throughout several major Palestinian cities, including the West Bank cities of Tulkarem, Nablus and Ramallah. Furthermore, Abbas has lost touch with civil society, avoiding meetings with mayors and other people who attend to the needs of local populations. Repression, rather than dialogue has been the PA's response under Abbas to any act of criticism or protest. A former head of the public employees' union pointed out that Abbas is "incapable of dealing with internal issues [97] A member of Fatah's Central Committee expects more protests to spread in the West Bank, as the "PA had conducted itself in a wrongful fashion."[98] Former members of Fatah have predicted that "the situation will explode. And once it does, no one will be able to contain us."[99]

It is reasonable to assume that the PA is fully aware that it is facing a legitimacy crisis exactly like the one the old Arab regimes have. As Samir Awed, a political science professor from Birzeit University has pointed out: "The Palestinian situation does not differ much from that of other Arab people and regimes, despite the fact that Palestinians have defined their major contradiction with the Israeli occupation. This does not mean that experiences of the neighboring Arab people will pass without affecting Palestine, entailing demands for more freedoms, democracy and fighting against corruption." [100]

The Palestinian leadership is in no rush to create a Palestinian state because there is no incentive to create one. Abbas is immune to international criticism, as the international community and even some in Israel itself view Abbas as the only hope against more radical groups such as Hamas.

Hence, in order to reduce the deficit of legitimacy, Abbas has avoided peace negotiations while at the same time launching a diplomatic war against Israel through the United Nations. The idea has been to secure a Palestinian state through a United Nations resolution knowing the Israelis will never accept a non-negotiated Palestinian state. In other words, a Palestinian state would exist *de jure* and not *de facto*. In this way, Abbas avoids the responsibility of being in charge of a troubled state while enjoying some legal and political advantages that such enhanced international status provides. Palestinians could then bring Israelis to the international court of justice, use the United Nations Educational, Scientific and Cultural Organization (UNESCO) to fight Israel's sovereignty over sites, and make use of other international mechanisms to delegitimize Israel.

In this way, the Palestinian leadership can gain points among its most extremist detractors and at the same time continue to enjoy the status of victim and avoid hard decisions. Israel has become an external scapegoat to be blamed for Palestinian failures to achieve peace. Furthermore, by delaying the creation of a Palestinian state, Abbas is able to enjoy the financial and political support of the international community and, ironically, the protection provided through its security cooperation with Israel. This attitude and behavior characterized Palestinian actions throughout the tenure of United States President Barack Obama, who tried hard to achieve a peace agreement and displayed sympathy for the Palestinian cause.

Peace Proposals under President Obama

President Obama's election in 2008 coincided with the election of Benjamin Netanyahu as Prime Minister of Israel after a ten-year absence from that office. Netanyahu was elected following an entire decade of Israeli Prime Ministers willing to compromise, and very much conscious of the need to separate from the Palestinians and maintain Israeli security. Barak and Olmert showed willingness to make big compromises. Sharon unilaterally withdrew from Gaza

without negotiation. All of these led only to further violence perpetrated by the most radical elements in Palestinian society.

President Obama did not understand the PA's fragile internal
situation. For Obama, Netanyahu appeared as the perfect symbol
of Israeli intransigency. The newly formed Jewish group, J-Street,
which began its ascendancy as a pro-peace lobbying group, believed that peace would become a reality once Israel stopped building settlements in the West Bank. Thus, the key to peace based on a
two-state solution should be the result of effective American pressure on Israel. In their view, the traditional pro-Israel lobby, the
American Israel Public Affairs Committee (AIPAC), is allied with
the Israeli right wing and too indulgent of Israeli settlement policy. AIPAC is an obstacle because it protects Israel from American
pressure, the key ingredient for a peace agreement based on the
two-state solution, in J Street's view.

Obama, who in principle agreed with the philosophy of
J-Street,[101] proceeded to promote peace by demanding a total freeze
on Israeli settlements. This freeze would apply to all territory taken
by Israel after 1967 and include natural growth, for example the construction of new houses and schools.[102] Jerusalem neighborhoods
such as Armon Hantaziv, Gilo, Ramat Eshkol, Ramat Shlomo, Neve
Yaakov, Pisgat Zeev and others, were built on empty lands taken
after 1967. They are extensions of the city and are homes to well
over half of the Jewish population of Jerusalem.[103] As we pointed
out earlier, Bush's letter to Sharon in April 2004 recognized the fact
that towns and regions built next to the 1967 Green Line should
remain part of Israel, as they contain the majority of the settlers and
constitute an important security buffer for Israel.

It is true that a settlement freeze was recommended by the 2001
Mitchell Report and was part of The Roadmap" established after
Bush's speech on June 24, 2002. It is also true that settlement construction has grown dramatically since the beginning of the Oslo
peace process. Indeed, in 1995 there were 120,000 Jews living in
the settlements, and by 2016 that number rose to 400,000. Yet, the
overwhelming majority of the settlers live in Jewish neighborhoods
in East Jerusalem or in towns close to the Green line, known as
"settlement blocs."[104] This territory could be exchanged for other
land in Israel proper as part of a peace agreement and in fact Israel

did offer quality land in exchange for the settlement blocs. Still, it is important to point out that the settlement blocs in some cases prevent the contiguity of Palestinian territory. Likewise, the roads built to connect these settlements have taken some Palestinian private property.

Bush recognized the fact that some of the settlement blocs would remain part of Israel in any arrangement. Even those Palestinians, many of them influential figures, who negotiated the non-binding Geneva Accords, agreed to Israel's annexation of some settlement blocs in exchange for equal land swaps. Yet, the Obama administration confronted the Israelis over construction in Ramat Shlomo, a Jerusalem neighborhood where Palestinians have never lived and that very few Israelis even remember was once part of Jordan. The Geneva Accords also established that Ramat Shlomo would be part of Israel.

The Obama administration also confronted Israel on construction of settlements in Gilo, a 40-year-old Jerusalem neighborhood with 40,000 residents. Obama's broad generalizations on settlements failed to distinguish between a well-established area in a legitimate part of a settlement bloc, and a remote outpost on a West Bank hilltop located in an area heavily populated by Palestinians.[105]

As the anti-settlement Israeli organization Peace Now has explained, the settlement bloc concept has not been properly defined and, as a result, remains somewhat ambiguous.[106] As we pointed out in the introduction, the Oslo agreements sought to delay issues and allow them to evolve with the negotiations. Therefore, nothing "in-between" was defined, and everything was postponed to the so-called final status. This is why the Bush administration tried to place geographical limits on settlement construction.

Yet, the settlement question is definitely part of the Oslo Accords' open-ended terms designed to postpone issues to the final status negotiations. This has led to abuses by Israeli authorities, including not only increasing the number of settlers, but also expropriating land to build public roads that often benefitted the settlers. Moreover, construction in Area C, where Israel has full military control, is open to Jewish settlers but is closed to Palestinian Arabs.[107]

In May 2015, Prime Minister Netanyahu suggested negotiating with the Palestinians on the issue of legitimate and illegitimate areas for construction in order to solve the problem of the definition of settlement blocs. Palestinians refused.[108] Furthermore, some have argued that settlement activity is killing the peace process, since those settlements are creating irreversible facts on the ground. However, as Middle East expert and former advisor on Obama's Middle East team, David Makovsky, has revealed, the settlements at this point have not created a *fait accompli*. Borders can indeed be adjusted to include the large majority of West Bank settlers and still reach a territorial compromise with the Palestinians where the latter can enjoy a state on a substantial piece of territory. In his view, the two-state solution remains viable, and it is still possible to establish a Palestinian state based on land swaps.[109]

Under the Obama administration timeline, the Palestinians hardly convened with the Israelis to discuss peace, despite an Israeli 10-month moratorium on construction. Secretary of State John Kerry went to great lengths to try to find reasonable proposals to increase momentum in the peace process. In March 2014, Obama presented Abbas with a proposal that was more generous than what the Israelis had agreed to and received no response from Abbas.[110] The proposal called for an arrangement based on the 1967 borders with mutually agreed on land swaps and for a solution to the refugee issue that would not come at the expense of the Jewish character of Israel. It also called for East Jerusalem to be the capital of the state of Palestine.[111] This, according to Tibon and Rumley, was "the best peace offer the Palestinians had received" since the Clinton parameters were presented in 2000.[112] As Steve Simon, a former director of the Middle East desk at the National Security Council in the Obama Administration pointed out:

> Kerry sketched out the terms of a grand bargain: Israel would release the fourth tranche (of prisoners), plus another 400 prisoners of its own choosing and forgo all new announcements of settlement construction throughout the West Bank (excluding Jerusalem). In return Abbas would agree to a nine-month extension of the talks… an agreement appeared to be within reach on April 23 (2014). One can

therefore imagine (the) surprise when Abbas repudiated the deal that evening in the most provocative way possible by signing a unity agreement with Hamas. [113]

Saeb Erekat, the Palestinian chief negotiator, had already announced to Israeli Justice Minister Tzipi Livni that the Palestinians had decided to take the UN route.[114]

In fact, it was on Obama's watch that the Palestinians effectively sought to delegitimize the role of the United States as a mediator in the conflict with Israel and began appealing to the UN instead. The Palestinians sought unilateral recognition of a Palestinian state by lobbying different countries. The Latin American region was the first to break with the traditional neutral position when then-Brazilian president Luis Inácio "Lula" da Silva stated that the United States had proven incapable of fairly mediating the Israeli-Palestinian conflict.[115] But the crux of the issue is that the settlement obsession ignored the real problem. As former United States negotiator Aaron David Miller, an opponent of settlements explained:

> But even if the settlement issue were resolved today, negotiations would still confront another galactic challenge: a crisis within the Palestinian national movement, with two authorities governing two discreet areas with two different security services, two different patrons and two different visions of the Palestinian future. The upshot of the battle between Hamas and the Palestinian Authority is that without a monopoly over the forces of violence in Palestinian society—without one authority to silence the guns and rockets—no agreement can be implemented.[116]

This is the reason why Obama and Kerry's peace initiatives failed.

Conclusion

Israeli opposition leader Isaac Herzog from the Labor Party presented a plan in early 2016 for unilateral disengagement from parts of the West Bank, acknowledging that, for now, there was no partner for peace.[117] The UN declaration of a Palestinian state has not led to a Palestinian state because the problem of Palestinian weakness would still persist. The idea of getting a Palestinian state recognized at the UN is a strategy to continue the propaganda war, take Israel to court, and even challenge its guardianship of the Temple Mount as happened in April and October 2016, when the PA managed to pass resolutions in the United Nations Educational, Scientific and Cultural Organization (UNESCO) erasing the Jewish connection to the Western Wall.

It appears that the struggle the Palestinian leadership faces is not about the future of the Palestinian people or a Palestinian state. It is about delaying any decisions to be made and perpetuating the status quo. A real Palestinian state would expose the PA to a "Palestinian Spring" like those that have broken out in the larger Arab world. The PA's crisis of legitimacy is expressed in the fact that it has not held elections since 2006 and has ruled by decree. This is an indication that the PA views any input from Palestinian civil society as a threat to its rule.

This situation of illegitimacy persists, as indicated in a 2017 survey conducted by the Palestinian Center for Policy and Survey Research, which found that two-thirds of Palestinians want Abbas to resign. Furthermore, and interestingly enough, the Palestinian public blames the Palestinian leadership, factions and political parties for the continuation of the Israeli occupation.[118] This shows not only the crisis of legitimacy of the Palestinian leadership on domestic grounds, but also that the Palestinian people hold it accountable for the failures of peace negotiations.

Thus, the continuation of the conflict, on the one hand, excuses the Palestinian leadership from the responsibility of taking the reins of a Palestinian state, thereby preventing its imminent downfall. The PA's weakness in the context of Palestinian society and politics remains the main obstacle to peace between Israelis and Palestinians.

The obvious fact is that the PA lacks the ability to rule over its own people. As a result, Abbas and the PA have adopted a strategy of survival in the face of internal threats. This strategy is based on turning against Israel and the peace process.

In the next chapter, we will discuss how the PA's policy of anti-Israel propaganda is aimed at appeasing those very forces that have defied it. This policy has exacerbated the crisis and led to the stagnation and virtual death of the peace process. In the next chapter, we will also analyze the long-term consequences that this PA strategy might have for future prospects for peace.

CHAPTER 2

THE PERMANENT
PALESTINIAN REVOLUTION

The weakness of the Palestinian Authority in the face of internal challenges led it to start a propaganda campaign against Israel. Desperately seeking to appease its overwhelming internal enemies and to regain popularity among fellow Palestinians, the PA turned its peace partner into a fierce enemy. Fear of Islamists and those who challenge the PA have forced the latter to adopt an even tougher tone towards Israel.

Palestinian mobilization and exposure to propaganda is not a new phenomenon. Palestinian public opinion has historically been galvanized by nationalists, and later by Islamists. This chapter will describe how the Palestinians have been mobilized into a state of perpetual revolution, and how this phenomenon adversely affects the chances of peace today.

Development of Palestinian Mobilization

During the early 20th century, Palestinian Arabs did not have a nationalist ideology. Palestinian nationalism is the product of the colonial period. Its content was determined by the confrontation with the Zionist movement and the rise of nationalism throughout the Arab world.[1] Residents of Palestine viewed themselves as either Arab or Muslim, but not necessarily as a people separate from the larger Arab or Muslim world. According to Palestinian American historian Rashid Khalidi, Palestinians were deeply attracted to Arab nationalism, first of all because Arab nationalism and later Pan-Arabism were similar to other supra-national ideologies that the Palestinians had identified with in the past: Ottomanism, when

Palestine was part of the Ottoman Empire; Arabism, which empha-sized Arab identity; and Pan-Syrianism, which stressed the identity of the former Ottoman province of Syria of which Palestine was a part. Pan-Arabism gave Palestinian refugees a sense of identity and protection because they were living in Arab countries. Like-wise, Pan-Arabism held the promise of liberating Palestine through a joint Arab effort.[2]

As Professor James Gelvin has pointed out, at the end of World War I, after the collapse of the Ottoman Empire, many, particularly among the Palestinian-Arab educated elite, adopted the idea that Arabs comprise one single nation. Yet, other inhabitants of Palestine saw themselves as Syrians since they were originally inhabitants of the Ottoman province of Syria, which was an economically inte-grated unit under the Ottomans. They had commercial and famil-ial connections to Damascus and other cities in the province, such as Beirut, where they travelled freely back and forth. The division created under the British and French mandate isolated Palestinian Arabs and contributed to the development of their later identity.[3] Thus, they advocated for a solution in which Palestine would be part of a larger united Arab entity.[4]

This is why local Palestinian Arabs fought the Jews in 1948. However, once the local Arabs lost the war, the conflict transformed into an Arab-Israeli war. In the aftermath of 1948, Palestinian Ar-abs, with the exception of those who stayed and became citizens of the State of Israel, became refugees.

Thereafter, the period beginning with the revolution of the free officers in Egypt (1952), was dominated by Pan-Arabism. This polit-ical stream, led by Gamal Abdel Nasser of Egypt, viewed the Arab world as united under one sovereign rule and not separated into different states. The idea of Pan-Arabism was based on the premise that the Arabs are a single people with a single language, history and culture. The existing divisions among Arabs, in the Pan-Ara-bists' perspective, are not the result of a natural order, but rather the result of imperialistic machinations and foreign rule.

Between 1949 and 1967, Egypt, which ruled Gaza, and Jordan, which controlled the West Bank, did not allow discussion of Pales-tinian self-determination in the territories.[5] The idea of Arab unity, in the words of Oxford scholar and Lebanon-born Albert Hourani, was that,

Arab states had enough in common, in shared culture and historical experience as well as shared interests, to make it possible for them to come into close union with each other, and such a union would not only give them greater collective power but would bring about that moral unity between people and government which would make government legitimate and stable.[6]

Pan-Arabism holds that the bonds uniting Arab countries are stronger than the bonds connecting Arab and non-Arab Muslim countries. This may explain why Pan-Arabism emerged originally from Christian Arabs and was embraced by Christian Arabs more than non-Arab Muslims. Michel Aflaq, a Syrian Christian considered the preeminent intellectual of Pan-Arabism and one of the founders of the ruling Syrian Baath party, asserted that there should be a single Arab nation living under a single unified state. According to Aflaq, the origin of the Arab nation is rooted in the founding of Islam by the Prophet Muhammad and "the society which embodied it."[7] However, "this experience belonged not only to Arab Muslims, but to all Arabs who appropriated it as their own, and regarded it as the basis of their claim to have a special mission in the world and a right to independence and unity."[8]

With this political philosophy and the political dominance of Pan-Arabism in Egypt and Syria, the most influential countries in the area, it seemed as though the Palestinians' destiny was to be part of the greater Arab nation. What mattered in terms of "Palestinian rights" were not national Palestinian rights *per se*, but rather the recovery of Arab sovereignty over the land.

In addition, this great Arab nation, which would be based on socialism and nationalism, needed to defeat the obsolete monarchies of the past. In Nasser's view, the Arab defeat in 1948 at the hands of Israel reflected the decadence of the Arab monarchies. Thus, the rally against Israel was in the name of Arab unity and against the outdated, inept regimes, and the existing monarchies that failed to defeat Israel. This may explain why Nasser's foreign policy within the Arab world was considerably aggressive toward other Arab regimes with ties to colonial powers. For instance, one of Nasser's aims was to remove any British influence from the protectorates in Sudan, Yemen, and the Persian Gulf.

Along the same lines, Nasser provided aid to the rebels fighting for Algerian independence from France. In addition, the Egyptian president challenged the Hashemite government of Iraq to end the Baghdad Pact, a strategic alliance formed with Britain in 1955 against the Soviet Union.

In 1962, Nasser dispatched 70,000 troops to wage war in Yemen against those groups that were supported by the Saudi Monarchy. He also conducted campaigns of subversion against the governments of Saudi Arabia, Jordan, and Tunisia. He backed the Adeni Marxist party in Yemen and the Algerian revolutionary Ahmed Ben Bella as well as Muammar Gaddafi in Libya.

For Pan-Arabism, anti-imperialism, anti-Zionism, and anti-monarchism were more important than any Palestinian right, whether individual or collective. This explains why most Arab countries, with the notable exception of Jordan, signed the Casablanca Protocol in 1965, which stipulated that Arab countries should guarantee Palestinian refugees the rights to employment, residency, and freedom of movement, while also denying them the right to citizenship. Indeed, not granting citizenship to Palestinians was an attempt to preserve their identity as refugees destined to suffer from the consequences of exile, thereby exacerbating anti-Zionist sentiment and justifying the continuation of war against Israel. Furthermore, Nasser orchestrated the creation of the PLO and appointed its first chairman, Ahmad Shukairy, who oversaw the Palestinian National Charter, a document that called for the establishment of an Arab Palestinian state over all of historical Palestine.

However, as Gelvin explains, "By making the PLO a wholly owned subsidiary of the Arab League, Nasser hoped to ensure that the liberation of Palestine would remain an Arab problem" and not an exclusively Palestinian problem.[9] Nonetheless, Israel's military victory over Arab countries in June 1967 obliterated the hopes of Palestinians who thought their problem would be resolved through the destruction of Israel by a Pan-Arab coalition. The Palestinians were condemned to live under Israeli military occupation or among other Arabs as second-class citizens. This was coupled with the disappointment over the Arab countries' inability to defeat Israel. Together, this provided a framework of consciousness through which the Palestinians began to organize their strategy to take back what they considered their land.

Under the PLO's leadership, the Palestinians sought to redefine their problem. The issue was now not just an Arab-Israeli conflict, where the Palestinians were merely displaced individuals requiring assistance. Now, the Palestinians were a nation and a people deprived of their land.

The Palestinian National Charter adopted in July 1968 emphasized the political and national rights of the Palestinian people, which transcended "the disasters which have befallen the Palestinians."[10] The Palestinian National Charter defined the Palestinian identity as:

> ... a genuine, essential, and inherent characteristic; it is transmitted from parents to children. The Zionist occupation and the dispersal of the Palestinian Arab people, through the disasters which befell them, do not make them lose their Palestinian identity and their membership in the Palestinian community, nor do they negate them.[11]

Likewise, the Charter identifies the existence of "a Palestinian community that has material, spiritual, and historical connection with Palestine."[12] Therefore, "it is a national duty to bring up individual Palestinians in an Arab revolutionary manner... [The Palestinian] must be prepared for the armed struggle and ready to sacrifice his wealth and his life in order to win back his homeland and bring about its liberation."[13] Collective goals supersede individual goals.

The Charter proceeds to adopt the language of the League of Nations by invoking the Palestinian people's "right to self-determination."[14] As Shaul Mishal and Avraham Selah point out, "The Palestinian national movement, like others in the third world, mystified the land that was defined by the British mandate from the Jordan River to the Mediterranean Sea, and gave the land a mythological status of a historical fatherland."[15] Thus, the Palestinians claimed to have rights over the indivisible territorial unit of British Mandate Palestine.

Before 1918 the area that became known as Palestine was part of a larger Ottoman province of Syria. The concept of the Palestinian people as a nation was introduced in the late 1960s, allowing them to transcend their refugee status and create a new identity. This concept became a focus for mobilizing Palestinians worldwide. The Palestinians also had a strong sense of mission, in which they held themselves to be spiritually superior and more motivated than the rest of the Arab world. This transformed the Palestinians into the most mobilized and determined group in the Middle East.[16] Article 10 of the Palestinian Charter is eloquent and clear about this revolutionary and militant character of Palestinians in the post-1967 era:

> Commando action constitutes the nucleus of the Palestinian popular liberation war. This requires its escalation, comprehensiveness, and the mobilization of all the Palestinian popular and educational efforts and their organization and involvement in the armed Palestinian revolution. It also requires the achieving of unity for the national (*watani*) struggle among the different groupings of the Palestinian people, and between the Palestinian people and the Arab masses, so as to secure the continuation of the revolution, its escalation, and victory.[17]

Shortly after the Arab defeat in 1967, Fatah tried to mobilize Palestinians by creating small guerilla networks in the West Bank. One episode offered an opportunity for the PLO to mobilize the Palestinian masses. In March of 1968, the IDF attacked guerilla positions in the West Bank, chasing the guerillas into Jordanian territory.

The Jordanian village of Karameh was one of the main bastions of the Palestinian guerillas after they were forced to retreat from the West Bank. In the Battle of Karameh, Fatah fought Israeli forces for 15 hours. In the end, 28 Israelis, about 170 Palestinians, and 100 Jordanians were killed. Israeli forces eventually retreated, likely to prevent escalation with Jordan.

However, for Palestinians, Karameh became a symbol of Palestinian superiority and generated the social myth that it was not the Arab but the Palestinian spirit that can bring Israel to its knees. As historian Mark Tessler noted, a few hours after the battle ended, Karameh became a legend, and Fatah succeeded in recruiting thousands of people in its aftermath.[18]

Karameh also generated mass recruitment for other Palestinian organizations. Karameh was portrayed as a victory and established the myth that Palestinians could do what Arab countries were unable to do, namely defeat Israel. That myth worked for them because it became a symbol of victory to the Palestinian masses and sent a message of "yes we can," even though there was no Palestinian military victory by any definition at Karameh.[19]

The collective excitement generated by Karameh among the Palestinians created a situation in which an attempt to takeover Jordan became a serious threat. King Hussein of Jordan, frightened by such a possibility, proceeded to brutally crush Palestinian organizations in the fall of 1970. He moved against the PLO and others following a string of plane hijackings by the Popular Front for the Liberation of Palestine (PFLP) and other Palestinian factions such as the Popular Democratic Front for the Liberation of Palestine (PDFLP). These groups openly called to remove the Jordanian King because he represented an illegitimate, reactionary force, was a "puppet of implerialism and a "Zionist tool."[20] Despite the unfortunate ending for the Palestinians, Karameh proved to be a myth of enormous psychological and political significance.

The importance of Karameh can be explained by French anarchist-syndicalist Georges Sorel's concept of the general strike. The general strike, according to Sorel, is an act of class war that engages every individual and is therefore more important than relying on ideals that, if not implemented, are likely to die. The general strike maintains the revolutionary momentum of collective action and mass mobilization, vital elements to the revolution. Sorel, whose ideas strongly influenced totalitarian movements, particularly communism and fascism, stated that, "The goal is nothing; the movement is everything."[21] In other words, the use of violence gives a general sense that the movement is active and can achieve victory. In application, this victory would mean the elimination of the state of Israel and the establishment of Palestinian hegemony.

Following this Sorelian logic, Palestinian terrorist activities aimed not just at intimidating the population they attacked, but also served as a propaganda tool to elevate the revolutionary enthusiasm of the masses via violence.[22]

But along with this galvanizing force, the PLO imposed a rule of terror in the occupied territories of the West Bank and Gaza. People suspected of dissent or collaboration with Israelis were severely punished by PLO operatives and supporters. As David Pryce Jones explains:

> [Since 1967] Palestinians have known a daily existence of intrigue and danger, of tacking and trimming, in an atmosphere of plotting each-for-himself, that rapidly turned sinister. Considerations of personal safety came first, as anyone could lose his life on an account of an unguarded remark or a hasty deed. The list of those murdered by the PLO extends to many hundreds, including lawyers and intellectuals who floated ideas of compromise, the Imam of Gaza, bankers and businessmen who took some step which the PLO judged to be against its interest, and of course a majority of peasants accused of collaboration and treason, usually on hearsay, always without a chance of appeal.[23]

The incitement to terror, subjugation, and the killing of fellow Palestinians were intimidation tactics used to coerce people into supporting the PLO. As will be discussed later, terror and fear became important components of what I define as a totalitarian situation, which has had egregious consequences for Palestinian society.

Like a typical revolutionary system, the PLO combined ideological motivation with terror and fear. This revolutionary euphoria also emboldened the PLO to act aggressively in other countries: first in Jordan, from where the organization was ultimately defeated and expelled, and then in Lebanon, where the PLO established and consolidated its base.

Specifically, in Lebanon the number of Palestinian refugees increased from 100,000 to 300,000 after their expulsion from Jordan. Lebanon served as a convenient location from which the PLO could attack Israel. The weakness of the Lebanese government favored the PLO, allowing its militants to move freely within the country without obstacle. The Cairo Agreements signed between the PLO and the government of Lebanon in November 1969 defined the Palestinian presence in the country, securing the Palestinians the right to work, reside, and domestic travel. Likewise, it secured local governing committees in the refugee camps and an internal Palestinian military presence. Finally, according to the agreement, the "Palestinians are to participate in the Palestinian revolution through armed struggle and in accordance with the principles of the sovereignty and security of Lebanon." [24] Subsequently, Southern Lebanon was overwhelmed by armed Palestinian militias.[25]

With the PLO's increasing militarization and presence in Lebanon, Palestinian militias emerged as an important armed force in that country. Armed Palestinian Fedayeen had a presence in the streets of Beirut, and, no less important, in the refugee camps. The Lebanese Army clashed a number of times with Palestinian militias, particularly as Israelis carried out retaliatory operations on the country's soil. The army was not able to control Palestinian militias, bringing about tensions between Arafat and the Lebanese government that angered not only the Lebanese government but also other Arab states. Such isolation brought the PLO closer to the Lebanese Druze. Muslims and Druze sought the assistance of the PLO to fight the Christians. Thus, the PLO joined the Muslim-Druze coalition during the Lebanese civil war that began in 1975. [26]

By breaking its neutrality in the Lebanese civil war the PLO aggravated the situation in the Lebanese civil war, aggravated the situation. As Middle East scholar Robert Rabil explains, "Although the Palestinians were not at the root of Lebanon's weak system, they were the catalysts of the system's downfall."[27] Palestinians controlled vast parts of southern Lebanon (the area became known as "Fatahland") as well as West Beirut. Thus, when the Syrians, with strong support from the Christians, entered Lebanon in 1976, they targeted Palestinians. The collapse of the Palestinian refugee camp of Tel al-Zaatar at the hands of the Christians was followed by an atrocious massacre of Palestinian refugees. At the same time, the Christians, distrustful of the Syrians, sought an alliance with Israel, the PLO's chief enemy. The animosity between Lebanese Christians and Palestinians had further consequences years later when Christian Phalangists massacred hundreds of Palestinians in the Sabra and Shatila refugee camps.[28]

The Palestinian euphoria was highlighted by the multiple terrorist attacks against Israeli civilian targets carried out by the PLO's different factions during the 1970s and 1980s. These included attacks at the Lod Airport near Tel-Aviv in 1972; the Munich Olympics Massacre in the same year; the attacks on the northern towns of Maalot and Kiriat Shmona in 1974; the hijacking of an Air France airbus and its diversion to Uganda in 1976; the coastal road massacre in 1978; and bombardments of Israel's northern populations from Lebanese soil. These terrorist attacks were key instruments that succeeded in generating massive excitement among Palestinians and Arabs alike.

The PLO combined terrorist attacks against Israeli civilian and military targets with political action. While its militants were planning and carrying out attacks, the PLO also obtained major political victories, such as the United Nations' welcoming reception of PLO chairman Yasser Arafat and its granting of observer status to the PLO in 1974. In 1975, the United Nations General Assembly (UNGA) also adopted a resolution calling Zionism a form of racism.

The PLO political offensive was not only supported by Arab and Soviet allies, but was also enabled by Western countries that began to feel the pressure of the 1973 Arab oil embargo. This was marked by votes of abstention and even support of anti-Israel resolutions at the UN by Western countries that were previously friendly to Israel. Those countries became more critical of Israeli policies and demanded that Palestinian rights be respected.[29] This shift was a major political victory for the PLO and the Palestinians.

But jubilation, increased international clout, and self-confidence were followed by disaster for the Palestinians. The Israeli invasion of Lebanon in 1982 destroyed the PLO infrastructure in that country. Close to 19,000 Palestinians were killed and 30,000 were wounded.[30] The subsequent expulsion of the PLO from Lebanon to Tunisia weakened the organization, which lost its capacity to mobilize. As Rashid Khalidi wrote, "This defeat and its aftermath were particularly painful for Palestinians, as it evoked for many of them the exodus of 1948, and the more recent expulsion from Jordan... [As in Jordan] the Palestinians had lost the support of the sympathetic local populations."[31] But as the PLO retreated, new forces began to emerge that capitalized on the Palestinian tradition of mobilization, the most important of them being radical Islam.

The Emergence of Radical Islam

With each passing year and military defeat of the PLO, most notably the destruction of their military infrastructure in Lebanon and the uprooting of their base in that country in 1982-1983, the Palestinian movement altered course.

After the First Intifada (1987-1992), a homegrown mass movement emerged without the active participation of the PLO. The PLO became fully aware that it could lose leadership over the Palestinians. As pointed out in Chapter One, in order to regain influence and control over the Palestinians in the occupied territories, the PLO moved to recognize Israel and agreed to initiate a new peace process in Oslo, Norway. By recognizing Israel and engaging in peace negotiations with Israel, the PLO leadership expected to return to the West Bank and Gaza and recover its leadership over the Palestinians.

As French scholar Gilles Keppel observed in the aftermath of the First Intifada, "The conditions appeared to be in place for Islamists to oust nationalists in Palestine, just as they had elsewhere. The *jihad* in the occupied territories now replaced the holy war in Afghanistan, which was gradually winding down, as the major focus and symbol of Islamist militancy."[32] The PLO was losing ground to other forces that emerged in the West Bank and Gaza.

However, by the time Arafat was allowed back into the West Bank as a result of the Oslo peace process in 1994, there were other forces operating in the territories. The Movement of Islamic Resistance, more commonly known as Hamas, was the most ominous of all. With the rise of Hamas and its gradual advance into the Palestinian territories, a new phenomenon began to take shape: an identity based on Islam rather than a Palestinian national identity.

Hamas, whose origins can be traced to the Muslim Brotherhood, had discredited the identity proposed by the PLO nationalists, instead stressing an Islamic component, adding religious ideals into the Palestinian narrative. Among them was the idea that Jerusalem is as important to Muslims as Mecca and Medina since it is where the Prophet rose to heaven. Hamas opposed and continues to oppose the regional divisions created in the Arab world in the aftermath of World War I, regarding them as artificial and pointing out that the Palestinian territory had never been a territorial unit during the thirteen hundred years of Muslim rule in the region. Palestinian identity, according to Hamas, was expressed mostly in terms of the sacredness of Palestinian territory rather than the rights of the Palestinian people.[33] This point is particularly important because Muslim *jihad* calls for Muslims to expel the occupying enemy. Therefore, the struggle of Palestinians turned into a struggle for all Muslims. Indeed, Hamas is concerned with Islam and not with a Palestinian identity or Palestinian independence per se. It is concerned with the liberation of the territory of Palestine and its Islamization—not necessarily with Palestinian freedom or Palestinian nationalism. The Hamas Charter states that "The Movement's program is Islam. From it, it draws its ideas, ways of thinking and understanding of the universe, life and man. It resorts to it for judgment in all its conduct, and it is inspired by it for guidance of its steps."[34] According to the Hamas Charter, Hamas is "one of the wings of the Moslem Brotherhood in Palestine."[35] The Moslem Brotherhood Movement (MB) "is a universal organization which constitutes the largest Islamic movement in modern times."[36] The MB is about embracing "all Islamic concepts of all aspects of life, culture, creed, politics, economics, education, society, justice and judgement, the spreading of Islam, education, art, information, science of the occult and conversion to Islam."[37]

Likewise, through accepting Islam as the way of life, "the Movement goes back to the time of the birth of the Islamic message, of the righteous ancestor, for Allah is its target, the Prophet is its example and the Koran is its constitution. Its extent in place is anywhere that there are Moslems who embrace Islam as their way of life everywhere in the globe. This being so, it extends to the depth of the earth and reaches out to the heaven."[38]

Hamas claims to have come into being because of a situation in which,

> Islam has disappeared from life. Thus, rules shook, concepts were upset, values changed and evil people took control, oppression and darkness prevailed, cowards became like tigers: homelands were usurped, people were scattered and were caused to wander all over the world ... Thus, when

Islam is absent from the arena, everything changes. From this state of affairs, the incentives are drawn.[39]

Therefore, Hamas has a universal message aimed at restoring Islam to a prominent place in society. Palestine is important because it is an Islamic land, not necessarily because of the national aspirations of the Palestinian people. The Hamas Charter continues,

> The land of Palestine is an Islamic Waqf [(religious endowment)] consecrated for future Moslem generations until Judgement Day. It, or any part of it, should not be squandered: it, or any part of it, should not be given up. Neither a single Arab country nor all Arab countries, neither any king or president, nor all the kings and presidents, neither any organization nor all of them, be they Palestinian or Arab, possess the right to do that. Palestine is an Islamic Waqf land consecrated for Moslem generations until Judgement Day.[40]

Hamas views Palestinian nationalism as an important component of the struggle but not its main thrust. "Nationalism...is part of the religious creed," according to Hamas, and "Nothing in nationalism is more significant or deeper than in the case when an enemy should tread Moslem land. Resisting and quelling the enemy become the individual duty of every Moslem, male or female."[41]

Thus, as stated in the Hamas charter, "Palestine is an Islamic land...liberation of Palestine is then an individual duty for every Moslem wherever he may be. On this basis, the problem should be viewed. This should be realized by every Moslem."[42] Hamas is not concerned with the Palestinian people, but with the revival of Islam as a totality that rules individual, social and political life. The problem with Palestine is that it is a land not ruled by Muslims, but by "usurper" Jews. Palestine is Muslim land. Thus, it is the liberation of the land that matters, not the Palestinian people, their aspiration to national independence, or their pursuit of self-determination. The Hamas charter talks about solidarity with other radical Muslim movements fighting elsewhere and regards itself part of a universal Islamic movement operating in Palestine. Most importantly, it views itself as a wing of the Muslim Brotherhood and not principally a Palestinian movement.

Regarding Palestinian territories, Arab journalist Hazam Amin has pointed out that, "The difference between Al Qaeda and other Islamic groups is mostly on the modus operandi not on the objectives to be reached."[43] In other words, Hamas is not simply another body representing the aspirations of the Palestinian people, but it is a Palestinian body that represents a local form of Pan-Islamism. Therefore, Hamas regards peace conferences as incapable of "realizing the demands, restoring the rights or doing justice to the oppressed. These conferences are only ways of setting the infidels in the land of the Moslems as arbitrators. When did the infidels do justice to the believers?"[44]

Thus, Hamas begins its covenant by reaffirming the principle established by the Egyptian founder of the Muslim Brotherhood, Imam Hassan al-Banna, who said "Israel will exist and will continue to exist until Islam will obliterate it, just as it obliterated others before it."[45] Along those lines, Hamas' leader Ismail Haniyeh has explained that Iran and Hamas have an "ideological compatibility that enables us to confront a plan whose objectives are to target Arabs and Muslims ... The Palestinian people are part of the Islamic nation. Iran supports us by providing us with strategic depth, and we support Iran in its confrontation against American and Israeli hegemony."[46] According to this point of view, Palestine has a mythological and sacred meaning, and the conflict over it is not merely a matter of recovering usurped land; rather, it is a confrontation between Islam and Judaism.[47]

However—and most importantly— it was the existing state of mobilization of the Palestinians that became a crucial determining factor in the transition from nationalism to Islamism among a large number of Palestinians. Islamists operate on a permanent, open-ended and nihilistic Palestinian revolution, justified by Islam, characterizing the Palestinian revolution as not just a Palestinian duty, but rather, an Arab and Muslim duty.[48]

The existence of grimy and polluted refugee camps exacerbated these extremist tendencies. The conditions in the refugee camps and their high concentration of Palestinians have made their residents vulnerable to absorbing extremist ideologies. According to a report by the International Crisis Group (ICG), it was precisely in the refugee camps where the harshest remarks in support of the "right of return" have been heard. The message has been to make clear that Palestinians will not accept anything less than the "right of return" [49]

The right of return is a crucial myth that has kept the Palestinians in a state of high mobilization and has been part of the Palestinian identity. Refugee camps hold a high concentration of Palestinians that have in the words of historian Howard Sachar, "vegetated helplessly in the squalor of their UNRWA[50] shantytowns,"[51]

Palestinians' experience of this permanent situation of conflict and constant mobilization make them into important players for other extremist causes. Indeed, many Palestinians have joined Salafi-Jihadist organizations such as Usbar al-Ansar, which grew out of the Palestinian refugee camps in Lebanon. Usbar al-Ansar supported the violent activities of al-Qaeda in Iraq. The organization grew as a result of the socio-political conditions in the refugee camps, mainly Ayn Al Helweh, but particularly due to the Palestinian grassroots' disenchantment with the PLO.[52] The fact that Shiite militias led by the Shiite Amal Movement eradicated the power of the PLO and Palestinian militias in Southern Lebanon may have also been a factor in the radicalization of the Palestinians.

Indeed, as Rabil explains, "the growing militarization of the Palestinian refugees in confessional-polarized Lebanon, together with the mounting call among Islamists that 'Islam is the solution,' conditioned a significant number of refugees to heed the politicized sermons of religious scholars."[53] These new religious scholars and leaders advocated armed struggle against Israel and Zionism, but in the context of Islamic activism. As Rabil again observes, "No longer was the Palestinian nationalist cause at the heart of Palestinian activism. The question of Palestine became subsumed under the transnational objective of establishing an Islamic state and protecting the *ummah* (Muslim community)."[54]

Islamists began to gain ground in Palestinian refugee camps. These new Islamic groups were cultivated in the 1980s and later strengthened as the PLO weakened and lost clout in Lebanon. Fatah began to express alarm over this phenomenon and ordered the assassination of the main Islamist leader in the refugee camps, Hisham Sharaydi.[55]

Such acts did not prevent Palestinians in the refugee camps from embracing Islamism, as it provided a new form of excitement and euphoria that the PLO could no longer provide. The fact that Islamism entered Palestinian society in the West Bank, Gaza, and refugee camps in Lebanon is not coincidental. We would argue that Islamism rides on the Palestinians' tradition of mobilization. Thus, it may not be accidental that Abdallah Azzam, one of the teachers and spiritual adviser to Osama Bin Laden, was also a Palestinian.

According to Amin, "Palestinians have been responsible for the radicalization of the majority of the Islamic movements where they join, from Egypt to Iraq via Jordan, Afghanistan and Chechnya."[56] For instance, an increasing number of Palestinians in Lebanon have joined the Islamic State, also known as ISIS or ISIL, as well as the Al-Qaeda affiliate al-Nusra to fight in Syria. The Lebanese government has made efforts to avoid an Islamist take-over of the Palestinian refugee camps.[57]

Palestinians are also at the forefront of those Jordanians who have embraced global jihad. According to one observer, Palestinians "who left Jordan have become the backbone of the global Jihad against the infidel regimes and the blatant foreign interference in the countries of Islam."[58] Likewise, Palestinians have provided the most influential and notorious terrorists, including people like Abu Qatada, originally from Bethlehem in the West Bank, who is considered to be the spiritual leader of al-Qaeda in Europe. Another is Abu Muhammad al-Maqdisi, originally from Nablus in the West Bank, who is known for having been the mentor of Abu Musab al-Zarqawi, the leader of al-Qaeda in Iraq (AQI).[59] In April 2017, King Abdullah of Jordan said in an interview with the *Washington Post* that 96% of ISIS terrorist attacks in the Kingdom in 2016 were perpetrated by Palestinians.[60] In Syria, hundreds of Palestinians are fighting for both sides. They have joined the opposition forces in the Yarmouk Refugee camp near Damascus, and, on the opposite side, with the pro-Assad Palestinian militias.

Likewise, ISIS has penetrated the West Bank and even Hamas-dominated Gaza. It has even carried out terrorist attacks in Israel.[61] This does not necessarily mean that the Palestinians are the precursors of extreme forms of Islamism, but it certainly suggests that they are effective agents of such extremism due to their tradition of high mobilization and permanent conflict. It is also worth mentioning that there are organized Palestinian forces supported by the PA that are trying to resist the penetration of ISIS in the refugee camps.[62]

Nothing reflects more powerfully the magnitude of the Palestinians mobilization and permanent state of revolution than the role children have played. Children participated very early on in Palestinian armed operations. Children took part in the terrorist bombing of the offices of El Al airlines in Brussels in September 1969 and were at the forefront of confrontation with Israeli soldiers in the Palestinian protests against Israel in the West Bank in the 1970s. They also played an important role in the First Intifada, and played a more violent role in the Second Intifada, where a large number of children joined Hamas, the Islamic Jihad and the al-Aqsa Martyrs Brigade, militant groups that were involved in the most heinous attacks and suicide bombings. Children as young as eight years old attacked Israeli settlements and military checkpoints with guns and knives, and participated in other acts of sabotage.[63] According to scholar David Rosen, "The steady stream of suicide attacks and suicide bombings has valorized the ideal of personal martyrdom in the name of Palestinian nationalism."[64] The fact that children and young people might be killed was justified by the need "to defend Islam and Arab civilization."[65] As Rosen affirms, "within this context Palestinian historical consciousness became defined by a sense of catastrophe."[66]

As Rosen again points out,

The militant Palestinian response to Zionism reflected an apocalyptic and millenarian view of the Jewish presence in Palestine that imbued the Palestinian Arab struggle with meaning. The involvement of children and youth in the Palestinian national cause emerged out of the sense of cataclysm and catastrophe that permeated Palestinian nationalism. In Palestine, apocalyptic views were nourished by two nascent forms of totalitarianism then found in the Middle East, Islamism and pan-Arabism.[67]

Again, it is the permanent, unending revolution and mobilization that makes Palestinians prone to radicalization, which often spills beyond the boundaries of the Israeli-Palestinian conflict. This is aggravated by the sense of marginalization as second-class citizens assigned to them in Arab countries, and the existence of refugee camps which seem to be incubators of mobilization and radicalization. In the West Bank, the only place where Palestinians enjoy a degree of civilian autonomy, radicalization is further aggravated by the attitudes of the PA itself. The PA's actions on the ground are indirectly providing legitimacy and justification to extreme views and actions.

The Effect of Propaganda and Indoctrination: The Role of the Palestinian Authority

Islamism has made serious advances in Palestinian society. A weakened Arafat tried to survive using two different discourses. One discourse remained committed to peace while the other advocated permanent revolution (or *jihad*). The latter nihilistic discourse took hold in the Palestinian educational system. The contradiction between Arafat's "good will" and the legacy of mobilization finally exploded in the summer of 2000 with the collapse of the Camp David conference and the ensuing outbreak of the Second Intifada, also known as the Al Aksa Intifada.

Chapter 1 explained how some sectors within the ruling Fatah party found themselves competing with Hamas during the Second Intifada. During that time both groups launched suicide attacks against Israeli population centers, causing a fierce Israeli reaction and subsequently ending in Yasser Arafat's house arrest.[68] But nothing reflected Palestinian weakness and competition with Hamas more than official Palestinian propaganda against Israel in schools, the media, international forums, public speeches and other outlets. As scholar Reid Weiner explains,

Incitement in Palestinian society is both authoritative and nearly omnipresent, and emanates straight from the top of the PA...Television and radio stations, religious sermons, school textbooks, newspapers and magazines, and even

summer camp curricula are all directly or indirectly controlled by the PA, which uses them to glorify martyrdom
and to convince Palestinian children to engage in dangerous behavior.[69]

Although it is Hamas that carries out most of the suicide bombings and other heinous acts (some are carried out by secular Palestinian factions), it is the PA that promotes propaganda that provides
justification for such acts even when the PA does not call directly
for the use of violence.

As time passes, radicalization persists. The Palestinian intellectual class has rejected a peace settlement without providing
any peaceful, positive alternative. Palestinian writer Fawaz Turki
claimed that the Oslo process robbed Palestinian refugees of the
idea of the return to the land they lost in 1948. Edward Said defined Oslo as "an American peace," "a Palestinian Versailles," and
"a Palestinian subservience," in which the Palestinians were forced
to surrender. He claimed that Arafat was an enforcer of Israeli rule
and described his behavior as "degradation." Said explained that
Arafat looked humiliated and almost apologetic when in fact he
should not have been, since Israel "expelled 800,000 Palestinians in
1948, conquered their land and property and destroyed over four
hundred Palestinian villages."[70]

With some notable exceptions, however, such as the Egyptian
poet Naguib Mahfuz and a few others, Arab and Palestinian writ-
ers alike expressed opposition to peace even after the Oslo peace
process with Israel began.[71] The Palestinian nationalist poet Mahmoud Darwish and others have spoken with nostalgia and pain
about the loss of Palestine, but little about compromise and accommodation with the Israelis. In fact, Darwish stated in a visit to Gaza
in 1995, when hopes on Oslo were still very much alive, that he was
disappointed with the process. Darwish claimed that he felt "that
his exile has not come to an end."[72]

Palestinian poets systematically highlight themes of exile and
nostalgia that help perpetuate a collective memory of loss. What is
worse, those who were born after 1948 not only target their anger
against Israelis, but also against their parents' generation, who so
"easily" fled Palestine and surrendered their birthright.[73]

Palestine seems like an irreplaceable place. The poet Abu Salma wrote a powerful and tragic poem that concludes, "Oh Palestine. Nothing more beautiful, more precious, purer."[74] Said, who rejected the Oslo accords as a setup aimed at serving Israel, also speaks about exile as a dreadful experience:

> Arafat and his dwindling number of supporters were turned into enforcers of Israeli security, while Palestinians were made to endure the humiliation of dreadful and non-contiguous "homelands" that make up about 10 percent of the West Bank and 60 percent of Gaza. Oslo required us to forget and renounce our history of loss, dispossessed by the very people who taught everyone the importance of not forgetting the past. Thus, we are the victims of the victims, the refugees of the refugees.[75]

Said proposes a one-state solution, in which historic Palestine would be one state where Arabs and Jews could co-exist under one umbrella. No such scenario is obviously possible as these two nations are at war and are unlikely to find peace through a common state. In fact, war could be expected to continue in the form of a civil war.

As part of the Hebron Protocol, concluded in 1997 between Israel and the PA, a note for the record reaffirmed the Palestinian commitment to end the anti-Israel incitement. That requirement was reiterated in the 1998 Wye River agreements. Yet, the PA did not comply with that requirement, and the situation has since continued to intensify. For instance, a 2015 report by Palestinian Media Watch, an Israel-based NGO that tracks incitement in Palestinian media, shows that the PA has actively promoted religious hatred by demonizing Jewish people and Judaism altogether. Jews have been portrayed as inherently evil, treacherous, corrupt, and bloodthirsty. An advisor to PA Chairman Mahmoud Abbas stated on PA TV that the conflict between Israel and the Palestinians is a conflict of "Allah's project versus Satan's project."[76]

Media and other official vehicles delegitimize Israel and the Jewish connection to the land.[77] Children's programming broadcast on Palestinian TV often includes poetry with strong anti-Semitic content. One of the programs features a poem recited by children that calls for "war that will smash the oppression and destroy the Zionist soul."[78] Another poem recited by a young girl on TV reads as follows: "Between me and them there are wars and bloodshed... so I shall buy a bullet at any price."[79] Likewise, according to this officially sanctioned propaganda, the Jews are a source of trouble and evil felt wherever they go or live. Czarist Russian pogroms and the Nazi extermination of Jews are justified by the Jews' actions and behavior. These are, therefore, legitimate persecutions.

A PA Minister of Tourism publicly stated that the final goal of the Palestinians should be to bring an end to Israel. Elements within the PA accuse Israel of spreading AIDS, drugs and prostitution among Palestinians. Likewise, they accuse Israelis of experimenting with Palestinian prisoners as Joseph Mengele did in Nazi concentration camps.[80] At the same time, honoring martyrs of suicide bombings, naming streets after terrorists, and welcoming murderers liberated by Israel as heroes, contributes to the poisonous atmosphere and sends the message that Israelis cannot be peace partners, or that violence and murder against Israelis is legitimate. The PA also deliberately targets places where young people gather. For instance, Dalal Mughrabi, who was responsible for the murder of 37 Israeli civilians in a 1978 bus hijacking, was honored by placing her name in two elementary schools, a kindergarten, a summer camp, a community center, a youth center, and a public square.[81] The Mughrabi case is one of the many cases where terrorists were honored and glorified.[82]

Abbas himself, who preached non-violence, pointed out in September 2015, "We welcome every drop of blood spilled in Jerusalem. This is pure blood, clean blood, blood on its way to Allah." A few weeks later, a series of terrorist and knife attacks began.[83] These attacks that began in October 2015, were carried out by "lone wolves." But the fact that young individuals are carrying out these assassinations so callously, displays a hatred that cannot only be attributed to the cold organizational capabilities of groups such as Hamas or the Islamic Jihad. It is the result of incitement, for which the PA is also responsible.

Such incitement has become a huge obstacle to the peace process. Indeed, the PA seems to perpetuate the myth of the Palestinian refugees claiming that it was an intentional act committed by the Israelis with no justification other than robbing Palestinians of their land. The "Nakbah" (Catastrophe), as Palestinians call it, seems to be the intellectual tool with which Palestinians claim the "right of return." Thus, the victimhood perpetuated by the Palestinians, and the general belief that the Palestinians were not responsible at all for their own catastrophe, automatically leads to unreasonable demands on Israel such as the "right of return".

The official Palestinian propaganda constantly stresses the right of return as a fundamental demand, knowing that peace with Israel and the right of return do not go hand in hand. This exacerbates Palestinian emotions.

Indeed, a poll taken by the Pew Research Center in 2011 indicates that 68 percent of Palestinians think that suicide bombings against civilian targets are justified. Even in comparison to other Arab or Muslim populations, Palestinians have proven to be the most supportive of this kind of murderous tactic; in Lebanon, 35 percent of those surveyed supported suicide bombings, while in other countries like Turkey, Pakistan and Indonesia, 10 percent or less did.[84]

To be sure, we are not denying here that often violence is encouraged by the reaction of the Israelis, which could unleash anger and feelings of revenge. Indeed, Israel reacted harshly in its attempts to control violence including raids, killings in confrontations, use of local spies, imposition of checkpoints, restriction of movement of Palestinians, prohibiting some Palestinians from working in Israel, and other measures.

Psychology professor Anne Speckhard, who has interviewed failed suicide bombers, claims that suicide bombings are the result of intolerable pain. This intolerable pain seems to be, according to those interviewees, caused by unemployment, loss of land, humiliating checkpoints that restrict their freedom of movement, or some sort of injustice or hardship that Palestinians suffer. [85] One of the people interviewed claimed that he is willing to kill himself, not for religious reasons, but in order to restore a normal life to Palestinians.[86] However, according to the research conducted by sociologist Bader Araj, the main reason that seems to motivate suicide bombers is not unemployment, social maladjustment or even nationalistic feelings. In fact, most of them were employed. What prevailed in their motivation was a sense of revenge.[87] A second motivator was religious convictions and fanaticism, [88] which was more prevalent among Hamas and Islamic Jihad members.[89]

Another psychologist, Mali Soibelman, interviewed five suicide bombers. What they all had in common were negative primary or secondary experiences with Israelis, such as witnessing Israeli soldiers shooting their friends or other similar incidents.[90]

Araj's and Soibelman's conclusion that suicide bombing is a response to Israeli repression and a feeling of revenge may be true. However, it is reasonable to conclude that the feelings of pain and vindictiveness have much to do with the indoctrination Palestinians undergo, combined with a deep feeling of victimization, which to a significant degree is the result of propaganda. In other words, the sense of injustice and vindictiveness that Palestinians feel is exacerbated by propaganda that demonizes Israelis, portrays Palestinians as victims, and, thus, exempts them from assuming any responsibility for the conflict or its consequences. For example, one suicide bomber who failed to carry out his mission during the Second Intifada pointed out that he was enraged by the fact that Israel killed Palestinians. He also blamed Israel for the Intifada, portraying the Palestinians as victims despite the fact that it was Palestinian groups who started the violence, including killing Israelis in mass, and sabotaging the peace process.[91]

This is why, the scholar Martha Crenshaw views acts of terrorism as being motivated by ideology, socially constructed reality, tradition and socialization patterns. Crenshaw places emphasis on the entire cultural and social dynamic that motivates violence: [92]

Both cognitive processes and motivational factors encourage reliance on a set of unchanging beliefs that inhibit flexibility and openness. This combination of factors explains the tenaciousness of terrorist beliefs despite their growing deviation from reality. It may also explain the bitterness and violence that control dissent within terrorist organizations. The dynamics of the group encourage cohesiveness and solidarity that stifle challenges to the dominant beliefs in the terrorist organization. [93]

This is the tradition of mobilization, encouraged by a Palestinian leadership that has not displayed public flexibility regarding anti-Zionist dogmas nor to the view that the peace partner is the enemy. This creates a collective social dynamic that perpetuates beliefs that lead to violence. This is what sociologists Charles Tilly and Sidney Tarrow called contentious performances and contentious repertoires. Contentious performances are familiar and standardized ways "in which collective claims are made". [94] Contentious repertoires are "arrays of contentious performances that are known and available within a set of political actors". [95]

The Palestinian use of violence constitutes a tool kit that worked well in the past. Violence is the method that is deeply familiar to them because of their tradition of mobilization. At the same time, the continued portrayal of Israel, not as a partner of peace but as a bitter enemy, makes the use of violence a logical choice. Therefore, the tool kit encompasses actions that Palestinians have known and inherited from the past, and are constantly being reactivated.

Marwan Barghouti, the leader of Fatah's Tanzim, the group that led the Second Intifada, epitomizes this point. Barghouti believes in violence and has criticized Abbas's policy of non-violence as a failure.[96] In Barghouti's own words, "The Palestinians have created modern times' longest revolution. We will renew it."[97] This statement reaffirms the belief that violence should remain part of the repertoire of this long-mobilized movement. It is this collective feeling of permanent revolution and conflict that prevails.

To be sure, it is Hamas and Islamic Jihad that incite violence; but the PA's anti-Israel propaganda enables the actions of these radical groups and helps sabotage any kind of discourse conducive to peace or even to a reasonable compromise with Israel.

Rashid Khalidi points out that, consistent with its revolutionary history, the PLO "produced the strategic incoherence that resulted from, on the one hand, accepting a two-state solution and renouncing violence in 1988, but not, on the other, drawing the logical conclusion that what was necessary was the reeducation of the Palestinians away from the armed struggle and toward a whole new approach of unarmed mass popular struggle." [98] What is interesting about Khalidi's remark is that since taking over the leadership of the PLO, Abbas has advocated for a strategy of non-violence. However, he made no effort to reeducate the Palestinians about the need to compromise with Israel, particularly on the right of return and the legitimacy of the State of Israel. While receiving praise from some leaders and media for his policy of non-violence, he continued to run a parallel negative anti-Israel propaganda campaign that has not advanced peace or reconciliation with Israel.

The PA's incitement began before the breakdown of the Oslo peace negotiations.[99] For example, in 1998 the head of the Palestinian Consumer Protection Association pushed a baseless conspiracy theory portraying Israel as deliberately spreading diseases to Palestinians.[100]

In August 1997, the Israeli Ministry of Foreign Affairs issued a memorandum that recorded nearly one hundred statements from Palestinian officials viewed as "incitement to violence and hostile propaganda against Israel." These statements included calls for violence against Israel and denial of the name Israel, using instead, the pejorative term "Zionist entity". Also included were claims that the territory of the State of Israel belongs to the Palestinian people, calls for the destruction of Israel, accusations that Israel intentionally poisons Palestinians, dehumanization of the Israelis by calling them "the enemy", and proposing violence as an alternative to the political process. [101]

As we pointed out in the previous chapter, Netanyahu was elected Prime Minister for the second time in 2009, after 10 years of moderate Israeli governments. By then, the PA had been already traveling down the path of incitement for several years, despite the fact, as we pointed out, that the 1997 Hebron Agreements and 1998 Wye River Agreements stipulated, among other things, that the PA must commit itself to stop incitement.

The basic condition for preparing the public for peace and reconciliation has taken a U-Turn. As Robert Danin, a former director of Near Eastern Affairs at the National Security Council pointed out:

> While talks are an essential element for resolving the Israeli-Palestinian conflict, other tools of statecraft are required to help instill confidence and build constituencies for a genuine peace...But they will only be able to do so when their peoples are prepared to support them. For Israelis and Palestinians to support such compromises, they must believe

that they have a real partner for peace on the other side and that the point of compromise is worthwhile. Negotiating success requires that the Israeli and Palestinian people believe that negotiations are desirable, that they can succeed, that they should succeed, and that their leaders should be supported and empowered at the negotiating table.[102]

In fact, however, sixty percent of Palestinians reject the two-state solution and believe that there should only be one Palestinian state.[103] A June 2014 survey commissioned by the Washington Institute for Near East Policy showed that fewer than thirty percent of Palestinians supported a two-state solution, and a clear majority of those interviewed in the West Bank and Gaza, more than sixty percent, believed that the final goal should be to "reclaim all of historic Palestine, from the river to the sea."[104] Two thirds said that "resistance should continue until all of historic Palestine is liberated."[105]The survey showed that the majority supported the takeover of land in stages. The Anti-Defamation League published a report in 2014 showing that ninety-three percent of the adult population in the West Bank and Gaza holds anti-Semitic views.[106]

This is hardly surprising if one carefully follows the generational consequences of propaganda and indoctrination. As French sociologist Jacques Ellul has shown, indoctrination and propaganda are not about manipulation; they are "no longer to change adherence to a doctrine, but to make the individual cling irrationally to a process of action. It is no longer to transform an opinion but to arouse an active and mythical belief."[107]

In the case of the PA, even if we give the PA the benefit of the doubt that it has no totalitarian intention, but that it only seeks to compete with and appease the most radical elements among Palestinians, it does not change the totalitarian effect of such propaganda. Indeed, scholars Nico Voigtlander and Hans Joachim Voth found that the effects of Nazi indoctrination continue to contribute to the intensity of contemporary anti-Semitism in Germany.[108] The research found that anti-Semitic attitudes are more pronounced among those born between 1930 and 1939, regardless of education or economic status. The study also suggests that "Nazi indoctrination in schools and youth organizations successfully instilled strongly anti-Semitic attitudes in the cohorts that grew up under the Nazi regime, and that the differential effect is still visible today, more than half century after the fall of the Third Reich."[109] The authors explain that these individuals were five and six years old while they were being indoctrinated with Nazi ideology and racial hatred. This shows how schooling and propaganda were so effective in shaping anti-Semitic attitudes among the youth, and how this phenomenon has had long-term cultural effects.

Something similar happened in the conflict between Serbs and Albanians over Kosovo in the 1990s. Serbian media systematically portrayed the Albanians as a demographic threat to the Serbs warning of the "diabolical proliferation" of Albanians in Kosovo. Propaganda provoked fear among the Serbian population, and in turn, this fear exacerbated Serbian animosity towards Albanians.

In other words, there is a dialectical relation between propaganda and the receptivity of the message among the population. Since the Serbian population was open to the message, conditions were perfect for absorbing the propaganda that its government was disseminating.[110]

Likewise, the genocidal massacres in Rwanda counted on mass participation. Thousands of Hutus joyfully participated in the massacre of their Tutsi neighbors. The scholar Robert Melson explains this was also the result of constant messages spread through the radio, in which the Tutsis were portrayed as collaborators with the Rwandan Patriotic Force, a group composed of Ugandan Tutsis that invaded Rwanda in October 1990. Tutsis were portrayed as a foreign group whose aim was to destroy the Hutus and steal their lands.[111]

What could be expected from the young generation of Palestinians, if not to live with the deep resentment that such indoctrination would inevitably cause? Can the peace process survive under such conditions?

The continuous incitement and systematic propaganda campaign in the Palestinian territories have created a dominant paradigm that is difficult to reverse. Marxist thinker Antonio Gramsci understood the importance of culture, language definition, semantics, normal prejudices, and routine aspects of everyday life to maintaining a socio-political paradigm. It is a set of premises and

practices in which the Palestinians take the demonization of Jews and Israelis, and all of the myths that have defined them as victims, as unquestionable truths. Thus, the killing of Jews and Israelis, the activation of suicide bombers and stabbers, even if we accept the premise that most Palestinians are not willing to commit these heinous acts, are understood as a natural outcome of reality as they understand it. In other words, the killing of a Jew or an Israeli is often justified. While a 2007 Pew research survey found a decline in the percentage of Muslims who justify suicide bombings in many parts of the world, including some Arab countries, the Palestinians have stood out in their support for such acts. Seventy percent of Palestinians surveyed believed that "suicide bombings against civilians can be often or sometimes justified."[112]
Eight years later in 2015, another Pew Research survey found negative views of al-Qaeda and other extremist groups prevail in the Muslim world. However, the most positive rating for al Qaeda was in the Palestinian territories, where twenty-five percent had a favorable view of the terrorist group.[113]

It is reasonable to assume that the difference between the Palestinians and the rest of the Arab and Muslim worlds in their attitudes towards al-Qaeda is a function of a stronger Palestinian subjugation to indoctrination. A poll conducted in 2011 indicated that fifty-three percent of Palestinian children found it appropriate to teach anti-Israel incitement, while seventy percent of Palestinians believed that Jews are the enemy, and that the conflict will end when the Jews are "defeated by Islamic Arab forces."[114]

An analogy can be found in the Nazi doctrine. For a large majority of Germans, a phenomenon like the Holocaust was inconceivable before and after World War II. However, during World War II those involved in such killings could commit these inhumane acts because they understood that doing so was "the right thing to do" for the German people, as well as for the cause for which they were indoctrinated.

Even if we assume that most Palestinians are not terrorists or not willing to kill or sacrifice themselves as suicide bombers, it is clear that they will find justification for terror and the demand for the right of return. The right of return is a formula for civil war between Arabs and Jews and the insistence on this point reaffirms the idea that the ultimate goal is to recover the entire land— not just pre-1967 land, but pre-1948 land as well. Given Israel's military might, there is no way it could be forced upon Israel without its consent. Since "the right of return" is a false hope, it remains solely an instrument of a nihilistic, uncertain, and open-ended struggle.

This state of permanent mobilization and revolution that Palestinians experience prevents them from living a normal life, outside the conflict, a life where they can enjoy individual autonomy unhampered by the interference of any institution, a life of family, home, work, and self-interest. Currently, Palestinian lives are largely determined by the conflict without positive outcomes.

A *New York Times* story tells of a Palestinian woman who expressed her desire "to have a normal life." She claimed, "the years before the Palestinian Authority came were better...Before that, residents were still under Israeli occupation but had more freedom of movement."[115] She pointed out that she would settle for living under Israeli sovereignty with equal rights "At least it would be a 'normal' life."[116]

There was likely a sector that supported peace with Israel and firmly believed in it. Palestinian signatures at the Geneva Initiative (see chapter 1) are a vivid example. However, the PA created its own contradictions by not promoting the peace process to their populations and thinking that, by maintaining the old rhetoric, they could contain their competitors and rivals such as Hamas. Thus, the harsh anti-Zionist rhetoric has poisoned the population, particularly its youth, causing what I consider an irreversible dynamic of hate that has closed the door to Israeli-Palestinian reconciliation.

This problem indeed will persist for a long time. This negative momentum is likely to transcend generations. It is against this backdrop that new solutions outside the Israeli-Palestinian bilateral negotiations must be sought out, particularly with the help of the greater Arab world. Thus, before proceeding in this direction, I will explore the Arab states' attitudes concerning the conflict and examine how the larger Arab community is positioned to help bring peace.

CHAPTER 3

THE ARAB WORLD AND
THE PEACE PROCESS

As we have seen in Chapter 1, the Palestinian Authority (PA) was unable to deliver a peace agreement due to its crisis of legitimacy and its inability to exercise a monopoly over the means of violence. These failures have crippled the PA's ability to make major decisions, including reaching a lasting peace with Israel.

Moreover, Arafat justified his inflexibility on Jerusalem's status by taking the role of negotiator on behalf of the entire Arab and Muslim world. Arafat's Jerusalem argument and his self-portrayal as representative of the Arab and Muslim world, gave the impression that Arab states were watching Arafat's actions. However, they were not necessarily helping the Palestinian leader reach an agreement with Israel. If, as we have argued, Palestinian weaknesses limit the peace process, then it is important to turn to the larger Arab community as a potential force that could support the Palestinians and guarantee the implementation and maintenance of a peace agreement between the Palestinians and Israel. Indeed, in the past, the Arab nations were expected to sponsor the peace process, an expectation that they have not met. Most of them walked away when President Clinton sought to encourage Arafat to accept Ehud Barak's parameters for a proposed peace settlement.

After Palestinian leaders walked away from negotiations in April 2014, former Israeli military officer and peace negotiator, Michael Herzog, rightly observed:

Following the failure of the latest round of peace negotiations, the two-state solution seems ever more elusive to more and more Israelis and Palestinians. This low point in their political relations after so many years of peace efforts demands fresh thinking. My first conclusion from these nine months is that the two leaderships cannot, at this stage, bridge the gaps to reach a full, comprehensive, conflict-ending deal....Lacking a willing and capable Palestinian partner, [Israel] should nevertheless seek regional and international partners (which it is likely to find), and apply some constructive unilateral measures in coordination with these partners (including ceasing settlement activity beyond the blocs)—all the while leaving the door open to a future negotiated settlement.[1]

Like Herzog, we start from the premise that a solution to the current Israeli-Palestinian conflict must come from some regional arrangement that includes the Arab world.

This chapter will analyze the attitudes and policies of the Arab states towards Israel and the Israeli-Palestinian peace process. This chapter will also examine some of the changing geopolitical circumstances in the Middle East with respect to Israel and the peace process, particularly, the role of Iran in fomenting instability in the region.

Iran is becoming an ever more serious threat to the Sunni Arab world, particularly Egypt, and the Persian Gulf countries, and especially Saudi Arabia. Iran has sought to become a nuclear power and has also supported subversive activities in countries such as Lebanon, Iraq and Yemen by backing proxy groups. It has also tried to gain ground by militarily supporting the survival of the Assad regime in Syria.   On the other hand, Sunni radicalism, mainly embodied in the Islamic State (ISIS, also known as ISIL), Al Qaeda and other groups also presents a threat to the same countries as these groups take advantage of the political turmoil and civil war that is taking place in places like Syria, Libya and Iraq.

The Historical Ambivalence of the Arab States

The Oslo Accords paved the way for Israeli negotiations with the Palestinians and the Arab world. The goal of the Accords was to include regional countries in the negotiations in order to guarantee a comprehensive peace process as well as cooperation on trade issues, water resources, and other matters. These multilateral talks were meant to address functional issues and to foster broader communication between the Israelis and Arabs.[2] The talks were received enthusiastically by then Israeli Foreign Minister Shimon Peres, who shared his vision in his book *The New Middle East*.[3] He envisioned a regional powerhouse based on Arab-Israeli cooperation and integration.

The multilateral negotiations came to an end following Egypt's abandonment of talks two years after the Oslo process began. Following Egypt, Arab countries essentially disengaged from their responsibility for the outcome of the peace process. This study addresses a number of complex political, psychological and sociological reasons for this Arab ambivalence.

Historically, Arab states opposed the creation of the State of Israel because they saw it as a non-Arab, non-Muslim entity in the heart of the Middle East, an area they considered naturally Arab and Muslim. The first expressions of the Arab rejectionist approach were voiced and led by Amin al-Husseini. Al-Husseini belonged to one of the most prominent and politically elite patrician families in Palestine. He came to prominence when he was appointed Mufti of Jerusalem by the British Mandate in 1921, a position he used to promote Islam and a radical nationalist anti-Zionist stance. From the outset, al-Husseini furiously rejected the Balfour Declaration, a British public statement issued in 1917, and later adopted by the League of Nations, in support of a "national home for the Jewish people" in Palestine. Al Husseini believed that the British had no legal authority over Palestine and therefore had no right to give Palestine to people who represented a minority of the region's population."[4]

It is important to note that al-Husseini convened the World Islamic Congress [5] in Jerusalem in 1931, attended by delegates from 122 countries. The Congress condemned Zionism and British colonial rule throughout the Middle East and India. During the meeting, Al-Husseini was elected president of the Congress and began to emerge as a powerful figure in the Muslim Brotherhood, a pan-Islamic movement founded in Egypt in 1928. [6]

Al-Husseini, along with the Muslim Brotherhood, called for the reestablishment of the caliphate, a political system eradicated years earlier following the collapse of the Ottoman Empire. The idea of the caliphate was to create a unified Arab state ruled by the laws of the Koran, sharia.[7] Based on this concept of the Caliphate and his Pan-Islamic view of the region, Al-Husseini's approach was clearly aimed at not only demanding the right of an Arab majority to rule over Palestine, but also to declare the inadmissibility of any Jewish sovereignty over any territory that should be "naturally" Muslim or Islamic.

While the partition of Palestine was being debated, arguments brought by different Arab delegates to the General Assembly of the United Nations in 1947 stressed the idea that a Jewish state in the Middle East would be like introducing an alien body into the Arab world. Indeed, the Syrian delegate stated, "the Syrian and Arab peoples…will never allow a wedge or a foreign hostile bridgehead to be driven into the heart of their fatherland."[8] The Iraqi representative pointed out that "Palestine is at the heart of the Arab world," and therefore,

> A Jewish state breaks that unity and endangers the peace and security of the Arab States. The Arab states cannot tolerate this break in their unity. They are entitled to have a decisive voice in all matters, which affect their regional interests. Therefore, they oppose the creation of a Jewish state in Palestine now or at any future time.[9]

This Arab view was also displayed during the hearings of the UN General Assembly by Albert Hourani, a Lebanese professor at Oxford. He stated that "the Arab opposition [to Israel] is based also upon the situation of the dangers of Zionism which threatens to distort the whole natural development of Arab peace, social, economic, political and intellectual, and threatens also, if not to dominate the Arab world, at least to disturb its life for generations to come.[10]

For Hourani, there was no way to compromise on what he considered to be an immutable principle. He declared, "if the Arabs object to a Jewish state, on the grounds of principle, in the whole of

Palestine, they cannot object to it and they cannot accept it in part. If they accept it in principle in part, they cannot oppose it in principle in the whole. The size and the extent of the Jewish state is irrelevant to the question of principle."[11] Eventually, he continued, Jews "will be forced into conflict with the Arab world by various factors— by the need to deal with their own Arab minority, which would not consent willingly to become the subjects of a Jewish state and which would rise and protest, and whose protest would be aided actively by surrounding Arab countries."[12] This type of anti-Zionism, which portrays a Jewish state as more than just a Palestinian problem, is embedded in Pan-Arabism and was eventually echoed by the Palestinians themselves, as Israeli scholars Alexander Yakobson and Amnon Rubenstein observe.[13] In the words of the representative of the Arab Higher Committee, a body that represented the Palestinian Arabs in Mandatory Palestine:

> The Arabs lived in a vast territory stretching from the Mediterranean to the Indian Ocean, spoke one language, had the same history, tradition and aspirations. Their unity was a solid foundation for peace in one of the most central and sensitive areas of the world. It was illogical, therefore, that the United Nations should associate itself with the introduction of an alien body into that established homogeneity, a course which could only produce new Balkans.[14]

In other words, the problem was not only about the Palestinian Arabs, but of the entire Arab world. The struggle against Zionism was viewed as a struggle for Arab regional hegemony This view explains why seven of Israel's Arab neighbors participated in the attack against the newly created state in May 1948.

The war against Israel and Zionism turned into a Pan-Arab war, as evidenced in Chapter 2. Indeed, prior to 1967, the Palestinian problem was subordinated to Pan-Arab ambitions. The Pan-Arab principle not only justified the unified Arab attack on the newly created State of Israel in May 1948, but also constituted one of the key pillars of Egyptian president Gamal Abdul Nasser's ideology in the 1950s and 1960s. These ideas justified Nasser and his Arab partners' eventual unsuccessful war against Israel in 1967. For Nasser, the problem of Palestine was not a problem of the right of return or of solving the refugee problem. Rather, he believed that Israel must be destroyed, because it is an imperialistic entity, a non-Arab sovereign entity, and a mere extension of the great Western powers. As he explained in a speech delivered to the Egyptian National Assembly a few years before the war, the issue of Israel was not merely about Palestinian refugees but about Israel's very existence:

> The small particles of the problem did not become separate battles. Totalities became connected and coherent... For instance, Israel became nothing before us. Imperialism around us is something different. There had been attempts for division which aimed at disintegration of problems (sic). These attempts tried to give illusions that Israel is a problem of refugees which, once it is solved, will bring an end to the Palestine issue. (Sic).... The danger of Israel is its existence as it now stands with all it represents...It stands for imperialism, for its service and its objectives of domination and exploitation...liquidating the imperialist existence cannot take place without affecting the Israeli existence (sic).[15]

Equally significant, the question of Israel and Palestine served as a unifying factor in an Arab world that was deeply divided. In the wake of Nasser's controversial military intervention in Yemen's civil war on the side of dissident Republicans—along with his hostility to what he considered reactionary pro-Western monarchies, such as Jordan and Saudi Arabia—Nasser saw the war against Israel as an issue that "supersedes all differences of opinion," and one for which, "we are ready to meet with all those whom we have disagreements."[16]

These ideas and actions are clear evidence that the question of Palestine transcended the problem of Palestinian refugees or the "Naqba" (Catastrophe). Israel was a foreign entity that served Western imperialism in a region that pan-Arabists believed was supposed to be under Arab domination and hegemony. Thus, early in 1964 Nasser proceeded to gather all Arab leaders, including the monarchies he abhorred, to create a United Arab Command (UAC). The UAC was charged with providing military aid to Jordan, Syria, and Lebanon, and enlisting the Iraqi air force to support the Arab military coalition against Israel. Thus, in the words of historian Michael Oren, "conditions were laid down for waging war: secrecy, unity, and total military preparedness."[17] At that time, the Syrian Army Chief of Staff, Salah Jadid, later the *de facto* leader of Syria pointed out that "every soldier in our army feels that Israel must be wiped off the map," and called on the Arab world to support the war against Israel.[18]

On May 16, 1967 Egypt requested the removal of the United Nations Emergency Force from Sinai (UNEF), whose charge was to secure the separation of Israeli and Egyptian forces following the 1956 Suez Crisis. It was then that Nasser disclosed his intentions over state-controlled Cairo Radio:

> The existence of Israel has continued too long. We welcome the Israeli aggression. We welcome the battle that we have long awaited. The great hour has come. The battle has come in which we shall destroy Israel."[19]

On May 31, less than a week before the outbreak of the 1967 War, the President of Iraq, Abdul Rahman Arif, clearly pointed out that "the existence of Israel is an error which must be rectified. This is our opportunity to wipe out the ignominy which has been with us since 1948. Our goal is clear— to wipe Israel off the map"[20]

Another element that further exacerbated Arab fury was the question of honor. This issue has also historically played an important role in the cultural values of Arab countries and has been a major obstacle in the search for peace with Israel. For example, not too long after the establishment of the State of Israel, King Saud of Saudi Arabia observed that,

> Israel to the Arab world is like a cancer to the human body, and the only way of remedy is to uproot it just like a cancer... Israel is a serious wound in the Arab world body, and we cannot endure the pain of this wound forever. We do not have the patience to see Israel occupying part of Palestine for long. We Arabs total about fifty million. Why don't we sacrifice 10 million of our number and live in pride and self-respect?[21]

Prior to 1967, the 1948 Arab defeat symbolized a wound to Arab honor. Nasser used this effectively as propaganda against Arab monarchies, including the Egyptian monarchy of King Farouk, whom he blamed for that defeat. On May 26, 1967, a few days before the start of Six Days War, Nasser referred to Arab mobilization for the war against Israel as a matter of restoring Arab honor:

> Brothers, the revolt, upheaval and commotion which we now see taking place in every Arab country are not only because we have returned to the Gulf of Aqaba or rid ourselves of the United Nations Emergency Force (UNEF), but because we have restored Arab honor and renewed Arab hopes. Israel used to boast a great deal, and the Western Powers, headed by the United States and Britain, used to ignore and even despise us and consider us of no value. But now that the time has come...we must be ready for triumph and not for a recurrence of the 1948 comedies.[22]

The author and journalist David Pryce Jones stresses the fear in the Arab world of being dishonored and disrespected, [23] where shame is a sort of living death that requires revenge. [24] The euphoria and triumphalism of Nasser's pan-Arabism found its limits in the 1967 war. The 1948 War was supposed to be avenged in 1967. However, Israel defeated the three Arab armies in less than a week and conquered territory that increased Israel's size. The war resulted in the loss of territory and was a major blow to Arab honor.

The rejectionist approach to peace adopted by the Arab world at the Khartoum Conference a few months after the 1967 War is evidence of an element of honor that cannot be dismissed. While Israel left open the option of returning these territories in exchange for a lasting peace, the Arabs adopted a different attitude. At the Khartoum Conference Arab League states adopted a resolution that called for what became known as the "Three No's"; "no peace with Israel, no recognition of Israel, no negotiations with it, and insistence on the rights of the Palestinian people in their own country."[25]

Not only did the Arab League refuse any engagement with Israel, Nasser clearly stated that, "what was taken by force will not be returned except by force."[26] This was consistent with the Arabs' obsession with honor suggesting that another war was inevitable. Moreover, the "Three No's" was consistent with the honor lost by the battlefield humiliation of Arab defeat. Thus, Nasser started a bloody War of Attrition (1969-70) that cost Israel 300 soldiers, while Egypt lost thousands and sustained considerable damage to its cities.

Even though Egypt and Jordan eventually accepted UN Security Council Resolution 242, which adopted the principle of exchanging land for peace, the humiliation of 1967 could not go unanswered. Anthropologist Raphael Patai has noted that the concept of honor in the Arab world has multiple dimensions. One of them is the ability to defend oneself with pride and bravery, and to behave with dignity and maintain a positive public image, and this "is extended from the individual, the family, and the tribe to the nation as a whole."[27] Thus, "once honor is impaired, great efforts are needed to restore it."[28]

That attitude remained consistent even under the rule of Anwar Sadat, who ultimately made peace with Israel. Sadat, who succeeded Nasser after the latter's death in 1970, surprised the world with a peace initiative in 1977. However, before that courageous step, he needed to restore Egyptian and Arab national honor. Thus, in October 1973, six years after the Six-Day War, Egypt and Syria launched a surprise attack against Israel that caused Israel thousands of Israeli casualties and brought about the eventual collapse of Prime Minister Golda Meir's Labor government. The war was known as the October War or the Yom Kippur War.

The recovery of Arab honor and dignity was the most important aspect of this war. Despite the military setback they suffered from Israel's impressive counteroffensive, the Egyptians largely viewed the war as a military victory and as a major symbol of national pride. While Egypt and Syria celebrated their victory, bitter disputes erupted among Israeli politicians and among Israeli generals over responsibility for Israel's military failures. Likewise, mass protests demanded the resignation of the government. The crisis in Israel created a spirit of jubilation in the Arab world, which was reflected in the writings of historians, poets, and others. "We were transformed from an honor-less existence, an existence of beasts and animals, into human beings possessed of honor," wrote Egyptian poet Yusef Idris. [29] Riad Ashkar, an Arab author based in Kuwait, explained that, "On the psychological level, the Arab people and soldiers have gained a new level of confidence…. The October war has thus created a sense of insecurity in Israeli society while boosting Arab morale, the Arabs have definitely emerged as the beneficiaries psychologically."[30] Moreover, a former Syrian Prime Minister and co-founder of the Arab Socialist Ba'ath party, Salah al Din Al Bijar, stated that, "The Arabs recovered their self-confidence and their honor, wiped out the blow to their self-respect and the disgrace that had befallen them in the June [1967] War."[31]

Sadat took advantage of this momentum to design a pragmatic strategy to develop Egypt economically and to strengthen relations with the West. Thus, peace with Israel, which surprised Israelis and the world as much as the Yom Kippur War did, was the next step that would facilitate those goals. A peace agreement between Israel and Egypt was signed at Camp David in 1979, but it did not suffice to secure a full normalization of relations with Israel. Egypt's behavior was distant, and at times hostile towards Israel following the peace agreements. Egypt purposely maintained a cold peace, particularly after Hosni Mubarak succeeded Sadat following the latter's assassination in October 1981. The reason for this was Mubarak's desire to break Egypt's isolation in the Arab world that resulted from the peace agreement with Israel. Official Egyptian media, such as the daily newspaper *Al-Ahram*, waged a campaign against normalization with Israel. Egyptian intellectuals were allowed to agitate against the peace. Mubarak also restricted the operations of the Israeli embassy in Cairo. As Fouad Ajami has described it, Egypt's policy towards Israel was dominated by continuous attacks through UN resolutions, particularly expressing opposition to Israel's nuclear program and other negative views. [32]

Egypt was finally reintegrated into the Arab League in 1989. [33]

Egypt also failed to promote bilateral commercial relations and tourism. Egyptian authorities discouraged contact with Israel, and Egypt's public sector even imposed a boycott on Israel. Likewise, professional associations and other groups prevented the development of bilateral relations. Israeli tourism to Egypt had also dramatically decreased. Israeli journalists were prohibited from obtaining visas to enter Egypt and the Journalists Union in Egypt issued a ban on Egyptian journalists who visited Israel.[34] These prohibitions continue to this day, although some progress has been made on economic cooperation and tourism under the government of Abdel Fattah El Sisi [35]

It is important to point out that this hostile attitude was due in part to tensions coming on the heels of Israel's failure to follow through with talks regarding Palestinian autonomy as agreed to in the Camp David Accords, the attack on Iraq's nuclear reactor in the summer of 1981, the passing of an Israeli law that enabled the annexation of the Golan Heights, and, finally, the 1982 Israeli war in Lebanon aimed at destroying the PLO's infrastructure in that country. Egypt also resented the building of Israeli settlements in the West Bank and Israel's handling of the First Intifada.[36]

As we will see, Egypt sabotaged and effectively put an end to the multilateral talks, which were supposed to be a key component of Arab support for the Israeli-Palestinian peace process. It is clear that this hostile relationship, even under conditions of peace, involves elements of honor and resentment that resulted from Egypt's acceptance of a sovereign Jewish state in the heart of the Arab world. A peace agreement was indeed signed. But it was the will of one man, Anwar Sadat, who enjoyed the absolute power of the Egyptian presidency. However, as we will discussed, the Egyptian/Israeli peace particularly disturbed the Egyptian Muslim Brotherhood, whose numbers and influence, as we shall see, grew considerably.

The Arab Failure to Support Multilateral Talks

The multilateral talks were part of a concept that was formed after the 1991 Madrid Conference and were designed to be implemented in parallel with bilateral talks between the Israelis and Palestinians. The idea was to have various Arab countries discuss regional issues and cooperation, "that among other things would also facilitate any concessions made in the bilateral Israeli-Palestinian talks."[37] In other words, the multilateral talks would discuss economic cooperation and development, arms control, water resource issues and refugee-related issues. These talks were supposed to provide stability in a volatile area.[38] But above all, they were supposed to facilitate and guarantee the peace process.

The multilateral talks began early in 1992 (before the Oslo agreements) with the participation of thirty-five countries, including thirteen Arab states, Israel and a Palestinian delegation. The talks continued as the Oslo process commenced. Significantly, the talks were supported by most Arab countries, but were undermined by Egypt, the pioneer of peace negotiations with Israel. By 1993 an Egyptian diplomat, Tahseen Basheer, warned that "some feel that there is a danger that Israel might be made into an industrial base for the region, while the Arabs will simply provide the market."[39]

From the beginning of the arms control negotiations, Egypt demanded that Israel adhere to the Non-Proliferation Treaty (NPT) and dismantle its nuclear capabilities, an unacceptable demand for Israel. Egypt feared that successful multilateral talks would integrate Israel within the Arab world. Such integration would enable Israel to use "soft power" tools, such as technology or economic performance to become dominant in the Arab world. The fact that several Arab Gulf states normalized diplomatic and economic relations with Israel after Jordan's peace agreement with Israel in 1994, heightened Egypt's anxiety about this.[40]

Because of its own security fears, the Israeli security establishment would not agree to discuss its nuclear program, particularly when Israel knew that peace agreements would require her to withdraw from territory. Equally, important Israel was fearful of the uncertainty of peace with the Palestinians and the Arab world.

Egypt's fear of regional peace with Israel also had several dimensions. Since the independence of the Arab countries from colonial rule, the Egyptians have seen themselves not only as the leaders, but as the strongest country in the region. Furthermore, the Nasserist and pan-Arabic traditions envisioned Egypt leading an Arab world without Israel. The multilateral talks involved significant changes in this vision. The multilateral talks imply an acceptance of the Jewish state and integration in the region. These two factors heightened Egypt's concern that Israel's advanced technology and economy would dominate the region. Egypt feared regional isolation due to Israel's newly established relations with Jordan and the Gulf States.[41] Consequently, Egypt abandoned the multilateral talks at the end of 1995.

Mubarak, who came to power in 1981, grew anxious about losing economic ground and political influence in the region to Israel's increasing soft power and influence. There was the feeling that if the 1950s and 1960s were an "Egyptian era" of nationalism, and the 1970s and 1980s were a Saudi era of petrodollars, then the 1990s would be an "Israeli era."[42] That idea obviously stemmed from the fact that Israel was emerging as a technological and innovative powerhouse in a cybernetic age. Israeli Foreign Minister Shimon Peres' idea of an economically integrated new Middle East, where Israel and the Arabs would form a common market similar to Europe, worried those Arabs who feared Israeli hegemony in the region.

The Egyptian government saw Peres' idea, as well as his call for a security conference in Casablanca, Morocco, as a sign of Israel's ambition to dominate the region. This Egyptian attitude was aggravated by Israel's refusal to discuss the subject of its nuclear weapons. According to scholars Said Aly, Abdel Monem, and Shai Feldman, Egypt interpreted Israel's intentions as an attempt to achieve peace from a position of "regional hegemony."[43] For that reason, too, Egypt withdrew from the multilateral talks.

Syria, the only country that did not participate in the multilateral talks and probably the most reluctant player in the region, shared Egypt's concerns. Like Egypt, Syria was troubled by Israel's military might by comparison to their own. The Syrians, like the Egyptians, were also concerned that Israeli integration would be a means for Israel to dominate the region. They also based this argument on Shimon Peres' concept of a new Middle East, a sort of economic integration like the European Union that may affect "our inner feeling of being a nation, and our national and social identity."[44]

It is not difficult to understand why Arab countries did not respond to President Clinton's appeal to encourage Arafat to accept, or even to entertain in good faith, Prime Minister Barak's offers and, later, the Clinton Parameters. Therefore, as the 1996 Israeli elections approached, some Arab leaders even preferred a victory by the more hawkish Netanyahu, in order to pour cold water on the warming prospects arising from the Oslo peace Accords.[45]

Interestingly, Jordan and the Gulf states had a different view. These countries were not concerned with Israel's economic strength or monopoly on nuclear power in the region. In fact, they viewed normalization with Israel as beneficial and resented Egypt's insistence on holding the multilateral talks hostage.[46] Jordan, was genuinely interested in peace and security cooperation with Israel in the region.

Several Gulf States such as Qatar and Oman allowed Israel to open trade offices in their countries. Oman reciprocated by opening a trade office in Tel Aviv. Likewise, trade with the United Arab Emirates increased. [47]The Gulf states are without any doubt the most business-oriented among Arab countries. For them, business and economic profit seem to be more important than political domination or national honor. The most important outcome of the multilateral talks was the peace agreement signed between Israel and the Kingdom of Jordan. King Hussein embraced the peace. He belonged to the Hashemite family, the same family that supported the British against the Ottomans during the Arab revolt, and that maintained secret contact with Israeli leaders since the time Israel was created. Jordan took no issue with non-Arab sovereignty over certain areas. Hussein emphasized the need to make normalcy and humanity the prevailing order in the Middle East. He wanted to put an end to the toxic state of affairs in which leaders could not meet to resolve their differences, or to subordinate other issues to the desire to secure peace for "all children of Abraham." Likewise, he stated that the "sovereignty over the holy places of Jerusalem resides with God, and God alone."[48] In this way, he did not exercise any direct or indirect pressure on Arafat to hold onto the issue of sovereignty over Jerusalem as other Arab leaders had done.

Indeed, Clinton asked Egyptian President Hosni Mubarak, Saudi Arabia's Crown Prince Abdullah, King Abdullah of Jordan and President Ben Ali of Tunisia to provide cover for Arafat's concessions. Only Ben Ali and King Abdullah of Jordan contacted Arafat.[49] Perhaps it is the dovish former Israeli Foreign Minister, Shlomo Ben-Ami, who described the situation best. He said, "the past is frequently the enemy of the future, and nothing in the Arab past has prepared them for the idea of a Jewish sovereign state in their midst. Hostages of their traditional way of dealing with the Jews as nothing more than a tolerated minority, the Arabs only fueled the paranoiac instincts of the Israelis."[50]

Crisis of Legitimacy and the Rise of an Islamic "Constituency" in the Arab World

Fear of Israeli hegemony in the region was not the only reason for the Arabs' reluctance to endorse an Israeli-Palestinian peace agreement. Deep domestic issues were also involved. Dennis Ross, former U.S. Special envoy to the Middle East and architect of most peace initiatives under Presidents George H. W. Bush and Bill Clinton, made the following key observation:

> Arab leaders have long sought to use the cause of Palestine without ever thinking that it imposed a price on them... they understood that it has tremendous resonance with their publics...Here was a justification for anger that could be useful in diverting attention away from the failings of any regime. Here was imagery that could be used to build internal legitimacy for regimes that had little.
>
> Nevertheless, it was their very lack of legitimacy that made Arab leaders reluctant to pressure Yasir Arafat to be responsible and seize opportunities. No Arab leader wanted Arafat to say publicly that he... had pressured [Arafat] to surrender Palestinian rights. Arab leaders may have used the cause of Palestine, but they also became trapped by it.[51]

Ross makes an important point. When Sadat visited Jerusalem in November 1977, the Muslim Brotherhood and other Islamic groups with whom Sadat sought cooperation to develop the country, broke relations with his regime. As a result, Sadat proceeded to dissolve the Islamist Egyptian student unions, closing their summer camps and confiscating their property, and censoring Muslim Brotherhood publications.[52]

Following Sadat's assassination, Mubarak began to persecute radical Muslims. He destroyed extremist factions, forcing the Muslim Brotherhood to distance themselves from the extreme Islamist groups. As a result, the Muslim Brotherhood kept a low profile for a few years. However, several years later Mubarak proceeded to lift restrictions on the Muslim Brotherhood. He called for legislative elections that allowed the participation of the Brotherhood, which

managed to elect a few representatives. The government also par-
doned a number of Muslim radicals arrested in the aftermath of
Sadat's assassination.[53]

Thus, the Brotherhood returned to the scene in a more active
fashion. They began to run for leadership of student unions and
professional associations. By the mid-80s, the Brotherhood dominated twenty-two professional associations. By penetrating professional associations, they were also able to reach into the middle
class, whose prosperity was aided by a system of Islamist banking.[54]

Islamist banks and investment funds, which expanded with the
help of Saudi capital, worked with a large portion of the business
class and other important sectors of the economy. Islamic banks
provided better interest rates for investors than other banks. Between 1980 and 1985, more than one hundred Islamic investment
companies were created that offered 25 percent return and attracted large deposits. The Egyptian government encouraged Islamist
institutions in order to co-opt the middle classes, whose eventual
prosperity they believed would secure loyalty to the regime. [55]

Politically, the Muslim Brotherhood increased their representation in parliament as well as in the media. They released more
than 14,000 hours of broadcast, "ceding moral primacy to [radical]
preachers."[56] Islamists secured a ban on alcohol on Egyptian Air
flights, and several provincial governors issued their own bans on
alcohol. Other Islamists in parliament encouraged laws influenced
by Sharia, Islamic law. Thus, Salafist clerics began to dominate all
domains of culture and public attitudes.[57]

However, as the Egyptian government came to understand
the role of the Islamist financial system in empowering Islamist
opposition, Mubarak once again launched an offensive against
them. Links between these banks and Islamic extremists were exposed, and accusations of fraud against Islamist companies began
to emerge. Such government campaigns led to the withdrawal of
deposits, and many of those financial institutions filed for bank-
ruptcy.[58]

These repressive measures were not enough to curtail the growing influence of Islamists, and Mubarak adopted an anti-Israel discourse to appease them. Egypt's attitude of disdain towards Israel
was a concession to the professional associations and other sectors

of civil society, mainly the Islamists, who rejected the peace agreement with all their might. As Robert Wistrich explains, "For the fundamentalists, the peace with Israel was, and still remains, nothing less than a poison threatening the lifeblood of Islam, a symptom of its profound malaise, weakness and decadence. The Muslim Brotherhood leadership has defined normalization with Israel as a dangerous cancer eating away our cells."[59] In other words, they spoke of a contamination within Islamic society that would come from interaction and normalization with Israel.

As previously mentioned, direct and indirect travel restrictions to Israel also characterized the Mubarak era. Mubarak himself abstained from travelling to Israel, and he discouraged any type of traffic with Israel. According to Ajami, "the intellectual class was given a green light to agitate against peace with Israel."[60] This included official newspapers, such as *Al-Ahram*. In *Al-Ahram's* view, "Israel is an enforcer of a *Pax Americana*," where Egypt's role is diminished, "severing Egypt from its natural hinterland in the Fertile Crescent and the Persian Gulf."[61] In the global political arena, Egypt attempted to curb Israel's nuclear capability and promote anti-Israel resolutions in the United Nations.[62]

Although the Muslim Brotherhood and the Islamists were kept at bay in a broader political sense, they still had veto power over decisions that could be understood as capitulation to Israel and the West. This point was very effective from the opposition's point of view because it converged with Egypt's ideological traditions of nationalism and pan-Arabism. As Middle East scholar Kenneth Stein has noted, "In perspective, the Camp David Accords were another interim step, another disengagement agreement just like Nixon-Ford had negotiated in 1974-1975. The Accords were a transaction of exchanging land for peace; they did not transform Arab attitudes toward Israel."[63]

Even today, Egyptian media officials continue to attack Israel and Jews in general. Despite the July 2013 overthrow of the government of the Muslim Brotherhood and the fact that the brotherhood was declared a terrorist entity, the official Egyptian media continues to attack Israel and the Jewish people despite some changes in attitudes towards Israel by the current president Abdel Fatah El Sisi. Jews are portrayed as expansionists and ambitious to the point that they want to control the world or force most nations to align themselves with Israel. The American Israel Public Affairs Committee (AIPAC), the pro-Israel lobby in the United States, seems to be the primary target of attacks. According to official Egyptian publications, AIPAC not only seeks to influence policy, but also decides who will be the next president of the United States. They also claim Jews are trying to destabilize the Arab world by promoting the Arab Spring.[64]

The same problem is evident in Jordan where a situation exists in which the monarchy supported and even promoted the peace process, but the presence of a substantial Palestinian population hostile to Israel has prevented full normalization. The Palestinian diaspora in Jordan is generally opposed to normalization and has expressed tremendous hostility towards Israel.

Palestinian influence has caused professional associations and other opposition elements in civil society to oppose normalization with Israel. In the last several years, there has been a movement in Jordan calling for the cancellation of the peace agreements. Occasionally, King Abdullah of Jordan makes a move that looks hostile towards Israel in order to appease public opinion. One example is the King's declaration that Jordan would not ratify an annex of the peace treaty that enabled Israel to renew the lease of lands located in Jordanian territory.[65]

Like the case of Egyptian-Israeli relations, the peace agreement is viewed by the Jordanian government through the lens of strategic interests, especially regarding security cooperation. Fear of terrorism and the threat from Iran constitute the backbone of the relationship between both countries. There have been some economic transactions, such as a natural gas deal, but cooperation at this level is lacking. Nor is there much civilian or diplomatic dialogue.[66] There is a gap between public opinion and the government's will to seek cooperation with Israel. Therefore, according to Jordanian scholar Abdullah Sawalha, the Jordanian government downplays the agreement in its communications with constituents. It falsely claims that this is part of an international agreement rather than a bilateral Israel-Jordan agreement.[67]

Furthermore, significant sectors of the Jordanian media publish anti-Israel stories and opinion pieces that include justification for Palestinian acts of terror against Israeli civilians as well as expressions of anti-Semitism. Classic anti-Semitic texts such as *Mein Kampf* and the *Protocols of the Elders of Zion* are visibly displayed in Jordanian bookstores. Media characterizations of Jews as fraudulent and deceiving are also very common.[68]

According to another Jordanian scholar, Wasfi Kailani, peace with Israel is perceived as an extension of the Arab defeat in 1967. In other words, it is interpreted as capitulation and, therefore, a stain on Arab and Jordanian honor. Jordanian media and other sources, particularly since the eruption of the Second Intifada, have portrayed the peace as an attempt by Israel to achieve regional superiority, something Israelis have not been able to accomplish through military means.[69]

Since the conclusion of the peace agreements between Israel and Jordan, religious leaders have issued *Fatwas* against normalization with Israel, which, according to Kailani, have influenced the opinions of thousands of people.[70] These perceptions were aggravated by the Second Intifada and Israeli military operations in Gaza and Lebanon. Hezbollah's show of power in Lebanon encouraged resistance as an alternative to a negotiated peace. However, more importantly, these negative attitudes, according to some observers, are the result of years of negative stereotypes and propaganda.[71] This point is a crucial one and similar to the point made in Chapter 2 about the long-term effects of propaganda on the Palestinians. Thus, the economic and other potential benefits that a Jordanian-Israeli peace could offer seem to be less relevant than the psychological and political questions of shame, honor, resentment and ideology. However, the main difference between Jordan and Egypt lies in the firm attitude of the Jordanian leadership, particularly the late King Hussein, in openly supporting the peace agreement with Israel and preparing his people. King Hussein's attitude contrasts sharply with Mubarak's.

In Saudi Arabia, the oil boom of the 1970s generated wealth that translated into modernization and an improved standard of living. Paradoxically, this situation increased tensions between the Saudi government and Islamists who perceived these changes in societal structures and social practices as inspired by the West and thereby anathema to traditional Muslim practices. At the same time, the traditional social bonds that produced a cohesive society began to unravel. Furthermore, the advance of modernization created an existential crisis and a breakdown of traditional ways that opened the door for Islamist teachings. This included the doctrines of Wahabbism, the Egyptian and Syrian Muslim Brotherhood, and eventually the Afghan Taliban.[72]

Paradoxically, the authoritarian and repressive character of these Arab states strengthened Islamist groups precisely because highly repressive Arab governments did not allow any type of political expression from their citizens. Lacking any other outlet, new and growing discontents found expression in one of the few vehicles Arabs and Muslims had, namely religion. Mosques became instruments of expression, mostly monopolized by the most extreme fundamentalists who exacerbated hatred of Israel, the West, and the Arab rulers who were portrayed as aligned with the "oppressive" West. The ease with which Islamic teachings penetrated the mindset of the regular citizen is not only because such teachings were spread in Mosques and schools, but also because, as Middle East scholar Bernard Lewis explains, "[religious teaching] is readily intelligible to both educated and uneducated Muslims. It offers a set of themes, slogans, and symbols that are profoundly familiar and therefore effective in mobilizing support and in formulating both a critique of what is wrong and a program for putting it right."[73]

Most importantly, Islamism, although it gained strength from the social transformation of the oil boom, succeeded in replacing traditional sources of legitimacy like pan-Arabism. Islamists effectively portrayed the Saudis and Egyptians as having sold out economically and politically to Western interests. Religious opposition groups were the only ones who had regular meeting places where followers could assemble and have at their disposal a network outside the control of the state.

Thus, the more dictatorial the regime, the more it enabled fundamentalists to virtually assert a monopoly on the opposition. In Saudi Arabia, high levels of repression and the predominance of Wahhabism[74] encouraged the rise of Islamic fundamentalists. For some perplexing reasons, Saudi Arabia greatly feared subversive activities in the kingdom and funneled money from state coffers to terrorist organizations in order to appease these insurgent groups.

Al Qaeda was a recipient of such funds in order "to pay off Bin Laden to cause trouble elsewhere but not in the kingdom".[75] The Saudi government suspected that it was failing to prevent the funding of terrorist organizations by Saudi Islamic charities. At the same time, Saudi individuals continued to fund these organizations despite U.S and international pressure to stop such activity. The Saudi government also provided funding to religious establishments that promoted Wahhabism, and used government funds to spread this doctrine all over the Muslim world. According to Farah Pandith, advisor to Presidents Bush and Obama on Muslim affairs, Saudi Arabia has spent close to $100 billion spreading Wahhabism in Muslim countries.[76] Before 9/11 Saudi Embassies had religious attachés that handed money to madrassas and mosques.[77] Such Wahhabi training, Pandith claims, "made young Muslims vulnerable to recruitment by extremist groups, including those unaligned with or even opposed to the Saudi regime."[78] All this was taking place while the Saudis continued to deliver speeches against terrorism.[79]

Much like Egyptians, Saudis believed that as long as radical Islamists do not endanger the Saudi regime, they should have money and freedom of expression. Similarly, Islamist news media, radical preachers, and financing of terrorism paradoxically existed in parallel with Saudi Arabia's antipathy towards al-Qaeda and other radicals living among them. Thus, making room for Wahhabism, the Muslim Brotherhood, and other Islamists is part of a vicious cycle where the authoritarian state makes ideological and economic concessions to these extreme groups. Israel became one of the main casualties of their fierce ideological offensive.

Syrian Legitimacy and the Question of Israel

Syria was less influential in the Oslo peace process. However, Syria's role differed from that of Saudi Arabia and Egypt because Syria has had an interest in maintaining a perpetual state of war with Israel. Although the Ba'ath party has traditionally been the vehicle of a strong pan-Arab and socialist ideology in Syria, the power of this ideology was vague and weak. According to some observers, this vagueness intentionally allowed different interpretations to include various groups and to generate consensus.[80] However, since

Hafez al-Assad's rise to power in1970, Syria has turned into a sectarian Alawite minority regime that has disenfranchised its Sunni majority and created a crisis of legitimacy.

In Syria, as in Iraq, which also experienced Sunni minority rule over the Shiite majority, the cult of personality surrounding Assad became more important than ideology. This lack of emphasis on ideology created anxiety among party leaders who were concerned about its impact on party cadres' confidence in its leadership.[81] Fomenting opposition to Israel was a perfect tool to cover over the lack of cohesion and unity of purpose. The continuation of war against Israel helped compensate for the regime's deficit of legitimacy and the intellectual weakness of its ideology. More importantly, the war against Israel kept the Syrian army in a state of mobilization. The mobilized army was used as an economic and political instrument,[82] and not necessarily as an instrument of war.

The militarization of Syria had further societal implications that were vital for the survival of the Assad regime. Indeed, war, whether actual or ostensible, helped to mobilize the people through its "rally 'round the flag effect." War keeps the army busy and increases the power of the state. As political scientist and Syria expert Steven Haydemann points out, "it is precisely the normalization of war, the routinization of urgent threats to the nation, the transformation of the extraordinary into the everyday that reflects the extent to which militarism organizes processes of state formation and state-society relations in a number of Middle East countries."[83] Indeed, wars help centralize the power of the authoritarian state, exacerbate nationalism, and create an economic complex that generates jobs, honor, status and careers. In other words, war is a producer of legitimacy.

Under the rule of Hafez al-Assad (1970-2000), the state and the armed forces were expanded, decision-making was centralized, and professional associations, unions and other civil society groups were reorganized into hierarchical, corporatist bodies. These groups became sources not only of representation in a corporatist state, but also sources of mobilization. This helped the regime penetrate deep into society. However, as German political scientist Volker Perthes points out, the ability of the Syrian regime to consolidate power, maintain its stability, and support its capacity to generate substantial external rents, is deeply related to the militarization of society. Most importantly, such enterprises are largely based on a constant preparation for war and not necessarily for the conduct of one.[84] Indeed, war preparation in the Syrian case was not only a means to launch a war, but, more importantly, an end in itself. Particularly after the Yom Kippur War, its last major military confrontation with Israel, "Syria's continued militarization did not imply that the regime intended to lead a war...Rather, it is the domestic social and political benefits of protracted militarization, subsidized by external resources that explain the regime's determination to preserve Syria's status as a security state."[85] Thus, Syria's state of war is linked to domestic preservation, regime enhancement, and survival.

The Syrian regime justified its state of war arguing that Israel's peace with Egypt had left Syria alone on the battlefield. Israel still retained the Golan Heights, which Syria considered hers. There was also fear that Israel could gain influence in Lebanon. In 1982, during the Israeli military campaign to root out the PLO, a short military confrontation took place between Israel and Syria on Lebanese soil that destroyed more than eighty Syrian planes and devastated the Syrian army. This confrontation forced Assad to withdraw from part of the Bekah Valley and accept a ceasefire. Recognizing that any war with Israel would result in humiliation and even regime collapse, Syria has avoided any further military confrontation with its southern neighbor since then. However, the state of political confrontation with Israel has fed a nationalist ideology that has helped the Syrian government create unity and justify militarization.

The Syrian military has played an important social role as well. Military and security apparatuses are agents of socialization for youth. Such inclusion of the youth serves the regime and helps "to politically contain the population."[86] Thus, in Syria, the "state of war" has served as justification for the creation of politicized institutions loyal to the regime. In the early 1990s, the security apparatus and the army provided employment to half of the state employees, not counting the tens of thousands of conscripts enlisted in compulsory service. The army offered opportunities for career advancement and provided conscripts the possibility of continuing their service in the army.

The army has penetrated deep into Syrian society. Education in Syria is militaristic. The military trains members of the Ba'ath party and runs mandatory military courses in high schools and universities. Given the military's penetration into national life, it has been pointed out that Syrian youth are seriously indoctrinated into the "values of sacrifice and martyrdom for the defense of the homeland against its enemies and for the liberation of the occupied territories."[87] Even non-military personnel, including those in the private sector, are forced to participate in the "war effort."[88] The priority given to bolstering legitimacy and survival of the regime can also be seen in the fact that Syrian troops are concentrated around Damascus, like a Praetorian Guard, a body in charge of protecting the safety of the ruler rather than a conventional army at the front lines. Syria has not made any serious effort to develop a strong military industry, even after the collapse of its main benefactor, the Soviet Union.[89] Since legitimacy has been tied to militarization, and militarization has depended on the state of war with Israel, it is clear that the need to maintain Israel as an enemy, at least on paper, has been vital to the stability of the regime. As we pointed out, actual war with Israel would be catastrophic.

There has been a plethora of literature about the Israeli-Syrian negotiations during the 1990s and 2000s, including by authors such as Martin Indyk, Dennis Ross and Itamar Rabinovich. Plain descriptions of the negotiations reveal differences of opinions and mutual distrust between the two sides. Syria has even made unreasonable requests, such as demanding the Golan as a pre-condition for peace talks, not an acceptable proposal for Israel who acknowledged the principle of land for peace not land for negotiations. The Hafiz Assad regime also expressed concern that a peace agreement would leave Syria at a strategic disadvantage. Perthes astutely observed that if the Syrian regime reached peace with Israel, it would be subjected to a pure domestic legitimacy and would be forced to bargain or confront opposition in Syrian society, something that could destabilize the regime.[90] This is why the aspiration of the late Israeli Prime Minister Yitzhak Rabin and former Prime Minister Ehud Barak, to reach a peace agreement with Syria,[91] was doomed to fail from the outset.

The events of 2011 confirmed the logic of Assad's policy. The Syrian situation proved to be extremely fragile and sectarian. Throughout its existence, Syria utilized slogans such as revolutionary nationalism, pan-Arabism and socialism to sustain some degree of internal unity. Nevertheless, Syria became a country ruled by Allawites, crony capitalists whose closeness to the state elite was the name of the game, with all the sectarian and corrupt implications of this kind of regime. Therefore, a state of war, either active or inactive, or normalization of war, was what provided a sense of unity. That ended with the outbreak of the Syrian civil war in 2011.

Positive Developments in the Arab World: The Arab Peace Initiative and the Rise of el-Sisi in Egypt

As we have seen, countries like Saudi Arabia and Egypt are trapped in a hostile relationship with Israel. However, an interesting development, particularly in 2017, is that of an increasing interest on the parts of Arabs and Israelis to support the 2002 Arab Peace Initiative. The Arab Peace Initiative was developed by then-Saudi Crown Prince Abdullah and adopted by the Arab League in March 2002. The initiative, which was reaffirmed by the Arab League in 2007 and also in 2017, expressed a willingness to end the conflict and normalize relations with Israel. Furthermore, the document proposes offering an end to the Arab-Israeli conflict, "to enter a peace agreement with Israel, and provide security for all the states of the region."[92] Moreover, it clarifies that the initiative is the result of "the conviction of the Arab countries that a military solution to the conflict will not achieve peace or provide security for the parties,..."[93] These points sharply contrast with the Khartoum Resolution issued after the Six-Day War, in which Arab countries clearly stated that no peace, no negotiations, and no recognition of Israel were acceptable to them.

Indeed, the Arab Initiative seems to display a different spirit, but it was first proposed during the Second Intifada, when Israel's population was being terrorized daily by Hamas and other Palestinian militant groups. Shortly after the publication of the Initiative, Israel launched Operation Defensive Shield to root out terrorist groups and restore order after a suicide bombing that killed thirty civilians in the Israeli city of Netanya. The Arab Initiative came at a precarious moment for the peace process and for the security of Israel. The Israelis were skeptical of the Arab Initiative since the Arabs themselves refused to cooperate with U.S. President Clinton to encourage the Palestinians to accept any sort of deal. Indeed, they ultimately walked away from that responsibility. As Bruce Weitzman notes, the violence of the Second Intifada may have been the result of Arab absence from the peace process, which proved to be damaging. Furthermore, Arab countries reacted to the Second Intifada by supporting the insurgency and blaming Israel for the outbreak of violence. They proceeded to cease all diplomatic and commercial relations with Israel and condemned Israel for war crimes at the United Nations.[94] Furthermore, the fact that the Arab Peace Initiative also proposed that Israel accept the "right of return" of Palestinian refugees and their descendants to Israel proper, was not seen as a serious negotiating point given the fact that this issue was previously a major obstacle to a peace agreement.[95]

After the 9/11 attacks, President George W. Bush reevaluated the old notion that Arab authoritarian states provided stability in the region. In his view, that concept was disproven by the regimes' inability to prevent the emergence of Islamic extremism. Thus, promoting democracy in the Middle East, which among other things paved the way for the invasion of Iraq, worried Arab countries, particularly Saudi Arabia, whose dependency on U.S. protection is crucial. In this context, the Arab Peace Initiative was an attempt by Saudi Arabia and other Arab countries to ingratiate themselves with an impatient American president ready to reevaluate the special relationships with those countries. Consistent with our earlier arguments, it was Jordan, which was the Arab state most conciliatory toward Israel, that suggested omitting in the Arab Peace Initiative, the provision referring to UN Resolution 194, which demands the return of all Palestinian refugees to their homes in Israel. The Jordanian rationale was that inclusion of "the right of return" provision, would indicate a lack of seriousness on the part of Arabs towards peace efforts.[96] However, it was Syria's insistence on its inclusion that prevailed, making it easier for the Israelis to dismiss it. Jordan tried again to secure a similar modification years later, but to no avail.[97] This decision made it discernibly harder for the Arab

Peace Initiative to be taken seriously. Fifteen years later, the Arab Peace Initiative was revived and even considered by Israeli Prime Minister Benjamin Netanyahu. However, this time, the resuscitation of the initiative was not the result of the need to demonstrate to the United States the value of the Arab world in light of American disappointment. This time, it was the result of new geo-political developments in the area.

Changing Circumstances in Arab Israeli Relations

First, Iran is becoming even more influential in the region, and there is a feeling, especially after the 2015 nuclear deal reached between world powers and Iran, that the United States is retreating from the region leaving Saudi Arabia and other countries at the mercy of the Islamic Republic. Indeed, the final nuclear agreement, also known as the Joint Comprehensive Plan of Action (JCPOA), did not require Iran to completely stop enriching uranium or conducting nuclear research. Furthermore, after ten years, restrictions on research and development would have been lifted, posing a risk of shortening the amount of time, by approximately one year, to produce enough weapons-grade uranium. After fifteen years, Iran would no longer be limited in its centrifuge operations or uranium enrichment.[98] This means that Iran could obtain a dangerous nuclear capability regardless of an explicit provision in the deal forbidding Iran from developing nuclear weapons.

The JCPOA negotiations did not consider Iran's destabilizing activities in different countries of the region or its support of proxy groups such as Hezbollah, the Iraqi Shiite militias or the Houthi insurgents in Yemen. The Obama administration also gave Iran an implicit guarantee that it would not interfere in Iran's hegemonic aspirations in the Middle East. In an interview with the American journalist Jeffrey Goldberg, Obama stated, "The competition between the Saudis and the Iranians, which has helped to feed proxy wars and chaos in Syria, Iraq and Yemen, requires us to say to our friends as well as to the Iranians that they need to find an effective way to share the neighborhood and institute some sort of cold peace."[99] This statement confirms Obama's willingness to cede Iran more regional control in exchange for the nuclear deal.

This position puts Saudi status as a U.S. ally in question. Obama himself expressed irritation over "the foreign-policy orthodoxy" that dogmatically viewed Saudi Arabia as an ally.[100]

Meanwhile, Iran continued to recruit Shiites in Iraq to fight in Syria for Assad, despite objections from Iraqi Shiite leaders such as the influential Ayatollah Ali al-Sistani.[101] Furthermore, Iran undermined nation building in Iraq by supporting former Iraqi Prime Minister Nouri al-Maliki's sectarian policies against the will of the Iraqi people, who in the 2010 elections, voted for Ayad Allawi from the nonsectarian Iraqi National Movement. Iran's interference in Iraq helped Maliki destroy any hope for Sunni/Shia co-existence in the country.

Iran has also interfered in the delicate situation in Yemen, supporting the Houthi rebellion and helping to depose the interim president. Iran's actions in Yemen in turn forced Saudi Arabia to intervene militarily in that country. The Iran-backed Houthi rebellion has caused a situation of anarchy and civil war that is potentially destabilizing. Iran's pan-Shiite strategy has also led to interference in Bahrain, the only Gulf state with a Shiite majority that is politically underrepresented and discriminated against. Bahrain is dominated by a Sunni ruling elite and is considered a protégée of Saudi Arabia, Iran's regional Sunni rival. Finally, Iran also added another challenge to the equation when its government, under the guidance of the elite Islamic Revolutionary Guard Corps (IRGC), test-fired three ballistic missiles, two in October and November of 2015, and one in March 2016.

Saudi-Israeli cooperation has increased as a result of the need to contain Iran's advancement in the region by what is perceived as former U.S. President Obama's dismissal of Saudi Arabia as a reliable ally, and his call on the Kingdom to "share" the Middle East, apparently with Iran. This kind of disregard from Obama generated a harsh reaction from Saudi Arabia. In an open letter to the U.S president, Prince Turki al-Faisal stressed why Saudi Arabia is an ally in fighting terrorism and counterbalancing Iran, asserting,

> [You and King Salman] affirmed the "need, in particular, to counter Iran's destabilizing activities." Now, you throw us a curve ball. You accuse us of fomenting sectarian strife in

Syria, Yemen and Iraq. You add insult to injury by telling us to share our world with Iran, a country that you describe as a supporter of terrorism and which you promised our king to counter its "destabilizing activities . . ." . . . is it because you have pivoted to Iran so much that you equate the Kingdom's 80 years of constant friendship with America to an Iranian leadership that continues to describe America as the biggest enemy, that continues to arm, fund and support sectarian militias in the Arab and Muslim world, that continues to harbor and host Al-Qaeda leaders, that continues to prevent the election of a Lebanese president through Hezbollah, which is identified by your government as a terrorist organization, that continues to kill the Syrian Arab people in league with Bashar Assad?[102]

The entire letter seems to suggest that the Saudis were suspicious and fearful of Iran and certainly did not wish to share the Middle East as Obama envisioned. This issue, so important for the Saudis, was understood better by the Israelis than the Obama administration. For Saudi Arabia and Israel, the Islamic Republic of Iran represents a real and vital threat. The Obama administration was so consumed with normalization of relations with Iran that it alienated traditional allies in the region such as Saudi Arabia. This situation created an important and unprecedented momentum for cooperation between Israel and Arab Sunni states that can be ultimately helpful to the Israeli-Palestinian conflict.

Yet, this momentum is not free of obstacles. Saudi Arabia and Israel indeed have had strong cooperation on intelligence as a result of these new threats. In May 2016 Prince Turki, a former Saudi intelligence chief, and Yaakov Amidror, a former Israeli general and head of the Israeli National Security Council, held a joint public meeting sponsored by the Washington Institute for Near East Policy. At the meeting, Prince Turki reaffirmed his view that the issue of Israel and Palestine has not affected the relationship between the United States and Saudi Arabia. Prince Turki spoke specifically about the need to fight terrorism.[103] He denounced the Israeli settlements, the roadblocks in the West Bank and the occupation in general, but he also spoke in terms that were unconceivable for Saudi leaders in the past. At one point, Prince Turki stated that,

> ... cooperation between Arabs and Israel can be fortified if there is peace between the two...I do not see any difficulty in achieving that cooperation. If we have two states with mutual land swaps, we can build this cooperation . . . mutual cooperation [between Arabs and Israelis] is possible not just on Iran . . . We could also cooperate on science, technology and humanitarian affairs.[104]

Prince Turki's words are significant insofar as he is talking not only about peace with Israel, but also about cooperation in the style envisioned by Shimon Peres, the same vision that unsettled Egypt with fears of Israeli technological and economic hegemony.[105]

In July 2016, retired Saudi General Anwar Eshki, along with a delegation, visited Israel and met with important Israeli and Palestinian leaders.[106] General Eshki had been in contact with a number of Israeli high officers since 2015. Furthermore, it was reported that, because of cooperation between the two countries, they might undertake small-scale economic ties.[107]

Despite these steps, the Saudi position is more complex and problematic. Both Prince Turki and General Eshki have denied the possibility that Arab countries will make peace with Israel before the Israelis sign an agreement with the Palestinians. While referring to the conflict, General Eshki pointed out that, "The Israeli-Palestinian conflict is not the source of terrorism, but it does create fertile ground for acts of terrorism in the region. If the conflict is resolved, the countries that exploit the Palestinian issue, namely Iran, will no longer be able to capitalize on it."[108] What is interesting about this remark is that it recognizes that the conflict is perpetuated by other countries in the region seeking to exploit it. Although Eshki referred to Iran, that has been the case also with Saudi Arabia, Egypt and other countries. Furthermore, Saudi Crown Prince Mohammed bin Salman stated in an interview in April 2018 that he recognizes the right of the Jewish people to have a nation-state of their own next to a Palestinian state. Such a statement is unprecedented for a Saudi leader. [109] In the same interview, he also spoke about cooperation with Israel, not only because of their shared enmity towards Iran, but also because, were peace to be signed, there would be common economic interests between Israel, Egypt, Jordan and the Gulf Co-operation Council.[110] In a meeting with American Jewish leaders, Prince Salman fiercely criticized the Palestinian leadership for rejecting opportunities for peace with Israel. He pointed out that, "It is about time the Palestinians take the proposals and agree to come to the negotiating table or shut up and stop complaining."[111] This statement could be an indication of the extent to which a new window of opportunity may open up for Arab/Israeli reconciliation, if we consider that Saudi Arabia is a regional leader and the architect of the Arab Peace Initiative. Although Prime Minister Netanyahu accepted the Arab Peace Initiative as a good starting point, Israel has not yet provided a meaningful response to the proposal.

In Egypt, after the social protests in Tahrir Square toppled Mubarak and the brief rule of the Muslim Brotherhood under Mohamed Morsi, Abdel Fattah el-Sisi designed domestic and foreign policies aimed at neutralizing the power of the Muslim Brotherhood. Sisi views the Muslim Brotherhood as the source of extremist Islamic ideologies.[112] For el-Sisi, the Brotherhood spawned Hamas, ISIS and even al-Qaeda. He views all these extremist ideologies as interrelated and essentially cut from the same cloth.

In January 2015, Sisi delivered a speech calling for Islamic reformation. In his speech, el-Sisi stated that "the corpus of [Islamic] texts and ideas that we have sacralized over the centuries" are "antagonizing the entire world" and could bring about the physical destruction of the Islamic world.[113] He blamed religious clerics for the spread of radical ideas and warned Arabs and Muslims in general "not to remain trapped in this mindset" and to "reflect on it from a more enlightened perspective."[114] Sisi called for a "religious revolution" and made Imams "responsible before Allah" to make that change. "The entire world is waiting for your next move because this ummah [Islamic world] is being torn, it is being destroyed, it is being lost, and it is being lost by our own hands."[115] Sisi is trying to change the predominant narrative of the educational system, which he views as favoring radical Islam and the most extremist groups. The Egyptian government has begun a process of reeducation using the education system and other means to counteract extreme religious ideas. The constitution recommends that education curricula focus on national identity and a sort of balance between modern educational materials and cultural heritage. According to these recommendations, schools must offer activities that promote citizenship and tolerance. Al-Azhar University, an institution associated with the Mosque of the same name, has approved new school curricula that reflect the constitutional provisions mentioned above. [116] In the past, Al Azhar remained silent in the face of religious extremism. Its curriculum contained religious teachings considered extremist, including the idea that religious offenders such as fornicators and those who do not pray, should be executed. Al Azhar was also known for being oriented to Muslim students and often demeaning Coptic Christians.[117]

As Sisi pointed out, "Religious rhetoric is a problem. It has certain ideas that just promote confused thoughts about religion when adopted by people. People resort to violence when they adopt these wrong religious ideas."[118] Whereas the Mubarak government and Saudi Arabia tolerated this type of rhetoric, Sisi seems to be intolerant of such discourse and therefore not likely to appease the Muslim Brotherhood as Mubarak did.

Sisi views Hamas as an offshoot of the Muslim Brotherhood. Thus, an Egyptian court announced in February 2015 that Hamas was a terrorist organization. Although this decision was reversed a few months later, the military wing of Hamas, the Al-Qassam Brigades, remains designated as a terrorist organization.[119] Tension between Egypt and Hamas intensified after the former accused the latter of murdering an Egyptian prosecutor in June 2015. Sisi views Hamas as a negative, destabilizing force. Sisi was also infuriated by the fact that Hamas allowed Iran to operate in Gaza. Likewise, Egypt strongly objected to Hamas' attempts at working with Turkey to build a port in Gaza, concerned that such a port could be used to smuggle weapons to *jihadists* who could endanger Egypt's national security. By the same token, Egypt resented Turkey's closeness to the Muslim Brotherhood. Sisi criticized Hamas for adhering to armed resistance and urged the group to weigh the balance of achievements and failures, effectively suggesting that Hamas' methods have failed. Thus, Sisi fought Hamas and applied pressure on the group to cease harboring and cooperating with the

Islamic State in Gaza. Tunnels that served to smuggle weapons and other items from Egypt to Gaza were flooded and destroyed. Additionally, Egypt aggressively battled *jihadists* in the Sinai Peninsula, something that neither Mubarak, nor Morsi, were willing to do.[120]

As previously mentioned, Egypt, like Israel and Saudi Arabia, is very concerned about the rise of Iran. Immediately after the deposal of Hosni Mubarak, the Supreme Council of the Armed Forces (SCAF), which ruled the country, attempted to ease tensions with Iran by allowing Iranian warships to transit the Suez Canal. After the Muslim Brotherhood came to power under the leadership of Mohamed Morsi, relations between the two traditional rivals warmed further. Morsi visited Tehran and then reciprocated by hosting Iran's president, the ultra-conservative Mahmoud Ahmadinejad. This was part of the revolutionary agenda of the Muslim Brotherhood that tried to break with the practices of past Egyptian governments. However, Sisi reversed course towards Iran. Sisi joined Saudi Arabia efforts to prevent the Iranian-backed Houthis in Yemen from taking over the country. Egypt and Saudi Arabia worried that a Houthi takeover would threaten free passage through the Bab al- Mandab strait, which connects the Red Sea to the Gulf of Aden and serves as major passageway for international shipments. Sisi expelled the Iranian ambassador from Cairo to protest Iran's subversive activities in the region.[121] In addition, security and intelligence cooperation with Israel against Hamas in Gaza increased exponentially. When the French launched a Middle East peace initiative in June 2016, Egypt enthusiastically supported it. What is important is the fact that Egypt accepted the idea of securing a peace treaty with Israel that would ensure Palestinian national aspirations and security for Israel. Netanyahu reacted positively to President Sisi's attitude. The Egyptian position is important because it appears to be a departure from the unconstructive attitudes Egypt displayed in the past towards Israel. Early in 2015, Sisi noted in defense of the Egyptian-Israeli peace agreements that "the hostile mood and skepticism [between Egypt and Israel] have diminished. This can happen with the other Arab countries and Israel if a two-state solution is reached."[122]

Furthermore, in February 2016 it was reported that Egyptian history textbooks used in schools would include the country's

1979-peace treaty with Israel for the first time. The textbooks reaffirm the fact that Egypt and Israel ended the state of war with "each side respecting the sovereignty and independence of the other." [123] This is part of a project being carried out by Sisi to revise about 1,300 textbooks.[124] In January 2019, Sisi acknowledged in an interview with CBS's *60 minutes* that Egypt now has the closest cooperation with Israel it has ever had, particularly over control of terrorist activity in the Sinai Peninsula.[125] Furthermore, Israel has allowed Egypt to double its military presence in Sinai beyond the terms of the peace treaty.[126] Moreover, in February 2018 an Israeli gas giant signed a fifteen billion dollar deal to supply sixty-four billion cubic meters of natural gas to Egypt for ten years. This unprecedented agreement[127] is likely to be followed by the construction of a pipeline and further infrastructure, where interdependence and cooperation could develop between Israel and Egypt, and also benefit neighboring countries, including the PA.[128] But what is more important is that Egypt is showing an unprecedented level of openness to Israel.

This move is significant, because it demonstrates a shift away from Mubarak's ambivalence towards the peace process and the Nasserist legacy of pan-Arabism, nationalism, and hostility towards Israel rooted in honor and shame as well as on anti-Western feelings and ideology. Whether this time Egypt will really have a different attitude and contribute to a final Arab-Israeli or Palestinian-Israeli peace agreement remains to be seen.

Saudi Arabia, like Egypt, is deeply concerned with the rise of Sunni radicalism, as well as with Iran's regional expansion. Such concerns have led Saudi Arabia to form a coalition of Arab countries aimed at applying pressure on Qatar to sever its ties with Iran, the Muslim Brotherhood and other designated terrorist groups. The coalition, which includes Saudi Arabia, Egypt, the United Arab Emirates (UAE) and Bahrain, demands that Qatar scale down diplomatic ties with Iran, expel members of the Iranian Revolutionary Guards (IRGC), and cut off all military cooperation with Iran. Likewise, these countries demanded that Qatar comply with U.S and international sanctions regarding Iran. They also sought an end to Qatar's funding of designated terrorist organizations and demanded that Qatar extradite individuals tied to these organizations. They also demanded that Qatar freeze the assets of members of these groups who found refuge in Qatar and that the government provide information about these individuals' whereabouts.[129] Although some of the demands presented to Qatar were not reasonable, such as the demand that Qatar shut down *Al Jazeera*, the pressure applied shows serious efforts to curb both the threat of Iran and extremist Sunni groups. In addition, it is significant that the foreign ministers of Israel and Bahrain were photographed together in public. However, most surprising were the words of the Bahraini foreign minister, Khalid bin Ahmed Al Khalifa, to an Israeli TV station: "Israel is a country in the Middle East. Israel is part of this heritage of this whole region historically. So, the Jewish people have a place amongst us. So, communication needs to be a prerequisite for solving all the dispute. We should talk."[130] Al Khalifa's statement is significant for its recognition of Israel as a "natural" part of the Middle East and acknowledging the connection of the Jewish people to the land. This is highly revolutionary.

Just as important, the Egyptian government instructed official media in the country not to oppose U.S President Donald Trump's decision to move the American embassy in Israel from Tel Aviv to Jerusalem. In fact, it instructed them to persuade the public to accept the move.[131] This shows how much the geo-strategic interest and calculations of Egypt have changed. New geo-political challenges might bring Israelis and Arabs together and could well be a catalyst to reconciliation. Furthermore, after President Trump recognized Israel's sovereignty over the Golan Heights in March 2019, the Arab League Summit, which took place the following month in Tunisia, made a weak statement opposing the move. Furthermore, the statement was not followed up with practical steps aimed at counteracting the effects of the move.[132]

Representatives from Bahrain, the United Arab Emirates, and Oman attended President Trump's unveiling ceremony for his Middle East peace plan, which was rejected outright by the Palestinian leadership (We will discuss this plan and the Arab reaction to it further in chapter 5).

Furthermore, as I am completing the writing this book, Israel has signed peace and normalization agreements with the United

Arab Emirates and Bahrain, which include the establishment of full diplomatic relations.

It is not clear to what extent Arab states will stop enabling Palestinian boycotts and anti-Israeli incitement even while cooperating and finding common ground with Israel. After all, hostility towards Israel is still a component of legitimacy for some Arab countries. Arab states may still rejoice over UN resolutions condemning Israel, organized boycotts, and threats of political isolation.

In chapters 1 and 2 we discussed why the Palestinians were unable to deliver a peace agreement and why it is undesirable that they no longer be the lead negotiating partner in the peace process, even if it is their own fate at stake. What is missing is a roadmap to peace that goes beyond the bilateral Israeli Palestinian track. Building an alternative path to peace requires developing new formulas that take the geopolitical context as well as the sociological contexts into account. Before we discuss this road map, we will analyze the Arab Spring, a set of events whose final political and cultural consequences are hard to predict but cannot be ignored given its overwhelming significance to the Arab community.

CHAPTER 4

THE IMPACT OF THE ARAB SPRING

The changes that are taking place in Arab society in the aftermath of the Arab awakening or Arab Spring are occurring slowly and are less obvious to the naked eye. In this chapter, we will explore the actual and potential impact of the Arab Spring on the attitudes of Arab civil society towards Israel and we will identify changes that may accelerate the process of Arab/Israeli reconciliation.

The Arab Spring: The Emergence of a New Social Contract

The Arab Spring was a chain of uprisings against authoritarian governments. These uprisings began in Tunisia, followed by Egypt, Libya, Yemen, Syria, Bahrein, and, most recently, in Sudan. These rebellions generated hopes for a fourth wave of democratization in the Arab world as happened in Eastern Europe in the late 1980's and early 1990's. However, with the exception of Tunisia, no Arab country experienced an actual transition to democratic rule. Arab states experienced either an authoritarian restoration (Egypt), civil war and anarchy (Syria, Yemen and Libya) or an effective reaction by the existing government that enabled it to stay in power despite protests (Bahrein).

Consequently, some scholars and observers have expressed skepticism about the Arab Spring and declared it a failure.

Scholars such as the Egyptian, Tarek Heggy, argue that Arab culture often resists western forms of democracy and human progress.[1] Other scholars of the Middle East as well as politicians have described their bitter disappointment over the outcome of the Arab Spring from a variety of vantage points. George Washington University political science professor Marc Lynch claims that the enthusiasm of the youth in Tahrir Square, the place of mass protests in Cairo and the symbol of Mubarak's downfall, has diminished due to a new authoritarian regime installed in Egypt after the summer of 2013. Lynch argues that charlatans and politicians who pursue their own interest have stolen the revolution. He also claims that foreign powers such as the Gulf States, Saudi Arabia and Iran have taken advantage of internal divisions created during the Arab Spring in order to foment proxy wars.[2] His disappointment extends to deposals and challenges to authoritarian rulers in countries such as Libya and Syria, which have turned into interminable ethnic and sectarian civil wars.

Steven Cook, a scholar with the Council on Foreign Relations, also expressed doubt about the Arab Spring based on current conditions in the Arab world. Cook argues that the oppressive structures of the state inherited from the authoritarian age constitute an impediment to the progress of democracy and civil society in the Arab world.[3]

Politicians such as Israeli Prime Minister Benjamin Netanyahu cite Muslim Brotherhood victories in Tunisia and Egypt as clear examples of what could happen in the rest of the Arab world as old autocracies begin to fall. In the Prime Minister's view, the Arab Spring uprisings were not like the upheavals against Eastern European communist regimes in the late 1980's that ultimately led to formal democracies.[4] Instead, from Netanyahu's perspective, the Arab Spring resembled Iran in 1979 when popular rebellion was hijacked by Islamic fanatics. In November 2011, Netanyahu lamented that "despite all our hopes, the chances are that an Islamist wave will wash over the Arab countries, an anti-West, anti-liberal, anti-Israel and ultimately an anti-democratic wave."[5] For this reason, the Israeli government viewed the defeat of Hosni Mubarak in Egypt as a threat to regional stability. Netanyahu expressed concern that Egypt was moving toward a revolution as had Iran forty years prior. He feared exacerbation of anti-Israel feelings that could bring about regional tensions and further instability.[6]

The initial Israeli nostalgia for Hosni Mubarak reflects the extent of Israel's fear of change in the Arab world. As we have seen in Chapter 3, Mubarak maintained the peace with Israel that his predecessor, the late Anwar El- Sadat, signed while also restricting Egyptians from traveling to Israel or deepening relations with Israelis. Likewise, he took an anti-Israel position in international forums and tolerated domestic anti-Israel and even anti-Semitic rhetoric. The term "cold peace" was coined precisely for this reason. As Middle East scholar Daniel Byman has rightly pointed out, "Mubarak never won the goodwill of ordinary Israelis as did Sadat."[7] As we also have seen in Chapter 3, in Arab countries dominated by autocracies, the Arab/Israeli conflict has served as a useful tool to make up for a deficit of legitimacy and build unity around an external enemy. Indeed, Arab public opinion has long been a mystery well-buried in the depths of a repressed society. However, authoritarian rulers encouraged Arab citizens to hold negative views of Israel and express them freely.

Radical Islam and Islamists also have a strong anti-Israel rhetoric and intolerance for the presence of a non-Muslim entity in the region. This is the case with the Islamic Revolution in Iran that openly advocates for the destruction of the State of Israel. Likewise, the Sunni Muslim Brotherhood vehemently opposed the Egyptian peace treaty with Israel and was also the mother of Hamas, a group that has conducted acts of terrorism against the Israeli population and has openly advocated for the destruction of Israel.

Because Islamists are the best organized opposition group in the Arab world, they may be seen as the natural beneficiary of the Arab Spring and the obvious successor to the Arab secular authoritarian regimes.

This book however, views the Arab Spring as a more complex phenomenon. In our view, the Arab Spring does not necessarily lead to the replacement of a secular autocracy with an Islamist autocracy. We will argue that the Arab Spring is an unfinished project. It has initiated a long, arduous process, which we are now witnessing in its early stages. Furthermore, we will argue that the Arab Spring is already in the process of changing the social contract between Arab civil society and the Arab state because we are for the first time seeing ordinary Arab citizens acting with agency.[8] In other words, Arab peoples have become actors whose needs and wishes can no longer be ignored. We will also contend that even if Arab states do not become full-fledged liberal democracies, an identifiable civil society is emerging in the Arab world. Furthermore, as Arab civil society undergoes a process of transformation, attitudes towards Israel and the Israeli-Palestinian conflict may also slowly change eventually challenging traditional views on the subject.

Our analysis will examine three elements. First, we will assess Islamism's actual impact in the Arab world and society. Then, we will analyze how civil society began to emerge in the Arab World and how culture and social discourse have begun to slowly change in post-Arab Spring societies. Finally, we will examine how all these elements together might further transform the views of Arab civil society regarding Israel.

Islamism, Civil Society and Democracy

Islamism

The election of Hamas in the Palestinian territories in 2006 raised the fear that Islamists were likely to win elections should the existing political system in the Arab world open up. The victories of Islamist groups and parties in Tunisia and Egypt after the Arab Spring further exacerbated these fears, appearing to confirm what Mubarak once said: "The choice is between me or the Islamists."[9] In this section, we are exploring two important questions. The first is whether Islamism is the same in every country and in every context. The second is whether Islamism is inevitably the only alternative to the old authoritarian regimes.

As explained in Chapter 3, in Egypt the Muslim Brotherhood (MB) established roots among the people, particularly among the middle class. The MB won the election in 2012 and elected Mohamed Morsi as Egypt's president. However, the Brotherhood government pursued an illiberal model of government. Like the leaders of many contemporary illiberal democracies, the MB believed that an electoral victory would be tantamount to a mandate to govern as they saw fit. Indeed, Morsi granted clerics the privilege of being the sole interpreters of the constitution. He also restricted the freedom of expression and repressed political opponents.[10] The president then proceeded to dismiss the military's top leadership, including the head of the armed forces, Hussein Tantawi, and the chief of staff

Sami Anan. He also cancelled the constitutional declaration made by the Supreme Council of the Armed Forces (SCAF) that limited presidential powers over the military and proceeded to purge the military of seventy generals. Then, Morsi also invited Tarel al-Zomor, a leader of the terrorist group Gamaa al-Islamiyah, to participate in the ceremonies commemorating the October 1973 War against Israel. Zomor spent almost thirty years in prison for actively participating in the assassination of Anwar Sadat three decades earlier.[11] Likewise, the MB government proceeded to appoint Abdel Nasser Salama, known for his anti-Christian views, to be the editor in chief of the government newspaper *Al Ahram* and appointed Gamal Abdel Rahim, who called for the murder of a Bahai leader, to be the editor of *Al Ghmouria*, another major state newspaper. [12]

Furthermore, by trying to dominate the state apparatus, the means of communications, and key positions, the MB government sought hegemonic control of Egypt. It issued a new constitutional declaration removing legal checks on the government and stated that all of its constitutional declarations were final, binding and not subject to appeal or to any type of legal challenge.[13] The Egyptian government claimed that these measures were necessary to "move forward with the goals of the revolution and eliminate all of the obstacles which are linked to the past we hate."[14]

Thus, the MB government positioned itself as a revolutionary regime. Indeed, a new proposed constitution increased the role of Sharia, or religious law, and expanded the role of the state in enforcing religious codes. The state would "safeguard ethics, public morality, and public order and foster a high level of education and of religious and patriotic values."[15]

These actions generated a negative reaction within Egyptian society. The Egyptian judiciary went on strike and street protests spread. Political parties came together to protest the government's actions. People took over streets and public squares demanding that a referendum organized by the regime to approve the constitution be terminated. The Brotherhood refused to compromise and proceeded to mobilize its supporters to defend the presidential palace by attacking the opposition and detaining protestors.[16]

Despite such public opposition, the constitutional referendum passed with a 64% vote of "yes." However, turnout was only 33%.[17]

The poor participation in the referendum reflected the weakness of the Brotherhood. However, Morsi conveniently saw the results as a green light to move his revolution forward. Therefore, he proceeded to give authority to the Shura Council, the upper chamber of the Egyptian bi-cameral parliament, to draft a new constitution. The Shura Council was dominated by the Brotherhood. This meant that the legislature would be nothing more than a rubber stamp for the MB government.[18] This prompted the Egyptian Supreme Court to invalidate the constitutional panel and the authority of the Shura Council. [19]

Morsi also punished instances of free expression, particularly those that were critical of his government or his policies. He took legal action against journalists, television stations, comedians and others under the guise that they insulted the president.[20] Likewise, the Brotherhood refused to negotiate issues of public interest with other parties. The MB counted on parliamentary elections to secure a legislative majority, thereby ignoring opposition parties. These actions generated a hostile reaction by Egyptian political parties and by the military. Public opinion began to turn against the Brotherhood as well and to express a desire for the return of the military to government leadership.[21] A military *coup d'état* did not take long to occur. Abdel Fattah El Sisi, who was the Army Chief of Staff led the *coup d'état* that deposed the eleven-month old MB government.

The rule of the Muslim Brotherhood seemed to have lost legitimacy as it became another coercive force simply replacing the old one. Protests and riots also raised the fear that Egypt, like other Middle Eastern countries, could face a civil war. As Jordanian scholar, Abdullah Swalha, who frequently travels to Egypt, said, "during Morsi's rule, chaos and insecurity dominated the Egyptian streets. Egyptians were now looking to restore order to Egypt. Furthermore, they were watching the events in Syria and in Libya and they turned fearful of the possibility of civil war in Egypt itself."[22]

In the aftermath of Mubarak's deposal, Egyptians lost their fear of the state. As Noah Feldman has pointed out, "Tahrir I, [the February 2011 uprising against Mubarak] did legitimately express the political agency of the Egyptian people for regime change. Having advanced that argument, I cannot avoid the conclusion that Tahrir II [the June 2013 uprising against the Brotherhood did the same].

If the people willed the end of the Mubarak regime, the people also willed the end of the Morsi regime just two and half years later." [23] Equally important, the monopoly of the Muslim Brotherhood or Islamists over alternative forms of government was also shaken. While the Islamist alternative lost the appeal it once had, the process initiated in 2011 in Egypt appears likely to continue in an albeit uncertain way. El Sisi's brutal repression of the Muslim Brotherhood may, in the long run, have a moderating effect on both the Muslim Brotherhood and the Islamist movement. As scholar Shadi Hamid has explained, historically, the fear of repression has had a powerful effect on Islamist behavior. He writes, "Fear creates self-enforcing norms that encourage accommodation with the state and discourage confrontation."[24] Therefore, it is likely that the events that led to a crisis of legitimacy for the Muslim Brotherhood as well as the ensuing El Sisi's repression may have a moderating effect on Islamism or may lead to a severe weakening of the movement. More important, the Brotherhood's methods were rejected by large segments of society.

By contrast to Egypt, the Islamist Ennahda party in Tunisia, under the leadership of Rachid Ghannouchi, presented a moderate platform that advocated for ideas such as the rule of law and individual freedom.[25] The platform also included respect for women's rights, improvements in public administration and commitment to combat corruption. Ennahda's program also sought to assure Tunisian voters that the party would not establish religious coercive rule like Iran or the Taliban. The Tunisian Islamic party, contrary to the Egyptian Muslim Brotherhood, rejected rigid and anti-modernist notions of Islam. Instead, Ennahda took a very pragmatic and tolerant approach. The party won the first election and transferred power when defeated. In Ghannouchi's view, political Islam was needed to fight the authoritarianism of the Tunisian state but was no longer needed in a democracy. As Tunisia became a democracy, Ennahda became concerned with continuing democratic consolidation and more interested in implementing a social and economic agenda devoid of religion. Ennahda does not consider Sharia a source of legislation and accepts the separation between Mosque and State.[26] In Ghannouchi's own words, "Ennahda is now best understood not as an Islamist movement but as a party of Muslim democrats."[27] The party also entered a governing coalition with secular parties, including labor unions, human rights groups and others.[28] The result was a government built on a consensus among different factions and views. It was not an illiberal arrangement where an electoral victory was viewed as a mandate to govern without restrictions and without consideration for electoral minorities. Such consensus despite differences has made Tunisia's democratic transition a stable one.

What is also remarkable about the Tunisian Constitution is its western inspiration, which includes provisions to limit executive power and provides for parliamentary oversight as well respect for human rights and the rule of law. As North Africa expert Duncan Pickard has observed, the central constitutional debate in Tunisia was, "how to constrain executive power without resorting to religious or military domination."[29] Pickard's point highlights the sharp contrast between the Tunisian and the Egyptian model.

Ennahda rejected the Egyptian Muslim Brotherhood model. Ghannouchi has also claimed that he has been influenced by Germany's Christian Democrats, a conservative, religiously oriented political party that remains liberal, supporting an open economy and a democratic system.[30] After Ennahda was elected, the economic situation in Tunisia continued to face high unemployment and rising Salafist terrorism. The latter perpetrated assassinations against members of opposition parties such as Chokri Belaya, a member of a left-wing party.[31] After the *coup d'état* in Egypt, the Tunisian opposition organized protests mimicking the Egyptian model of a coalition of opposition parties asking for the resignation of Ennahda. Nevertheless, the Tunisian government, instead of responding with repression, initiated a national dialogue that included political parties and representatives of various sectors of civil society such as the trade unions. Similarly, it agreed on a set of additional demands from opposition parties.[32] The fact that Ennahda recognized political and social forces beyond itself saved Tunisian democracy.

Another factor that distinguishes Ennahda is, as Ghannouchi pointed out, there is no need to have a religious party in Tunisia because the state no longer imposes secularism through repression. As a result, Ennahda "can finally be a political party focusing on its practical agenda and economic vision rather than a social movement fighting against repression and dictatorship."[33] Ghannouchi's understanding of democracy comes clear in the following passage:

> Our priority was not to remain in control but to ensure that the National Constituent Assembly, the supreme representative body, could complete the work of drafting a constitution that would establish the political foundations of a democratic Tunisia... Confronting violent extremism requires an understanding of the true teachings of Islam, which reject black-and-white views and allow for interpretations that accommodate the needs of modern life. The genuine separation of mosque and state and the effective governance of religious institutions will facilitate better religious education and reintroduce moderate Islamic thinking to Tunisia.[34]

It is reasonable to think, as the expert on Islamist movements Monica Marks does, that Ghannouchi learned the lesson from the abrupt end of Morsi's regime in Egypt, especially that inflexibility and political arrogance can topple a government, including an Islamic one.[35] Along those lines, Morocco's Justice and Development Party (PJD) also accommodated the country's secular urban class; it focused on the economy and fighting corruption and even showed flexibility on the issue of abortion. [36] As in Tunisia, in Morocco the Islamist Party of Justice and Development (PJD) fell short of an outright majority and sought to build a coalition with secular parties. That was an indication that in Morocco, like in Tunisia, an extreme Islamist agenda was rejected. Islamist parties realized that it was incompatible with the people's will and the choices they had made.

In Libya and Syria, the chaotic disintegration of government created conditions, which enabled extreme Islamists to gain some political control. Libya held elections in the summer of 2012 with high participation. A major victory for the Islamist parties was expected. However, almost half of the votes and parliament seats were won by the National Forces Alliance, a non-Islamist coalition. The Islamist Justice and Construction Parties won only seventeen seats and many other parties each won a few seats. One of the most extreme Islamist parties led by Abd al Hakim Belhaj, a man who had ties to al-Qaeda, won just one seat, despite having conducted a well-financed campaign.[37] Indeed, the emerging political crisis in Libya was not the result of popular support for Islamism but of the aggressive penetration of ISIS that took advantage of the country's post-Ghadaffy's anarchy.

Likewise, in the case of Syria, radical Salafist organizations became major players in the context of civil war. This is mainly because the violent and ruthless repression carried out by the Assad regime forced protesters to resort to armed clashes with state forces. The Free Syrian Army (FSA), which consisted mostly of defectors from the Syrian army, was initially the main opposition force. However, a divided and weak opposition gave way to resistance by local organizations that resulted in the creation of one hundred and fourteen uncoordinated militias. Some of these militias were co-opted by Islamists and enjoyed more financial and military support from countries like Qatar.[38] However, the years of ISIS' brutal rule over parts of Syria ultimately turned the population against it.[39] The atrocities committed by ISIS, such as burning, drowning, decapitating, and summarily executing people, frightened Arab communities that came under ISIS domination. Furthermore, in territories occupied by ISIS, everyday life was profoundly brutal and dehumanizing. People were forced to watch decapitations and executions. Sometimes minor infractions such as speaking to foreign parties resulted in executions. Female patients, regardless of the urgency of their health situation, could not be treated by male doctors or health care workers. ISIS members would intentionally provoke citizens in order to trigger reactions that would allow them to respond with cruelty.[40] The experience under ISIS generated a reaction across the Arab world. According to polls taken among Arabs, groups such as ISIS and Al Qaeda, have minimal support.[41]

In Iraq, moderation also seems to be the most popular political preference. During the 2010 election, the party known as Iraqiya received most of the seats in parliament. The party was led by Ayad Allawi, a Shiite, but it included a diverse representation from Shiites and Sunnis. Allawi was able to draw votes from millions of Sunnis as well as Shiites. He was clearly considered non-sectarian.[42] However, the Shiite Prime Minister of Iraq, Nouri Al Maliki from the State of the Law party, did not allow Allawi to implement his right to be the first political leader to try to form a government. As a result of this manipulation, Maliki succeeded in securing a second term as Prime Minister while Iran pressured Muqtada Al Sadr, a Shiite extremist and an enemy of Maliki, to join Maliki's coalition.[43] Maliki formed a government characterized by sectarian rule. Maliki's behavior created internal conflict as well as Kurdish and Sunni alienation. The latter's resentment eventually empowered the Islamic State that capitalized on such Sunni bitterness. Kurdish alienation, on the other hand, expressed itself by their support for secession from Iraq. Maliki, with the help of Iran, promoted a Shiite-centralized state. Iran even trained Shiite militias in Iraq to add coercive and para-military elements to complement the government.[44] After Maliki won elections in 2014, he proceeded to crush political opponents, particularly Sunnis. He arrested Sunni tribal leaders, and even issued an arrest warrant for Tariq al Hashimi, his former Sunni vice-president.[45] Thus, Maliki politically sidelined the Sunnis.[46] His actions backfired when ISIS portrayed itself to the Sunni population as their protector. Maliki also politicized Iraqi institutions, such as the military, by removing certain officers that had good relations with American troops and replacing them with Shiite loyalists.[47] As the political situation in Iraq became less sustainable, and under pressure from the United States, Al Maliki resigned and was succeeded by Haider Al Abadi.

Al Abadi's administration was more inclusive. He resisted Iranian attempts to recruit armed Shiite groups to fight in Syria and worked diligently to prevent the advance of Iran's influence in Iraq,[48] especially Iranian training of Iraqi Shiite militias. Al Abadi made alliances with diverse groups, which included both Sunni and Shiite as well as a sector of the Kurds.[49] He sought public support from the Grand Ayatollah Sistani, who is widely respected by the Shiite community and secured the support of the Patriotic Union of Kurdistan (PUK).[50] By contrast to Al Maliki, Al Abadi's conciliatory approach was more inclusive, despite the fact, that he was unable to fully control the different militias.

The flourishing of Islamist elements in countries like Syria, Libya and Iraq is partly the result of anarchy and sectarian war. ISIS took over territories and positions in Syria and Iraq at a time of civil war and intense polarization. Indeed, rejection of radical Islam is extensive in the Arab world. As scholar Robin Wright has observed, "Clerics and theologians have begun to challenge bin Laden and Al Qaeda with their own *fatwas* in what has been dubbed the 'counter *jihad*,' and Sunni tribal leaders turned on Al Qaeda cells after they went too far in kidnapping and killing local populations."[51]

Radical Islam lost influence in the Arab world because of the coercive nature of Islamist regimes, the brutal actions of ISIS, and the need to build coalitions with other non-Islamist political parties.

Islamist parties cannot rule without legitimacy or a substantial degree of popular support. As Ghannouchi has stated, "The most dangerous thing for the Islamists is to be loved by the people before they get to power and then hated afterward."[52] It is in this sense that scholar Oliver Roy pointed out that in many cases Islamists have no choice but to adjust to the democratic process. This is the result of the complex social and political environment in which they operate.[53] The scholar Adeed Dawisha has pointed out that it is important to separate religious values from the needs of society. If Islamist parties fail to deliver the goods in the social and economic sphere, they are not likely to survive.[54] After the Arab Spring civil society is no longer easily manipulated. The result is that the coerciveness of radical Islam clashes with a society that is now different. As Marwan Muasher, a former Jordanian diplomat and foreign minister observed, "[Arab] Society has claimed the right to bring in or remove anyone from power. Religious parties can no longer claim a monopoly on faith or doctrine as a rationale for taking power or indulge in pretensions of sainthood. Slogans such as 'Islam is the solution' will not fly long if they do not bring people a better life."[55] Thus, we can say that civil society has emerged in the Arab world as a factor in the equation that defines political reality.

Civil society

The Arab Spring has enabled Arab societies to defy decades-long tyrannical rule. When authoritarian regimes have been challenged once, they are likely to be challenged again. This is confirmed by the fact that opinion surveys and polls taken between 2012 and 2016 show Arabs continuing to support democracy as the best system of government. Likewise, Arabs see "lack of representative democracy as being the major obstacles to peace and stability in the Middle East."[56] The findings of these polls and surveys do not necessarily mean that Arabs know exactly what real democracy means or how it is supposed to be implemented in practice. However, these polls clearly indicate a break with the past, even if the new future remains unknown.

It is obvious that a true democracy, with a democratic culture and a full enforcement and implementation of the rule of law will not happen overnight and probably not in this generation. There are not enough liberals in the Arab world, as scholar Samuel Tadros has rightly pointed out.[57] Nor is there a party structure capable of absorbing, integrating and properly representing societal factions. The security apparatus inherited from the authoritarian era is still strong enough to intimidate people and autonomous enough to undermine the development of a democratic regime. As Steve Cook has defined it, it is the "stickiness" of institutions in the Arab world such as the rules, laws, decrees, and regulations shaping people's expectations and behaviors in society that have so far remained authoritarian and repressive in some of these countries.[58]

Yet despite obstacles, the Arab Spring has broken the barrier of fear and created a sense of vulnerability among Arab and regional authoritarian governments. While they may not be entirely democratic, Arab governments will certainly have to consider the needs and concerns of their citizens. For instance, Jordan has accelerated its own reforms as a consequence of the eruption of the Arab spring. Morocco did the same. Even Saudi Arabia is considering reforms even though the country was not directly affected by protests or rebellions. The following statement by the young Saudi crown prince Mohammed Bin Salman is a case in point.

> What happened in the last thirty years is not Saudi Arabia. What happened in the region in the last thirty years is not the Middle East. After the Iranian revolution in 1979, people wanted to copy this model in different countries, one of them is Saudi Arabia. We didn't know how to deal with it. And the problem spread all over the world. Now is the time to get rid of it.[59]

The Prince proposed a moderate and more open Islam and pledged "to destroy" extremist thought. He broke the alliance between the Kingdom of Saudi Arabia and hardline clerics and reduced the power of the religious police.[60] Most importantly, the Saudi Prince stated in early 2016 that,

> The Arab Spring has put to test the authoritative form of government and non-authoritative form of government, and the regime that represents its people versus the regime that does not represent its people. Any regime that did not represent its people collapsed in the Arab Spring, and the other regimes we saw what happened to them.[61]

The scandal faced by the Saudi monarchy due to the assassination of Washington-based Saudi journalist Jamal Khashoggi and the arrest of human rights activists, cast some doubt on Saudi reform intentions. However, Bin Salman's words are an interesting evaluation of the Arab and Saudi state of affairs. The fact that the Crown Prince has made a public statement is significant in so far as it recognizes that political authority should rest on political legitimacy and the participation of civil society and not just on divine right or monarchical heritage.

Even in the case of Egypt, where El Sisi ascended to political power after a *coup d'état*, civil society is not dead. El Sisi has indeed ruled with an iron fist, arguably increasing repression and violating human rights. But this *coup d'état* took place after a civil rebellion against the Muslim Brotherhood.[62] According to Waleed Haddara, former advisor to Morsi, the coup that deposed the Brotherhood was possible because there was a coalition of Egyptian groups that agreed to bring an end to it.[63] It is our prediction that the El Sisi government, unlike the Mubarak government, may not last a long time. The El Sisi government's legitimacy relies on the need for domestic stability.

The events of January 2011 unleashed a process that made Egypt under El Sisi different from the Mubarak era.

After the events of Tahrir Square of early 2011 and the subsequent deposal of Mubarak, there was an awakening of civil society that required some sort of legitimacy or social contract between civil society and the state. In April 2016, there were demonstrations against El Sisi demanding his resignation amid economic failure and police abuse.[64] In February 2019, twenty-three amendments were added to the constitution without much discussion. The opposition was not allowed to organize, and thirty-four thousand websites were blocked. The parliament approved the amendments and then a popular referendum on the parliament's decision was convened. Without descriptions of the amendments on the ballots, people were required to vote "yes" or "no."[65] The amendments included allowing El Sisi to remain in office until 2024 and then to run for re-election for another six-year term.[66] They also included a series of clauses that de-facto subjugated the judiciary to the president. The latter has been defined by experts as "the worst attack on judicial independence since Nasser's 1969 massacre of the judiciary."[67] By making the judiciary surrender to executive prerogatives via constitutional amendment, El Sisi attempted to crush any resistance to his decisions or policies that may come from the courts.[68]

However, this time there was a reaction on the part of the general public. A grassroots campaign called *Batel* ("void" in English) organized a petition opposing the amendments, which gathered sixty thousand signatures in a single day.[69] A coalition of eleven parties including liberal and left-leaning parties rejected the constitutional changes calling them an "assault on democracy". They publicly urged people to vote "No" on the referendum.[70] To appease the opposition, El Sisi included some articles that appear benevolent such as the establishment of a twenty-five percent parliamentary representation for women and adequate representation for workers, farmers, youth and Coptic Christians.[71] However, Nazra, an Egyptian organization that supports women's rights, issued a statement arguing that "Symbolic rights for women cannot replace their active participation in a true pluralist democracy, rooted in a firm belief in women's diversity and voices and the values of pluralism, and equality and freedom for both women and men."[72]

This kind of action by organized groups in Egyptian civil society may well be an indication that the government may no longer be able to rule without properly engaging civil society. A government of the military and by the military will be more difficult to sustain once the perceived threat of civil war clears. In addition, it is important to point out that El Sisi lacks the infrastructure Mubarak possessed. While Mubarak relied on the military, on a party apparatus, on a plethora of economic sectors and a large network that benefited from their relationship with the president, El Sisi relies only on the military.[73] Under El Sisi, the military has become the main referent for every economic activity, acting as gatekeeper for private investors and multinationals. According to the Italian scholar Gianni De Pianta, "such a context tends to be barely stable, often sidelining partially critical businessmen and sometimes transforming former allies into vociferous critics. It is interesting to note that this was exactly the dynamic that led to massive, though short-lived, protests in September 2019. These protests were indirectly put into motion by the declarations of Mohamed Ali- a former building contractor subsequently marginalized by the generals- against the allegedly improper use of public funds by El-Sisi and his inner circle. Today's Egypt is a giant with feet of clay."[74]

If the El Sisi take over was initially legitimate, this legitimacy could not be sustained unless it opened to the players that have been activated since the anti-Mubarak uprisings. Sooner or later El Sisi will face stronger resistance unless he is willing to open the system and accept a transition to democracy.

Iraq presents a more complex situation, but it is no different in principle. As we have seen in the 2010 parliamentary election, a great number of voters rejected the idea of sectarian rule by supporting Allawi. Maliki managed to prevent Allawi from enjoying that victory and proceeded to establish sectarian rule with Iran's help. However, as this policy brought about Sunni alienation and the rise of ISIS, Al Abadi, who replaced Maliki, adopted a different attitude, promoting inclusion and peaceful solutions to conflicts. In fact, Abadi expressed interest in forming alliances with former foes.[75] Abadi also included Sunnis in his cabinet and mitigated some of the sectarian tensions created by Maliki.

Yet, rebellions in Iraq erupted in 2019 against the backdrop of resentment of political corruption and government failure and mismanagement. In the words of the Iraqi analyst Ghassan al-Attiya, "the young generations no longer believe in political parties and leadership. Instead, they have increasingly resorted to trade unions and professional syndicates to voice their opinions.[76]

Furthermore, Al Attiya argues that these types of protests were generated in those regions where support for Iran was stronger, indicating that sectarian divisions may be set aside as Iraqis join together to place demands for more concrete resolution to issues that affect everyday life.[77] This phenomenon is not unique to Iraq. Lebanon, a country characterized by sectarian divisions and with a history of a bloody civil war, has been swept by mass protests demanding that everyone in government resign. Protests are widespread and are mostly against repression and corruption. As in Iraq, protests in Lebanon are not only post-sectarian but also constitute a revolt against clientelist politics and the corruption created after the civil war where sectarian leaders created patronage networks.[78] This momentum has intensified with the explosion of 2,500 tons of ammonium nitrate in a warehouse located at the Port of Beirut in August 2020. In that tragedy, 191 people died and about 6,500 people were injured. [79] The government was widely accused of negligence and subsequently resigned. Now civil society is unified against a system that has been rejected as corrupt and unacceptable.

As we pointed out at the beginning of this chapter, the Arab Spring is an unfinished project. State repression does not necessarily mean that the Arab Spring has come to an end.

As scholar Maha Yahyah pointed out,

Something fundamental has changed. Arab governments have traditionally rested on what political scientists call an "authoritarian bargain," in which the state provides jobs, security and services in exchange for political loyalty. This bargain assumes that ordinary people will remain passive. However, today, that assumption no longer holds. Citizens no longer fear their governments. Now more than ever before, ordinary people across the Middle East are politically engaged and willing to voice dissent.[80]

Regardless of whether democracy arrives now or in the next generation, what is important is that Arab civil society is a factor that Arab states can no longer ignore. In the aftermath of the Arab Spring, the Arab people have reached a Tocquevillian moment. The idea of equality of conditions and freedom has been planted in the Arab world and powerful autocrats have been deposed. The powers that be have weakened. As Tocqueville wrote: "The evil that one endures patiently because it seems inevitable becomes unbearable the moment its elimination becomes conceivable. Then every abuse that is eliminated seems only to reveal the others that remain, and makes their sting that much more painful. The ill has diminished, to be sure, but sensitivity to it has increased."[81]

The Arab Spring has not produced a new regime or a full-fledged democracy. Nevertheless, it has triggered a change in the social consciousness of Arab civil society and created conditions that allow for a new, modified mindset to emerge. People may demand more equality and may be more aware of injustices and privileges denied to them by the government or by the dominant classes. They may gradually challenge social norms or prevalent ideas in their society. What we want to check next is how, in the meantime, new ideas and new conversations are penetrating Arab society and what kind of impact they may have on the Arab/Israeli relationship.

The Arab Spring, the Public Sphere and the Question of Israel

The Arab Public Sphere

As Arab rulers have been challenged, we are witnessing other developments that may be less visible. Despite the chaotic situation we have seen since the Arab Spring erupted, there are other important elements that need to be explored. The decline of authoritarian regimes often gives way to an evolving public sphere. Following the philosopher Jürgen Habermas, we refer to an emerging public sphere as a transitional stage in which the citizen is no longer a passive object of manipulation or domination by political elites. He or she is no longer the submissive subject that participates in referendums aimed at reaffirming the thoughts and actions of the ruler. Instead, the citizen may have more room to express opinions. These opinions can evolve into a debate that may eventually help shape civil society. This can be expressed in informal settings such as cafés or in the development of new reading habits accompanied by the proliferation of publications such as books and journals.[82] In this sense civil society begins to develop alternative opinions to the narrative of the authoritarian state, even if the state is not yet a liberal democracy. Furthermore, civil society begins to evolve as a body separate and distinct from the state apparatus. State policies are discussed among members of civil society and critical thinking emerges. This pre-liberal development could open the way to a pluralism and diversity of opinions.

Some observers, like Egyptian author Basma Abdel Aziz, believe that this literary proliferation is a positive phenomenon because "it has given people the courage to find their voice."[83] Furthermore, Aziz claims that "breaking down the political walls of fear also had the impact of breaking down personal fears of being judged."[84] Thus, self-censorship is beginning to fade away. While Arab societies are still far from becoming full-fledged democracies, a new Arab public sphere may further intensify.

As Habermas points out when analyzing the historical evolution of the public sphere in Europe, "the public sphere in the political realm evolved from the public sphere in the world of letters; through the vehicle of public opinion that put the state in touch with the needs of society."[85]

One of the important elements in this transitional stage today, is precisely the use of the internet and social media. Both have already played an important role in the uprisings of 2010 and 2011. Indeed, the Arab Spring unleashed an industry of political analysis, opinion pieces, talk shows, Facebook status, twitter and other forms of modern social media.[86]

We have seen a change in the way media have been operating. The arrival of Arabic language satellite television in the 1990's broke the state monopoly on media. The creation of *Al Jazeera* in 1996 offered a broader set of topics and programming that differed from official state television. Despite the fact that *Al Jazeera* is owned, and to certain extent, also directed by the government of Qatar, it allowed the Arab public to watch politicians, analysts and others presenting different and conflicting points of view for the first time. People interviewed on different programs and talk shows were not merely carefully selected cheerleaders for the government.[87] Even though *Al Jazeera* embraced the classic official anti-Israeli position,

Israelis were nonetheless interviewed. Furthermore, *Al Jazeera* also was able to engage many viewers by opening the microphone to people to express their views without censorship.

Al Arabiya, a Saudi-based TV station, emerged as a competitor to *Al Jazeera*, covering economic issues, but independently from the edicts of the state.[88] This introduced an element of democratization into public discourse. For instance, in 2008 there was a major strike in the Egyptian town of Al-Mahalla Al Kobra organized by textile workers. Thanks to the work of bloggers, seventy thousand people provided their signatures in support of the strike within two weeks. Since then, blogs have multiplied, escaping the censorship of mainstream newspapers. Between 2005 and 2011, the number of internet users in the Arab world quadrupled.[89] British journalist Rachel Aspden collected testimonies from young Egyptians that are indicative of this development. In 2000, only one percent of Egyptians was connected to the internet. By 2009, twenty-five percent of the Egyptian population were connected to the internet. As people gathered to chat online, they met a plethora of diverse individuals with similar interests. In the protected safety of these chatrooms, people began to discuss all kinds of subjects, including those considered taboo, such as matters related to religion and political change.[90] Egypt and other countries suppressed and blocked the internet in order to prevent exposure and communication between potential dissidents. However, such whole suppression of the internet could adversely affect the economies of these countries. As political scientists Kevin Wagner and Jason Gainous have indicated, the internet is needed today to make business competitive. If the Arab world is seeking to stimulate and advance business and economic activity, the use of the internet is vital. Once the internet is open, chances are that it will be used for purposes other than business.[91] Again, as Wagner and Gainous point out "in the absence of effective filtering, the Internet has the potential to shift and reshape the nature of politics in the Middle East because it transmits ideas and images that were unimaginable just a few short years ago."[92] Furthermore, the authors observe, the internet changes "what people know, when they know it, and who is doing the speaking," thus creating "a new universe of political actors that are hard to anticipate and identify."[93]

In other words, the internet enhances the public sphere and the way people communicate with each other. This may have an important effect on the way people adopt political attitudes. People may embrace Islamist ideas, maintain the beliefs instilled by the old authoritarian regimes, or assume Western, liberal attitudes. It is true that the internet could serve as an instrument of manipulation of ideas or even as a tool for the recruitment of terrorists. However, the fact remains that social media also enable communication that fosters critical thinking. Egypt began to block internet access to websites critical of the regime and in July 2018 passed the Anti-Cyber and Information Technology Crimes Law. This law grants the government the power to restrict digital activity and interfere with online activities.[94] The government censored Muslim Brotherhood and Human Rights websites as well as international media such as *The Huffington Post* in Arabic. Egyptian censors also proceeded to block websites used to circumvent censorship. Egyptian citizens, however, were prepared for these types of measures and managed to use several Uniform Resource Locators (URL) that remained accessible to the public to carry on their discourse. Additionally, the use of Google Drive has not been effectively blocked by Egyptian authorities. Google Drive allows storage of files online making them accessible anywhere. Since Google Drive requires the user to connect through a secure link, it makes the work of censors harder. Several crucial news websites and human rights reports that have been blocked in many Arab countries can be found on Google Plus and in Google Drive. Furthermore, users also disseminate information on how to gain access to alternative sources to combat censorship.[95] Electronic communication produces alternatives to state discourse. It generates communication and dialogue between individuals and enables the spread of multiple views and voices. This development uncouples the people from the state. Under these conditions, the state may lose control of the people's thoughts and its monopoly on the definition of what constitutes the public interest and national priorities.

As Egyptian scholar Ashraf El Sherif has noted:

> ...It used to be very difficult to speak against El-Sisi in public, but now there is a steady flow of insults on social media.

El-Sisi does not enjoy the public deference shown to Egypt's previous strongmen, even to the unpopular Mubarak. This erosion of presidential prestige is just one sign of our deep crisis of governance and state-society relations.[96]

However, even if there is an effective censorship of the internet in the future, the peoples of the Middle East have already started a conversation that is likely to continue within the walls of private salons, informal gatherings and other settings beyond the reach of the state. A millennial journalist from Egypt, who shares her time between Egypt and Spain, pointed out to me that Egyptian society has changed dramatically since the Arab Spring. People may be fearful of the regime and may not be that visible in social media. "However, they talk politics as never before. People cannot be fooled anymore. People scrutinize what the government says. The government can no longer win the hearts of the people with speeches."[97] These changes affect mainly Arab youth. They are a growing population that has played an important role in the protest movements that launched the Arab Spring.

Canadian researcher Bessma Momani points out that it is not infrequent to hear Arab youth challenge their older family members. This phenomenon is very much contrary to previous generations where questioning parents would be considered disrespectful. As they challenge the older generation, Arab youth also challenge clergy and government.[98] In a survey conducted among three thousand youth across nine countries, sixty-three per cent are demanding more freedom. Likewise, Arab youth is a key population group generating information that has had some socio-political impact. Young Saudis for example have used YouTube to attract millions of viewers to voice their opinions. Most of the themes expressed in these videos demand more political and economic accountability from government.[99] The United Nations "Arab Human Development Report" views Arab youth as important agents of change.[100] Statistics show that two-thirds of the Arab region's population is below thirty years of age.[101] This sector of the population is likely to suffer the most from the poor economic infrastructure that exists in the Arab world. About fifty percent of the Arab population is rural. However, agriculture, which also constitutes the main economic activity of the Middle East, represents no more than fifteen percent of GDP in Arab countries.[102] The Arab region has the highest rate of unemployment among developing nations.[103] This includes people who are not part of the formal economy. Furthermore, young people feel deeply anxious about their futures. They lack adequate education, opportunity for social mobility and decent health care. They feel excluded and without any political voice that can represent them. The situation is even worse for young women who also suffer the burden of being discriminated against because of gender.[104]

The UN report, prepared with the participation of Arab experts, draws two important conclusions. First, the need for change in Arab countries can no longer be contained. Secondly, the precarious situation of youth in Arab countries are consequences of failed public policies over many decades that gradually led to the exclusion of large sectors of the population from economic, political, and social life, depriving many people of appropriate health care, good education, and suitable livelihoods. This exacerbated the problem of the slow growth in incomes from which the region had suffered for a long time.[105]

The report provided validation to the Arab Spring without naming it and faulted Arab governments for a systematic policy of exclusion, based on an economic model of state development and expansion of the public sector. This policy, while it improved rates of employment and secured a small safety net, did not increase economic productivity because the governments invested mostly in unproductive bureaucratic jobs or unnecessary government jobs. The fact that the state was the ultimate engine of this economic model created a system of nepotism that benefitted economic elites associated with political elites. This also led to lack of transparency and corruption[106] as well as to high unemployment rates.[107]

Lack of quality education is another factor that affects youth. Modern economies are knowledge-based societies and education in the Arab world does not meet the requirements to develop such economy.[108] Since the Arab Spring, Arab states are much more aware of the need to pay attention to their societies, but the work is far from complete. It is reasonable to assume that Arab states will have to focus on domestic needs and move further away from external conflicts, The UN report also notes that military spending between 1988 and 2014 amounted to approximately two trillion dollars. Such spending has come at the expense of investment in education, infrastructure and other civilian priorities.[109]

Young people have become more conscious of the need for change. As an Egyptian journalist observed,

> We young people realized we were different than our parents. We are still afraid of talking certainly on TV or to the press. However, in the Arab coffee shops young people get together to exchange ideas. In other words, the revolution has succeeded at the ideological level even if we still face authoritarianism or other fear factors.[110]

And then she continued, "Now, people, especially the young people have higher expectations. Contrary to the old generation, who expected nothing from the government, people now believe that their voice counts and they can make a difference."[111] People talk politics everywhere and express their opinion [not so much on internet but in private]. In Egypt prices of basic products go up every day and people talk about it. People talk about issues that affect them and that are directly connected to government policies and politics.[112] "There is also a generational difference between those today in their 20's and their parents," as young people want a more liberal life and they are expressive. "They consume alcohol and hang out in places previous generations did not; young people are more secular and tend more to reject religion as way of life."[113] Furthermore, we are seeing minority groups such as LGBTs and atheists speaking more freely about their opinions and feelings.[114] What we are witnessing in the Arab world is that secretive, private and intimate conversations are beginning to make civil society and public opinion relevant: exchange of information, opinion formation, critical thinking, and normative transformation. It is against this background that many of the ideas planted by the old autocracies may be challenged. In the next section, we will discuss how these actual and potential challenges to the state now affect and may further affect the traditional Arab view of Israel.

Israel and the Arab Spring

Israeli scholar Esther Webman has stated that, "the image of the Jew as an irredeemable destructive agent, hostile to Arabs and Muslims as well as to the whole of humanity has struck roots in Arab society."[115] This perception may be attributed to a combination of several elements: the image of the Jew in the Quran; European and Christian literature present in the Middle East since the 19th century; the rise of Zionism; and the founding of the State of Israel. This has created a spark that blended religious and political motives and resulted in the creation of a "trans-historical symbol of evil."[116] Furthermore, anti-Zionism became a major element of Arab states' public discourse and national identity as we have seen in chapter three. The fight against Zionism was supported by the intellectual community that saw such struggle as an existential challenge.[117] It was a struggle against colonial imperialism, the continuation of the struggle against western powers.

The Islamist discourse, from which the Muslim Brotherhood, Wahhabism and other religious sources also draw, project the image of Jews as arrogant, cowardly, attached to money, descendants of apes and pigs, warmongers, and other unflattering names. The struggle against Zionism is the struggle of the entire Muslim world.[118] Zionism is viewed as "the political and colonialist aspect of the Jewish faith."[119] Between the anti-Zionism of the Arab political leadership and the anti-Semitism of the religious establishment, the uprooting of those sentiments from the Arab mindset looks like an impossible task. This conclusion, however, is too simplistic. Scholar Roy Olivier observes that:

> The demonstrators [of the Arab Spring] referred to no Middle Eastern geopolitical conflicts, burned no U.S. or Israeli flags. [The new Arab rebels] simply would not follow the script which holds that the centrality of the Arab-Israeli conflict is fostering an ever-growing Islamization within Arab society, a search for charismatic leaders, and an identification with a supranational cause...This is why the ritual denunciations of imperialism—including the usual condemnations decrying Zionism as the source of all the Arab

world's troubles—were so remarkably absent from the demonstrations. Similarly, global jihad is no longer a model for young activists.[120]

A breakdown of authoritarian regimes could diminish Arab states' hegemonic control of public discourse. It is this domestic dialogue or balance and the breakdown of the authoritarian state that may potentially reduce the role that Israel or Zionism could play in distracting the Arab public from focusing on their domestic needs. As civil society demands its place at the center of state action and policy, Arab governments will no longer be able to ignore them. To be sure, Arab public opinion has never been considered in Arab governments' decision-making process. Arab civil society was muted and non-existent. Arabs were subjects of powerful states, not real citizens. As discussed in Chapter Three, antagonism towards Israel was promoted to the Arab public by governments. However, post-Arab Spring conditions and the prospect of a new social contract in the Arab world, may have also affected the centrality of the Israeli-Palestinian conflict in the eyes of the Arabs and perhaps even a change of attitudes toward Israel.

In a survey conducted in 2015 across the Arab world, only twenty-three percent of those interviewed considered the Israeli-Palestinian conflict as the biggest problem in the Middle East. The survey was conducted in six Gulf Cooperation Council (GCC) states, Bahrain, Kuwait, Oman, Qatar, Saudi Arabia and the UAE, as well as in Algeria, Egypt, Iraq, Jordan, Lebanon, Libya, Morocco, Palestine, Tunisia and Yemen.[121]

Khaldoon Bakhail, a scholar from Yemen who travels across the Middle East, has pointed out, "less and less people believe that Israel is the enemy. Intellectual elites begin to understand that our main problem is not Israel. People care about poverty, security and terrorism, not Israel."[122] Furthermore, Bakhail commented that people are beginning to question the practice of Arabs killing other Arabs. Bakhail, referring to the Houthis'[123]call for "death to Israel" and "death to America," questions "how is it that the only ones dying are us and not the Israelis and the Americans?"[124] Bakhail added that people in Yemen pay less and less attention to the Palestinian issue. Moreover, negative feelings about the Muslim Brotherhood have led to negative feelings about Hamas.[125]

Mohammed Al Samawi, also a young man from Yemen and the author of a book that describes his struggle for social change in his country, describes similar feelings as he talks about a conversation with his mother about Israel. He asked her "why [do] we Yemenites hate Israel when in fact Yemen never engaged in a war with Israel?" She responded that the question of Yemen and Israel was not the issue. The issue is "our Palestinian brothers." [126] Al Samawi responded to his mother with the following answer:

> I understood the Palestinians were suffering. I have pain for them. But were they our only brothers who matter? Why didn't we unite against the Saudis when they beheaded their own people? Or the Syrians when Bashar Assad massacred innocent men and women? Why did we only care about Palestine at the expense of everything else? [127]

Likewise, the young Egyptian journalist I interviewed pointed out that, "Israel has benefitted from the Arab Uprisings. The Israeli / Palestinian conflict is no longer a priority for the Arabs since they are more focused on their own needs."[128] She also pointed out that there is less hostility toward Israel because it is not the enemy anymore. In other words, "[The Israelis] don't attack us like they used to; the threat is now from terrorists and extremists. However, the attitude towards Israel has not changed. The only difference is that people don't care anymore. Israel will always remain an occupying power and I don't think this will change."[129] A member of a group of young Syrian refugees from the civil war mocked the fact that Assad was treated as God in a Christian School and students were forced to pray for Jesus and Assad. He scornfully referred to the fact that "power outages and other technical difficulties or disasters were blamed on Israel."[130] In this case, Syrians who witnessed the massacres perpetrated by Bashar Al Assad on his own people were voicing their awareness of the fact that the Assad regime is their real problem. Israel was being used as an excuse and a scapegoat for everything wrong that happened in their country. Although these comments were made in the U.S. to a mixed audience of Muslims and Jews, it is reasonable to think that such critical thinking, whether it is openly expressed or not, is shared by others inside Syria. This point can be best illustrated by the spontaneous reactions of some in Syria to the case of Ahed Tamimi, a Palestinian teenager. Tamimi was portrayed in the Arab media as a hero because she spent eight months in an Israeli prison for slapping an Israeli soldier. However, a handful of Syrians observed that Tamimi gained substantial weight and pointed out that she would not have survived Syrian imprisonment. Dozens of tweets repeated the same argument. A Syrian journalist observed "Ahed Tamimi is a lucky girl because she was in Israel's prisons, not in Assad's prisons." Other journalists added that she was not raped, and "she looked more beautiful than before." Others tweeted photos of Tamimi next to a dead Syrian woman.[131] Obviously, the brutality displayed by the Assad regime toward Syrian citizens and other cases of Arab on Arab cruelty have made many in the Arab world aware that fellow Arabs can be more harmful to them than Israel.

Lebanese scholar Nadim Shehadi, an expert on the Arab world and the Israeli-Palestinian conflict, reaffirms this point, observing that the Palestinian question is on the "back burner" because a lot worse is happening in Syria. In Shehadi's own words:

> The Assads, the Sadams, the Gadhafis, and the Mubaraks derived legitimacy either by making war or making peace in the name of the Palestinians. In addition, there has been states of emergency where the Constitution has been suspended; civil rights have been suspended in the region since the 1960s, because of the Israeli- Palestinian conflict, or at least taking the Israeli-Palestinian conflict as an excuse or a struggle with Israel as an excuse. So, youth who are revolting against the system are also revolting against these components. This is a conflict from the past. This is what their parents were exercised about.[132]

Shehadi is describing the decline of the idea of Israel as the external enemy and the possibility of younger generations of Arabs challenging this view. Indeed, Arab Spring protests often demanded politicians to leave the Palestinian problem and external conflicts aside and focus on the needs and aspirations of their own societies. In Iran, which is not an Arab country but is definitely involved in the Israeli- Palestinian conflict, demonstrators chanted the slogan "Not Gaza, Not Lebanon, I give my life for Iran."[133] These slogans suggest that Iranian society is demanding attention to domestic issues and at the same time rejecting Iran's adventurous external wars and funding of foreign conflicts. Indeed, the Iranian regime, which has viewed itself as the exporter of an Islamic revolution, has provided Hezbollah *alone* some seven hundred million dollars a year and another hundred million to various Palestinian terrorist groups.[134] Furthermore, in the aftermath of the U.S elimination of General Qassim Soleimani, head of the Quds Force, who was in charge of all Iran's subversive and destabilizing activities abroad, the Iranian government attempted to create a sense of national unity around his martyrdom. However, a few days later protests against the government resumed. In an act of unprecedented defiance against the Iranian government, university students refused to comply with the Iranian government's traditional act of walking over American and Israeli flags.[135]

Moreover, as social protests increased in Morocco, just as in Iran, the slogan "Taza [a city in Morocco] before Gaza" was chanted, sending a clear message to the authorities that domestic issues and Moroccan citizens' well-being should take priority over the Arab-Israeli conflict.[136]

There are additional examples of voices that question traditional Arab axioms blaming the United States, Israel or the West for their own problems. Abdulrahman al Rashed, a former General Manager of the Saudi-owned *Al Arabiya* News Channel, wrote in 2014 that, "in the overwhelming majority of cases [criticism of Israel] is an excuse used as a card that is brandished by various factors in the Arab world to justify failures or emergency measures, and we [Arabs] have only ourselves to blame."[137] Basim al-Jisr, a Lebanese journalist, also wrote in a 2014 article that, "the real plot is that of the Muslim and Arab world against itself because it has not been able to put an end to the religious, ethnic, social and political divisions within it."[138] In 2013, Abd al Salam Wa'il, a Saudi writer, referred to Israel as an "Arab Treasure." He called Israel "a card used and manipulated by Arab rulers for their purpose on issues that Israel had nothing to do with."[139] Another Lebanese journalist, Samir Atallah, wrote in 2014 in the influential regional publication

Asharq al-Awsat that, "Arab regimes that led the Arab nation with slogans, speeches and proclamations and revolutions left the Arab nation poor and dependent, and now these regimes that oppress and exploit their people are sending their subjects to drown in the sea or to drown in the mud or turn to prostitution in the bitterness of their despair."[140] Along similar lines, another Saudi journalist noted that Arabs never blamed the Arab system for its failures: "We talk about Sykes-Picot,[141] imperialism and Zionism, but we never look at the mirrors on the wall."[142] An Iraqi journalist used more direct language, "time and time again Arab media brainwashed us that Israel desired to occupy the Middle East regardless of the fact that Israel withdrew from Egyptian, Jordanian, and Lebanese lands and is willing to negotiate withdrawals from other lands as well."[143]

According to Shehadi, "the anti-Zionist narrative does not work anymore. The Arab Spring's voices as we are seeing in social media focus on those elements that were suppressed in the name of the Arab/Israeli conflict."[144] Moreover, in countries where there is complete rejection of the despot's discourse, it could positively affect attitudes towards Israel. As scholar Salma Masalha has explained, the Arab Spring took place in countries where regimes voiced empty slogans of nationalism, freedom, socialism, Arab unity, and called for the destruction of Israel. None of these slogans ever materialized but instead those regimes created a nepotistic state that benefitted certain sects and tribes at the expense of others.[145] That resentment against the despot could have a deconstructive effect on those empty slogans that have dominated the Arab world including enmity towards the State of Israel.

Indeed, Ofra Bengio has shown how the collapse of Sadam Hussein and the new challenges Iraq has faced, have significantly changed Iraqi attitudes towards Israel.[146] Indeed, in the Iraqi state, under the Baath Party, Israel was portrayed as the symbol of evil and anathema to Arab civilization. It was basically defined as an existential threat to Iraqis and the Arab nation.[147] Iraq's military aid to other Arabs during the various wars with Israel, the launching of missiles towards Israel's population during the first Gulf War (1991) and the obsessive anti-Zionist and anti-Semitic rhetoric of the regime, exemplified this phenomenon. Furthermore, Saddam Hussein became the main funder of Hamas' terrorist activities until he was removed from power in 2003. As Saddam's regime collapsed, new voices began to emerge. The vicious rhetoric and propaganda spread by Saddam Hussein and his children through their control of media outlets and the educational system, began to diminish. Several unprecedented events followed. In 2004, then Prime Minister Iyad Allawi shook hands with Israeli foreign minister Silvan Shalom. Between September 2004 and September 2008, the head of the Democratic Party of the Iraqi nation and a member of the Iraqi parliament, Mithal Al Alusi, visited Israel. Upon his return, the Iraqi parliament voted to remove his immunity to allow for his prosecution. However, Al Alusi appealed to the Federal Supreme Court that decided to overturn the decision of the parliament, stating that he had committed no crime by visiting Israel.[148] Furthermore, Iraqi delegations that include local leaders have visited Israel, met with government officials, academics and others. These delegations were mostly comprised of influential Shiite and Sunni figures.[149] Moreover, Arab and Iraqi citizens responded favorably to a post by the Israeli Foreign Ministry welcoming the Iraqi delegations.[150] Significantly, the number of approving responses overwhelmed the number of responses indicating disapproval.

For example, a "welcome" from an Israeli citizen wishing good and respectful relations between the two countries received one hundred twenty-eight votes of approval. Another comment by an Iraqi citizen expressing his "hope to see the Israeli Embassy one day in Baghdad" received eighty-five votes of approval or "likes." Another comment congratulating the visiting delegation and expressing the desire "to develop relations with Israel and benefit from the successful Israeli experience in the cultural, scientific, military and political realms" and "to move towards lasting peace between the two countries and open the doors of investment for Israeli companies in Iraq," received forty votes of approval. Another comment calling "to resort to love and mercy," clearly calling for reconciliation between the two countries-received thirty-five votes of approval. Another comment praising the delegation visit as "tribute to the moderate voices in Iraq and outside Iraq," received twenty-nine "likes."[151]

By contrast, a comment citing Quran passages that define the Jews as close to Christians and not to Islam, received only one vote of approval. Another calling Israel a "usurping entity" and asking to reject Israel until its removal "from the map" received seven votes of approval. Another comment saying that anybody who helps promote "Zionist principles," "shall be sentenced to death" received only two votes of approval or "likes."[152] We can see in this small sample that the positive reactions outnumber the negative ones. The overwhelming majority of respondents were Arab.[153] Furthermore, the Facebook page of the Israeli Foreign Ministry mentioned earlier has reached 1.7 million followers. Thirty-three percent conveyed positive sentiments towards Israel and another seventeen percent were considered "neutral."[154] Two young Israeli citizens, descendants of Iraqi Jewish refugees, took the initiative to connect with young Iraqis in order to build better future relations between Iraqis and Israelis.[155]

In Tunisia we find an interesting situation. This country, whose founding leaders such as Habib Bourguiba, supported the idea of recognizing Israel in the mid 1960's, has shown a mixed reaction towards Israel. On the one hand, the Tunisian government, including the Islamist Ennahda, reiterated its support for the Tunisian Jewish community and for Jewish sites. The government also condemned acts of terror and vandalism against the Jewish community and made a call to Jewish pilgrims to visit Tunisia. During the visit by the Hamas leader Ismail Haniyeh in 2012, a group of Salafist fanatics greeted Haniyeh with the slogan "kill the Jews." Ennahda issued a strong condemnation of such statements claiming that this type of slogan was against the spirit of Islam.[156] Yet, in spite of this, Tunisia included a clause in the first draft of its constitution against normalization of relations with Israel and opposition to Zionism. The first draft published early in 2012 highlighted the importance of the Israeli-Palestinian conflict and the need to resist Zionism."[157] However, the final draft of the Tunisian Constitution although it maintained the reference to the Palestinian question, it removed the anti-Israel and anti-Zionist language. According to Israeli diplomat and former Israeli Ambassador to Egypt, Shalom Cohen, Tunisia kept the moderate version because of pressure exercised by the Americans.[158]

Chhaibi Abderrhaim, a professor at King Mohamed V University of Rabat in Morocco, observes that people were mute before the Arab spring. Now they express themselves and participate in demonstrations. According to Abderrhaim, people are not intellectually prepared to talk about politics but they discuss social issues that affect their lives. People have more freedom to express themselves in the media. More books are available and there is more freedom of research.[159] In addition, since the Arab Spring began, there is more recognition of ethnic groups that were not recognized before, such as the Berbers. [160] According to Abderrhaim, Moroccan authorities now recognize Morocco as an Arab and Berber country. The acknowledgment of Berber identity has also generated more sympathy towards the Jewish people and Israel. Berbers have historically struggled for social and cultural rights in Morocco. According to scholar Bruce Maddy-Weitzman, members of the younger generation of Berbers view Israel as sharing a common cause in so far as Berbers are fighting against the hegemonic tendencies of the Arabs. Israel is viewed as an important counterforce opposing the Arab hegemony against which they are struggling in their native Morocco.[161] Berber-Jewish friendships were established, and Moroccan delegations visited Israel. Berbers represent about forty percent of the total Moroccan population.[162] As Berber culture and identity become more integrated in Morocco, it is likely that the anti-Israel hostility may be considerably reduced. In one instance, Hamas leader and Israel's archenemy Khalid Meshal faced massive protests mostly from Berbers when he visited Morocco.[163]

Joseph Braude, a journalist and Middle East analyst, believes that the need to combat Jihadism, or religious extremism, has led to an Arab policy of media openness the purpose of which is to counterbalance the Jihadist's message. As a result, diverse views have begun to emerge in the Arab media. The diversity of these views may be seen in calls for religious pluralism and more tolerance. Braude observes that such discussion could potentially open up a window of tolerance for Israel and the Jews.[164] As an example, Egyptian journalist Ahmed Hidji, described three Egyptian professors who complained about the fact that their students expressed a desire to meet Israelis.[165]

There is another element that could mitigate relations between the Arab world and Israelis. This is the fight against Jihadism, itself.

As Braude has pointed out, the views of those holding "revision-ist" ideas of Israel or Israelis "appear to stem from broader cultural changes, which arose in turn from the globalization of media, the region's shifting politics, growing awareness of local Jewish histo-ry, and the youthful impulse to rebel against authority."[166] Accord-ing to Braude, these people knew that autocrats who oppressed and harassed them championed the Palestinian cause.[167]

In November 2019, a group of Arab intellectuals, journalists, artists, politicians, diplomats and Quranic scholars expressed con-cern about the continuation of boycotts against Israel and isolation of the country. These individuals support engagement with Israel. In the words of Mustafa el-Dessouki, the Egyptian managing editor of the Saudi-funded newsmagazine *Majalla*,

> [I met]'like-minded' Arabs who had kind of been waiting for somebody like me to come along…Arab news media and entertainment have long been programming people to-ward this hostility while political leaders were intimidating and scaring people into manifesting it. But many Arabs … actually want to connect with Israelis.[168]

The interesting fact about this is that these views were expressed by a group of intellectuals engaged in a conversation where alter-native ideas were debated outside the realm of the state and Isla-mist circles. In this sense we believe that Arab intellectuals could play a special role in this process of Israeli-Arab reconciliation as we shall see in the next chapter.

Conclusion

This chapter does not argue that Arab views on Israel have radi-cally changed. Braude points out that rejection of Israel is not dead and in fact still constitutes a predominant form of discourse. Re-jectionists were not purged, and still anti-Israel discourse is very much alive.[169] Those who speak more warmly about Israel are still a minority. This is why it is important to point out that we are not suggesting here to relegate the Israeli- Palestinian conflict to obliv-ion or to ignore it as a real problem. However, as civil society becomes an emerging actor in the Arab world, Arab rulers are forced to reconsider their priorities, which may have very little to do with foreign policy. Arab society's focus on fighting for freedom or attempting to solve the domestic problems affecting them, is likely to force Arab governments to focus their energy there and away from the strawman, Israel. As different social and political actors make demands, the national agendas are becoming more complex. Arab leaders will have to prioritize constituents' needs and respond to these demands. Because of this reorientation, the entire foreign policy agenda could change. The legitimacy of the Arab regimes can no longer be sustained by the Israeli-Arab conflict and the external enemy ideology. Secondly, new voices in the public sphere may, by opening a forum of critical thinking, also open themselves up to a different view of Israel. This is not a fait accompli. It is a process that could evolve as the Arab Spring continues along its unfinished course.

These new critical voices may not be sufficient for the time being, but it is still a new phenomenon that may expand and whose consequences are not clear. The Palestinian leadership may sense that the Israeli-Palestinian conflict does not resonate with Arab public opinion as it once did. Former Palestinian Prime Minister Salam Fayyad observed that because of the Arab Spring "people are preoccupied with their own domestic affairs" and suggested that the Palestinians have been sidelined.[170]

This situation could reaffirm a sense of weakness in the Palestinian leadership who hold onto old anti-Zionist rhetoric that may no longer be effective.

Israel, however, will also be required to help in the process of reconciliation. Israel's common enmity with Iran may not be enough to change the Israeli/Arab conflict's negative dynamics. As we will see in the next chapter, most Israeli academic experts and observers agree that normalization with Arab countries is unlikely to come into being without a solution to the Palestinian problem. A change in attitudes towards the Israeli-Palestinian conflict is more likely to happen as the Arab world moves in the direction of improving its internal governance and as its public sphere develops, even if such governance remains far from perfect in the short run.

Israel therefore must take proper steps to complement those developments in the Arab world. We will discuss this in the next chapter. A chance of another Arab-Israeli war is minimal. Israel's security is not threatened by Arab armies but by anti-Israeli and anti-Zionist discourse, international isolation, incitement, terrorism, and a potential nuclear Iran. The key issue is how to diminish the rhetoric and policies that perpetuate the Israeli-Palestinian conflict and instead transform Arab countries into entities that cooperate in achieving peace between Israel and its neighbors. In the next chapter, considering the analysis presented throughout this book, we will offer some possible solution.

CHAPTER 5

THINKING ABOUT SOLUTIONS

As we have noted in the first two chapters of this book, unless the Palestinian leadership can finally impose order in the territories, there is no possibility to establish a stand-alone Palestinian state, side by side with Israel. In addition, we have pointed out that Israeli-Palestinian reconciliation seems less likely as long as the Palestinians, especially the younger generations, are subjected to systematic anti-Israel propaganda and indoctrination. Furthermore, conflict and mobilization prevent normalization of Palestinian everyday life. Thus, it seems that a solution to the Israeli-Palestinian conflict must take into consideration the need to restore stable governance to the Palestinians and normalcy to their everyday lives. Although we are not ruling out a two-state solution in principle, such a solution does not seem viable or plausible unless dissident factions like Hamas and the Islamic Jihad cease to threaten the government of the Palestinian Authority.

Given the analysis we provided throughout the book, we will examine different potential solutions to the ongoing Israeli-Palestinian in this conclusive chapter. We will argue that any solution must bring about order and stability in the Palestinian community and economic improvement for Palestinians in ways that stimulate economic initiative, restore civil society and individual empowerment and dignity. Likewise, any solution must involve the Arab world.

The Trump Plan

In June 2019, The Trump Administration introduced the first phase of a plan to resolve the Israeli-Palestinian conflict. This phase consisted of a proposal to resolve Palestinian economic problems before implementing any political solution. The plan sought an investment of 50 billion dollars over ten years to substantially improve the Palestinian economy. It aimed at opening the West Bank and Gaza up to the regional economy, building infrastructure, creating enough business confidence to encourage investment in the Palestinian territories and promoting private sector growth.[1] In principle, the plan seeks to double the Palestinian GDP, reduce Palestinian unemployment rates in the West Bank and Gaza and cut the Palestinian poverty rate by fifty percent.[2] The plan's goal is to open the West Bank and Gaza to regional and global markets through investments in transportation and infrastructure, increase Palestinian exports and reduce barriers to transport and travel. Under the deal, the Palestinians are expected to cooperate with Egypt, Israel, and Jordan and regulatory barriers to the movement of Palestinian goods and people would be reduced.[3] Likewise, new opportunities would be expanded through online educational platforms, vocational and technical training, and international exchanges. It is also proposed to improve access to health care for Palestinians by establishing clinics and hospitals equipped with the most advanced medical technology. The plan also proposes to enhance Palestinian governance and long-term economic success through administrative reforms[4]

The Trump Administration's ideas were presented at a conference in Bahrain, attended by several Arab finance ministers, heads of international financial organizations, private sector business executives and investors from many countries. The American strategy constitutes, to a certain extent, the revival of the regional multilateral talks aimed at creating regional economic prosperity and facilitating a peace agreement. It could also be viewed as a rebirth of "Fayyadism," referring to the government of Prime Minister Salam Fayyad, who was Prime Minister of the PA from 2007 to 2013. Fayyad believed that the establishment of a strong economic infrastructure and Palestinian self-reliance could establish the institutions needed to build a stable Palestinian state. Indeed, under Fayyad there was an economic boom. Under his rule, three new hospitals were built, fifty healthcare centers were rehabilitated, and electricity networks were expanded, benefiting nearly all Palestinian households.[5] No less important, Fayyad established a timeline for creating a Palestinian state once the Palestinian economic and institutional infrastructure were put in place.

Fayyad's goal was to introduce an efficient administrative system that would provide basic services and pay the salaries of civil servants in the West Bank and Gaza. At the same time, his plan encouraged fiscal responsibility and transparency. These actions generated support and donations from the international community but caused fear and discontent among Palestinian leaders precisely because of the accountability and transparency requirements.[6] Fayyad was also perceived as a puppet of America because his policies were welcomed and enthusiastically supported by the US Administration.[7] It is reasonable to believe that Palestinian opposition to the economic phase of Trump's plan has similar motivations.

Fayyad faced opposition from both Fatah and Hamas. He created a system that opened greater foreign financial support to the Palestinians, but in doing so, challenged traditional elites that used foreign money to maintain their patronage.[8] Some of his opponents accused him of giving up political independence for neo-liberal economics.[9]

Fayyadism, like the Trump plan, focused on stimulating the private sector and creating an independent economy open to regional and global markets. The development of a private sector and the globalization of the Palestinian economy have the potential to reduce Palestinian society's dependence on the PA and its bureaucracy. This is obviously a reason for the Palestinian leadership to oppose the Administration plan. However, the fact that fifteen Palestinian businesspeople attended the Bahrain conference is not a coincidence. Echoing Jared Kushner, advisor to the American president and the architect of the Trump Plan, a businessperson from the Arab emirates pointed out,

> By generating jobs, income opportunities and filling gaps in delivering basic services, the private sector can help build momentum behind a fragile economy and instill hope in the people of the region. Indeed, when a steadfast peace plan is eventually put in place, the private sector will be the important catalyst that kick starts the transformation of the West Bank and Gaza.[10]

An economic boost, if successful, could provide Palestinians the hope to conduct a normal, safe, healthy and prosperous life.

Political Solutions

Seven months after proposing its economic plan, the Trump administration presented a political proposal that differs from previous attempts to resolve the Israeli-Palestinian conflict. According to the design, Israel would keep existing settlements but would discontinue building new settlements for the next four years. These four years would be the period during which Palestinians and Israelis should negotiate final status issues. Likewise, Israel would be granted full security control of the Jordan Valley, the western edge of the future Palestinian state and an area Israelis consider vital for their own security. Israel would annex 30 percent of the West Bank, which would mostly consist of Jewish settlements. In return, Israel would agree to land swaps and possibly to absorb a limited number of Palestinian refugees into Israel. These land swaps should provide the newly created Palestinian state land reasonably comparable to the land taken away from them in the West Bank.[11] After annexation, Israel would abolish its administration in the West Bank. A Palestinian state would be created on the entire Gaza strip and on 70 percent of the West Bank.[12] There would be physical connections between different parts of the Palestinian state through roads, bridges and tunnels (including a connection between the West Bank and Gaza). Holy sites would remain under Israel's control, but Muslims would have free access to the Al Aqsa Mosque.[13] It is expected that approximately 97 percent of Israelis in the West Bank would be incorporated into Israeli territory, and 97 percent of the Palestinians would live in the contiguous Palestinian state. [14]

Under the proposed terms, Jerusalem would remain the capital of the State of Israel, while the Palestinian capital would be in the section of East Jerusalem located in all areas east and north of the existing security barrier, including Kafr' Aqab, the eastern part of

Shuafat and Abu Dis.[15]

If the Palestinians refuse to negotiate with Israel, the US would support a unilateral Israeli annexation of the settlements.[16] The second largest party in Israel, the centrist Blue and White Party, supports the plan in principle, although thus far it has not supported unilateral annexation. However, the Palestinian leadership rejected the plan, characterizing it as a "new Balfour Declaration."[17] Thus, Abbas has pledged to continue the struggle to end the occupation and has joined Hamas leadership in trying to sabotage the Trump plan.[18]

According to the proposal, Israel would still have control of Palestinian airspace and would be responsible for security on the Palestinian state borders.

The most remarkable aspect of the publication of the Trump peace plan has been the initial reaction of the Arab world, which constitutes a major player in our analysis. Key Arab countries including Saudi Arabia, Egypt, Qatar, and the United Arab Emirates (UAE) were initially willing to consider the plan, even if they did not openly endorse it.[19] The Egyptian government's statement was significant: "The Arab Republic of Egypt appreciates the continuous efforts exerted by the US administration to achieve a comprehensive and just settlement of the Palestinian issue, thereby contributing to the stability and security of the Middle East, ending the Palestinian-Israeli conflict."[20]

Arab ambassadors from Oman, Bahrain and the UAE attended the White House event unveiling Trump's political plan. Saudi Arabia and the UAE urged the Palestinian leadership to negotiate with Israel based on the plan.[21]

Furthermore, days after the Trump plan was announced, the Prime Minister of Israel and the Chairman of Sudan's Sovereign Council met to discuss the possibility of normalizing relations between the two countries. Sudan's move also happened shortly after mass protests forced the ouster of longtime Sudanese dictator Omar al Bashir. This development was remarkable when considering that Sudan had earlier provided training camps for Al Qaida and Hezbollah and established a strategic alliance with Iran including providing from which weapons were shipped to Hamas and other Palestinian terrorist groups, as well as to ISIS in the Sinai Peninsula[22]

Sudan also broke its alliance with Iran and established a new alliance with Iran's rival, Saudi Arabia.[23] Most significant of all, the Sudanese example seems to confirm the connection that exists between changes brought by the Arab Spring, geopolitical alliances around the Iranian regional threat and Israeli-Arab reconciliation.

After a cautious reaction to the Trump plan, the Arab League adopted a resolution rejecting the plan and urged Israel and the United States not to implement it. They reaffirmed the principle of a two-state solution that included a Palestinian state based on the borders and with its capital in East Jerusalem.[24] Yet, during the Arab League meeting, Arab foreign ministers who spoke, refrained from criticizing the Trump Administration's proposal. Envoys from the UAE, Oman, and Morocco even suggested that the plan could be a basis for negotiations.[25]

It is reasonable to think that the Arab League is likely to reaffirm the principles established by the Arab Peace Initiative, which we discussed in Chapter 3, and to renew negotiations to solve the conflict with a different attitude than twenty years earlier. How Arab leaders behave in the future towards the Israeli-Palestinian conflict, however, will depend not only on how they weigh their own domestic and geo-political interests, but also on the degree to which they are pressured by the United States.

Indeed, with robust American mediation the UAE and Israel signed an agreement of full normalization of relations between the two countries. The Palestinian leadership reacted negatively to this development invoking the principles of the Arab Peace Initiative that state there should not be normalization between Israel and the Arab states until the Palestinian question is not resolved. The Palestinians introduced a proposal in the Arab League condemning the Israel-UAE agreement. However, the Arab League rejected the Palestinian initiative. [26]

This shows the important momentum that the Arab-Israeli relation is experiencing and it means that Israel should be judicious and cautious if it wants to maintain this momentum.

One of the provisions of the UAE-Israel agreement is that Israel should abstain from annexing territory in the West Bank. If Israel moves towards annexation there would be serious complications.

Not only peace with the UAE will fall apart. When the Israeli government voiced its intention to begin annexation in July 2020, Arab countries expressed opposition to such a move and Jordan's cabinet members threatened to reconsider their peace treaty and security cooperation agreements with Israel. Egypt, Saudi Arabia and Bahrain also expressed opposition to annexation.[27]

Therefore, it is reasonable to think that a solution to the Palestinian issue is still required to achieve full peace and normalization between Israel and the rest of the Arab world.

Possible Solutions to the Israeli-Palestinian Conflict

Since we do not know whether the Trump plan will succeed, it is vital to explore alternative solutions.

One alternative to the two-state solution has been the one-state solution. Extreme hawks in Israel who claim Israel's sovereignty over the entirety of historical Palestine (the Greater Israel), have proposed a one-state solution. Radical anti-Zionist Palestinians also favor a one-state solution because they believe that if Palestinians populations merge into one single democratic state, they will eventually recover all of Palestine from the Mediterranean Sea to the Jordan river through electoral means. Both the Israeli center right and the center-left reject a one-state solution because they view such a solution as a way to dissolve the Zionist dream of having a Jewish state. It may also be the case that the binational character of its society would lead to bitter conflicts over material and symbolic resources. Such a scenario could well end in civil strife, or even civil war.

As we have seen in Chapter 1, even a man of such hawkish views as Ariel Sharon, understood that retention of the West Bank and Gaza could threaten the Jewish character of Israel, and thus it is important to end the Israeli occupation of Palestinian lands. These calculations shaped Sharon's decision to unilaterally withdraw from Gaza and prepare for a unilateral withdrawal from the West Bank as well.

Former Israeli negotiator Yossi Beilin believes that two states, Palestine and Israel, could form a confederation to cooperate on issues such as zoning, infrastructure, and security. According to

Beilin, the West Bank area is so small that it is impossible to conceive its infrastructure separate from Israel or deal separately with common challenges such as agricultural diseases or water supply.[28] Belin conceived of two separate states possessing joint authorities only over specific sectors, including the administration of the Old City of Jerusalem and its historic sites. Such an arrangement would not require evacuating Jewish settlers so long as they complied with the laws of the Palestinian state. At the same time, Beilin suggests, "the same number of Palestinian citizens should be allowed to live in Israel as permanent residents, vetted by Israel."[29] In terms of security, Beilin suggests that Palestinians would be totally in charge of their own internal security that would end the use of the Israeli Defense Forces (IDF). Israel, however, would be "in charge of strategic defense, against threats from third parties."[30] The borders between the two states would have to be defined.

This solution is problematic. A confederation arrangement may increase Palestinian demands for the "right of return." Likewise, it could create a nationalistic confrontation, litigation and similar problems like the ones the one-state solution may generate, indicating that various solutions should be found through different venues.

Another idea is a unilateral withdrawal from the West Bank. This option is highly problematic given the results of Israel's withdrawal from Gaza. Such step made southern Israeli towns vulnerable to Hamas' bombing. Should Hamas begin to bomb Israel from the West Bank, the highly populated Israeli central region would be vulnerable to attacks. Equally troubling would be if a Palestinian state falls into a state of anarchy or falls victim to a *coup d'état*. Such state could become a totalitarian entity like the one created by the Islamic State in Iraq and Syria.

Furthermore, even assuming that a unilateral annexation and disengagement from the West Bank would be successful from a security point of view, international campaigns of propaganda aimed at isolating Israel could intensify, as happened after Israel's withdrawal from Gaza. Gaza has been often perceived not as a free and autonomous Palestinian territory but as an "occupied territory" and an Israeli "open prison."[31]

A Jordanian/Palestinian Confederation however, may present a more feasible opportunity. Jordan has a historical connection to the Palestinians because Palestinian migrants and their descendants comprise a large part of the Jordanian population. As opposed to the PA, Jordan is capable of exercising the monopoly on the means of violence, negotiating with Israel and providing Palestinians with the possibility of living normal and free lives. Either Gaza could be incorporated into the Confederation through a tunnel or, alternately, Gaza could be annexed to Egypt.

The West Bank

In February 1985, Jordan and the PLO signed an agreement proclaiming that "Palestinian self-determination" was to be exercised through the formation of "a Palestinian state in the occupied territories that would be linked to the Hashemite Kingdom of Jordan in a political confederation."[32] The Arafat-Hussein agreement stipulated that Palestinian self-determination would be exercised through a Palestinian state on areas occupied by Israel but linked to Jordan. Many Palestinians then accepted this agreement. Although such a project deepened divisions within the PLO, it was seen as an important movement toward reaching a settlement.[33] The then Israeli Prime Minister Shimon Peres also welcomed the agreement as long as the PLO was not included in the negotiations. [34] Even though Jordan declared in 1988 that the country wanted nothing to do with the West Bank residents, the idea of a Jordanian-Palestinian confederation was resurrected in the last several years. [35]

In May of 2016, former Jordanian Prime Minister Abdelsalam al-Majali visited the West Bank and announced that such a confederation could be good for both the Palestinians and the Jordanians. Majali proposed a confederation that would have a 'joint legislature and joint government with equal representation whereby the upper authority would have three main missions –security, economy, and foreign affairs-- and the rest would be the jurisdiction of the joint government."[36] Majali pointed out that the Palestinians were not "fully qualified to assume their responsibilities, in wake of the failures of Arab countries to support them."[37] Interestingly enough, a delegation of Palestinian notables was sent to Amman to call on the Jordanian King "to protect the West Bank and reactivate the confederation,"[38] thereby reflecting the Palestinian awareness of chaos and aspiration to normalcy.

In early 2018, the Trump Team discussed with PA president Abbas the idea of a Jordanian/Palestinian confederacy. Abbas seemed to open to the idea. [39] This may reflect Abbas' admission of Fatah's inability to take charge of a Palestinian state and that he may need the protection of a larger Arab entity against Hamas and other dissident groups. In fact, Adnan Abu Amer, a professor of political science at the University of Ummah in Gaza, reported early in 2019 that Israelis, Palestinians and Jordanians were seriously entertaining this idea. According to Abu Amer, the idea was to establish "one state for two peoples after the Palestinian state is established on the territories occupied by Israel in 1967. This single state will have two capitals, Jerusalem for the Palestinians and Amman for the Jordanians, as well as a central judicial authority and joint armed forces led by the Jordanian monarch. It would also include a central council of ministers and parliament elected by both nations, while both populations would be allowed to move freely between the two areas."[40] Abu Amer points out:

> We are entitled to ask why there is growing Palestinian support for a confederation with Jordan. It may be because the Palestinians have lost all hope of having an independent state and no longer have much trust in the PA after witnessing its successive political failures in its dealings with Israel. Jordan may also be seen as their gateway to the world, bypassing the tools of the occupation, which have kept them behind the hated Apartheid Wall and endless military checkpoints.[41]

A Palestinian/Jordanian confederation of course would not exempt Israel from making territorial compromises. The process of establishing such a confederation would need Israeli participation and would require Israel to make compromises similar to those it would have had to make in a bilateral Israeli- Palestinian negotiation like withdrawal from territory in the West Bank and/or compromises on Jerusalem. The confederation would add Jordan to the Israeli- Palestinian equation as a credible and stable partner that could guarantee an enforceable peace.

Another person who proposed this idea was a high-profile moderate scholar and former President of the East Jerusalem-based Al Quds University, Sari Nusseibeh. Nusseibeh spoke about the need to adopt the idea of a Jordanian/Palestinian confederacy to overcome the impasse in the negotiations and the increased pace of Israeli settlement construction in the West Bank. Although Nusseibeh acknowledges that it would be difficult to get acceptance of such a proposal from Jordan, he sees this as a real alternative to settlement activity and the vacuum in Palestinian leadership. Those who support the confederation, demand first, the creation of a Palestinian state, and then a confederacy.[42] Again, such a solution is possible if these two elements occur simultaneously. However, a Palestinian state must be guaranteed by actual Jordanian enforceable state power. Indeed, a confederation would protect Palestinians from further chaos and make it easier for Israel to negotiate, since peace would be ensured by a reliable Arab country capable of offering her security guarantees. Furthermore, the governance capability of Jordan could offer the Palestinians the order and normalcy they desperately need.

However, it is important to remember that in Jordan there is widespread skepticism and opposition to this idea for fear that the Palestinians may take over Jordan as they tried to do in 1970. Jordanians fear that such a scheme could dilute the Jordanian identity and create insecurity and instability in Jordan.[43]

Nevertheless, there are reasons for Jordanians to consider a Jordanian- Palestinian Confederacy positively. Scholar Asher Susser points out that relations and ties between Jordanians on the East Bank and the West Bank of the Jordan River are not new. In the aftermath of 1948, Palestinians who fled to Jordan were assimilated to integrate them into Jordanian society and promote the idea of Arab unity.[44] That is also consistent with the Palestinian conception that existed even before 1948, where Palestinian Arabs saw themselves as an integral part of the Arab world. Jordan was the only Arab country that provided full citizenship to Palestinians. Jordanians and Palestinians are both Sunni Muslims who share language and a common cultural and religious identity. There are also bonds of marriage between Jordanians and Palestinians. Susser also explains that despite Jordanians and Palestinians falling out during the Jordanian crackdown on Palestinians in September 1970, tensions between Israeli Jews and Palestinians are worse by far. Many Palestinians in Jordan have been successful and today they represent about fifty percent of the total Jordanian population. Whereas it is true that there are Jordanians who reject the idea of a Jordanian-Palestinian confederation, others believe that a joint Jordanian-Palestinian political order would enable Palestinians to exercise their political rights in Palestine and simultaneously continue to be residents of Jordan.[45] Furthermore, as Israeli historian Benny Morris has noted, given the fact that Jordan has large empty territory, the proposed confederacy could enable the redistribution of overcrowded Palestinian populations, such as in Gaza, and the absorption of refugees.[46] Such movement and migration of population have the potential to contribute to economic growth, particularly if the Arab and international community invests or contributes. The Jordanians may well benefit from an enlargement of their market and labor force and increased investments that are likely to flow because of a more peaceful and stable environment.

A compromise between the PA and the Jordanian government could give birth to a central authority capable of exercising the monopoly of the means of violence and establishing an order the PA is unable to currently secure. A new government tied to Jordan could provide some peace and tranquility to those Palestinians seeking a more stable order and an effective counterbalance to Hamas' putschist attitudes. Confederation would allow an autonomous Palestinian political entity to connect with a larger economic area of operation and thus reduce Palestinian dependency on Israel and on foreign aid. It would be easier for the Israelis to withdraw from the West Bank knowing that the Jordanian army would be responsible for guarding the borders between Israel and the Jordanian- Palestinian entity. Above all, the idea of a confederation could finalize a political arrangement that would demobilize the Palestinians. If the Palestinians adopt the habit of living under an orderly regime as politically autonomous, they are likely to move away from being permanent revolutionaries and towards becoming citizens that contribute to the well-being of their society. Even though it is not a western-style liberal democracy, the Jordanian state leaves enough room for civil life and personal security.

The challenge here would be to convince Jordanians to accept this option. Indeed, one of the key Jordanian objections to the Trump Plan is precisely that "once full annexation takes place all eyes will be on Jordan to assume a role in running Palestinian population centers. Jordanians, too, fear that the demographic problem that could arise from the Israeli annexation of the West Bank would be resolved at Jordan's expense through the fulfillment of an Israeli far-right claim that Jordan is Palestine."[47] Although what is suggested is Jordanian control of these territories and the placement of the Palestinians under a confederacy, Jordanians still fear a Palestinian take over [of Jordan] given the history of PLO/Jordan relations, which we described in Chapter 2.[48] However, Jordan has the capability to effectively fight sedition and combat groups like Hamas. As Morris has pointed out, "the unification of the Palestinian National Authority and Jordan, with its relatively powerful army and security services, would provide the possibility of reining in the militants, much as Jordan has easily and successfully reined in its own Palestinian and Islamist militants over the past decades."[49]

The Case of Gaza

Some scholars, like Morris, have proposed that Gaza should be part of the Jordanian- Palestinian Confederation. [50] Gaza could be physically connected to the Palestinian/Jordanian confederation via a West Bank/Gaza corridor. However, it would be difficult to convince Jordan to accept the idea of a confederation that incorporates Gaza, a territory that has been ruled by Hamas since 2007. That is why it would be worthwhile to also consider the possibility of incorporating Gaza into a confederation with or some sort of tie to Egypt. In fact, American scholar Daniel Pipes has championed this idea, as thousands of Palestinians entered Egypt in the aftermath of the Hamas takeover of Gaza in 2007. [51]

Over the years, Egypt has been able to toughen its position on Hamas' subversive and terrorist activities, which have included construction of tunnels linking the Gaza Strip to the Sinai Peninsula and smuggling of weapons between the two areas.[52] Hamas indeed fears Egypt more than any other force, in the region, including the Israeli army. Egypt has also proved itself very aggressive towards Hamas. Its military destroyed most of the twelve hundred tunnels used to smuggle food, cars and weapons to Gaza from Egyptian territory. [53]

Hamas is intimidated by Egypt's aggressive posture. The group's leadership even assured Egyptian authorities that they no longer had ties to the Muslim Brotherhood.[54] It is remarkable that Hamas would deny a connection to the organization that inspired its creation just to maintain peaceful relations with the Egyptian government. Equally noteworthy, in order to maintain good relations with Egypt, Hamas cracked down on Salafist extremists, an action that caused tensions between Hamas and ISIS.[55] It is significant that while Hamas does not fear the PA or Israel, the group is fearful of Egypt. Therefore, it is possible that Hamas could be constrained by Egyptian power in the region.

In general, Palestinians have not maintained a state of permanent animosity against any Arab country, even those it has fallen out with. In September 1970, the PLO was brutally repressed and forced to relocate to Lebanon by the Jordanian government, which suspected the PLO of attempting to overthrow the Hashemite monarchy. Despite Jordan's harshness towards the Palestinians, Jordanians and Palestinians did not break ranks. Even if tensions and distrust persisted, Palestinian animosity was always directed mainly towards Israel. The same applies to the 1976 Tel al Zaatar massacre of Palestinians in Lebanon at the hands of Christian militias with the indirect help of Syria. Syria also arrested and expelled PLO leaders from Damascus. Yet, the PLO and Syria eventually reached a rapprochement. Similarly, the Palestinians never held Kuwaitis accountable for the expulsion of hundreds of thousands of Palestinians from that country after Arafat sided with Iraq during its invasion of Kuwait in 1990. What made the difference is that Arab governments have historically stood as a legitimate entity in Palestinian eyes regardless of their often oppressive character. In practice, this means that an Arab state offers an effective deterrent to insurgent actions. The Palestinian leadership is not interested in causing problems for an Arab country. From this perspective,

Egypt could restore sovereignty in Gaza and contrary to what occurred in 1948, it could also establish civilian rule in Gaza and grant Gazans Egyptian citizenship.

The fact that Hamas traveled to Cairo to beg for clemency from el Sisi - the man responsible for the ouster of its ally, the Muslim Brotherhood- shows that Cairo has the ability to neutralize Hamas and even subdue it. If Egypt were to succeed in controlling Hamas in Gaza, restoring a normal life to the Palestinians living there and opening the Egyptian economy up to the Palestinians, we could potentially witness a fundamental change.

However, a regional solution is not only the responsibility of Jordan and Egypt. It is also the responsibility of the remaining Arab counties. The Clinton Parameters recommended "rehabilitation in the host countries" and "resettlement in third countries" to help solve the refugee problem.[56] Thus, Arab countries should offer patriation to the Palestinians, which in practical terms means doing what Jordanians did with the Palestinians decades ago, when they provided the Palestinians with citizenship and a life of dignity. The acquisition of citizenship must be an integral part of the process of Palestinian normalization. Indeed, experience has shown that in Jordan, Palestinians underwent a relatively successful process of integration. Despite suffering discrimination in certain sectors, like public administration and in the army, Palestinians there have obtained citizenship and have largely enjoyed equal rights. In other Arab countries, the situation is different. Most Arab countries have followed the 1965 Casablanca Protocol, which stipulates that Arab countries should guarantee Palestinian refugees rights to employment, residency, and freedom of movement while preserving their Palestinian identity by maintaining their refugee status.[57] Thus, the Casablanca Protocol does not grant the Palestinians citizenship. It reflects the Arab states' view of Palestinian refugees' presence in their territory as being temporary.[58] Egypt has denied the Palestinians access to nationality and required very high fees to attend public schools and universities. Likewise, free health care has been denied to them.[59] In Lebanon, Palestinian residents have been denied access to citizenship after decades of residency.[60] Indeed, it is clear that the idea of not granting citizenship to the Palestinians is an attempt to preserve Palestinian national sentiment and to justify the continuation of war against Israel. West Bank Birzeit University professor Asem Khalil, has pointed out: "To empower stateless Palestinians, most of whom are refugees, displaced and/or denied re-entry to their homeland, and/or to the territories that are currently under the PA control and which is a candidate, together with those Palestinian territories occupied in 1967, to become the territory of the state of Palestine, it is absolutely necessary to grant them citizenship in and of an independent and sovereign state."[61] Thus, Khalil continues, "given the lack of alternative options, one cannot but conclude that granting Palestinian citizenship to Palestinian refugees in host countries seem to be the most suitable and probable solution whenever the condition of statehood is satisfied."[62]

The principle of the Arab League that forbids the Palestinians to acquire citizenship has not only perpetuated their misery but has continued to fuel more conflict. As historian Howard Sachar explains that "the ordeal of these hundreds of thousands of bitter exiles was complicating the task of peace in the Middle East; the unrest it threatened was not between Israel and the Arab countries alone, but among the Arab nations themselves."[63]

The presence of Al Qaeda groups in the refugee camps in Jordan and Lebanon as we described in chapter 2, is an example of the great magnitude of the problem. This is why full integration of Palestinians into the different Arab states could mitigate the radicalization of the Palestinians. It is also very important to eliminate refugee camps in all these countries and at least review the role of the United Nations Relief and Works Agency for Palestine (UNRWA), which is in charge of providing services to relieve the conditions of Palestinian refugees. It is important to point out that Palestinian refugees receive unique treatment and UNRWA exists exclusively for them. With all its achievements providing health care, education and other services, UNRWA has also helped perpetuate the Palestinians' status as refugees and has kept the belligerent spirit of the refugee camps alive.

Arab states should be encouraged to provide citizenship and equality of rights to Palestinian refugees and absorb some of them as part of a "Patriation" process. As late Israeli scholar Jacob Talmon rightly pointed out decades ago in a letter to British Historian Arnold Toynbee, "it is inconceivable that Arab states would behave towards Palestinian refugees without any regard for their suffering just to turn the blame on the Jews and thus "keep that [Palestinian] sore running."[64] Furthermore, patriation could be justified also on the grounds of "exchange of populations" as happened in many countries after WWII, including in Europe, India, and Pakistan. This principle could be applied in this situation, since a large number of Jewish refugees from Arab lands resettled in Israel to flee from the vengeful wrath of the Arab governments following their military defeat at the hands of Israel in 1948.

Arab States must help solve the Palestinians' problem and minimize their suffering. They need to take responsibility to advance that peace. It is not enough to present the Arab Peace Initiative. As Farah Pandith, who was President Obama's Special Representative to the World Muslim Communities, has pointed out:

> The Arab states must recognize that the Arab Peace Initiative was an important beginning, but not the end of their responsibilities. The Arab-Israeli conflict should no longer be used to distract the people of Arab nations from other problems. Instead, it must be a cause for action to help the Palestinian people develop their institutions that will sustain the state.[65]

The role of the Arab world should be to give the Palestinians support for any peace agreement or step the Palestinians need to take to achieve peace and co-existence with Israel. If the Jordanian/Egyptian option we described above works, Arab countries should throw their support behind it. For the same reason, the United States and Western countries should encourage and even press them to do so.

Politically, the Arab League would do well to remove the principle of "right of return" from the Arab Peace Initiative. The international community needs to pressure the Arab states to relinquish this demand, invoking the precedent of previous exchanges of populations.

Despite progress, the cooperation of Arab states may not be fully guaranteed, as Israeli scholar Uzi Rabid points out.[66] In fact, Saudi Arabia, a country that has supported normalization of relations of the UAE and Bahrain with Israel, has made clear that without a Palestinian state there will not be normalization between Israel and Saudi Arabia. In fact, King Salman reaffirmed the need to see a solution to the Palestinian issue based on the principles established in the Arab Peace Initiative. [67]

Likewise, it is in Israel's interest to end the Israeli-Palestinian conflict, as scholars of the Israeli institute "Mitvim," argue. These scholars seem to agree that if the Palestinian issue does not get resolved, Israel's chances of reconciliation and peace with the Arab world are minimal.[68] For example, Dr. Nimrod Goren, head of the Mitvim Institute, argued that although relations between Israel and the Arab world are changing,

> Israel's ties with its neighbors in the Middle East remain limited in extent, focusing mainly on security issues (Iran, Daesh, Sinai and Gaza) and secret in nature... Likewise, "currently, Israel stands before exceptional opportunities to fulfill this potential. This is expressed, for example in gas export agreements, business cooperation, visits by delegations, and contacts in the cultural domain, which are already taking place between Israel and Arab countries. However, to fulfill this potential, progress in the Israeli-Palestinian peace process is vital.[69]

Goren is correct. However, one of the main arguments of this book is precisely that the solution of the Israeli-Palestinian problem cannot result from the continuing pursuit of a bilateral solution. There is no such a thing as having peace with Arab countries after a peace agreement with the Palestinians. The Arab states must be involved along with and simultaneously with the Palestinians in finding a solution. Arab states must guarantee normalcy and order to the Palestinians, and peace with Israel. If, for some reason, the two-state solution is still viable (which I doubt), the Arab states must serve as guarantors to the Palestinians that it is safe to sign an agreement with Israel. A situation like the one that happened at Camp David when Arafat feared compromising, cannot happen again. Whatever move the Palestinians make, it will have to be backed by the Arab states.

Yet, we remain skeptical that the Arab states can guarantee that a Palestinian state would not unravel in a two-state solution agreement under current circumstances. Unfortunately, as Ross and Makovsky observed more than a decade ago, nobody has elaborated on how Arab guarantees against a Hamas take-over, anarchy or threats against Israel's security would work out.[70] This is why we are proposing the idea of solving the problem through Jordan and Egypt.

The Role of the International Community

The international community is also complicit in perpetuating the Israeli-Palestinian conflict by allowing itself, through the United Nations, including some Western countries , to be used by the Palestinian/Arab propaganda machine. In the words of a renowned American Jewish leader, these countries allow themselves 'to be a tool at the United Nations to fight against the one country with a Jewish majority.'[71]

Many Western countries in the UN support anti-Israel resolutions or- in the best-case scenario-, they abstain. If European countries took a less biased position, this could discourage the Palestinians and other countries from using the United Nations against Israel. This could improve the environment and engender the mutual confidence Oslo intended to build to advance peace. It is important that European countries and world democracies demand that Arab governments as well as the Palestinians play a constructive role in promoting peace.

Such a demand would also signal the Arab world that the international community would no longer tolerate their self-exemption from responsibility for the ongoing conflict in the Middle East. As Daniel Pipes has suggested, "as long as the Arab and Palestinian worlds continue to enjoy diplomatic and political success in the international arena, the chances for achieving peace are minimal."[72]

The idea is not to exempt Israel from responsibility but to stress that the war of propaganda plays into the hands of those who seek to perpetuate the absence of peace. For the Palestinians, it raises the expectation that by isolating Israel and delegitimizing it, they will break Israel down. For Israel, those international resolutions further delegitimize the international community and encourage the factions that oppose any peace agreement with the Palestinians. Such international resolutions encourage anti-Semitism and alienate Israelis and Americans alike.

Indeed, even in light of multiple Israeli concessions to the Palestinians throughout the years, including the unilateral Israeli withdrawal from Gaza, many European leaders often sided with the Palestinian harshest positions. Thus, some European countries have created an environment adverse to peace. As an example, during Operation Defensive Shield in 2002, an Israeli military operation aimed at preventing terrorist attacks against Israeli citizens during the Second Intifada, the European parliament proceeded to adopt a non-binding resolution calling for economic sanctions on Israel and an arms embargo on both parties. Years later, the European parliament embraced the Goldstone Report, a controversial UN. Report later disavowed by its own author, the South African jurist Richard Goldstone.[73] The report accused Israel of war crimes during its military operation in Gaza in the winter of 2008- 2009, which aimed at eliminating Hamas' Gaza-based terrorist infrastructure.

Furthermore, countries such as France have taken international peace initiatives intended to recognize a Palestinian state if negotiations between Israel and the Palestinians do not make progress.[74] The French initiative originally proposed the renewal of the peace process with the goal of creating a two-state solution. However, if this goal were not met, France would unilaterally call for the creation of a Palestinian state without Israel's consent. This type of proposal only exacerbate Palestinian anger and animosity towards Israel. This attitude dates back to 1973 when, during the Yom Kippur War the Europeans came under a heavy Arab oil embargo aimed at pressuring them to withdraw support for Israel. This led European members of NATO to deny the United States fly-over rights and the use of their bases and airports to airlift supply weapons to Israel during the war.[75]

Europeans may change their views in the future as they become less dependent on oil from the Middle East. The United States is now a dominant energy power surpassing both Russia and Saudi Arabia. The power of OPEC is already diminished.[76] In addition, in July 2018, the United States and the European Union signed a trade and energy cooperation agreement that allows energy sup-plies to go from the United States to Europe.[77] In fact, Standard & Poor reports that exports of U.S. crude to Europe have increased since the agreement was signed.[78] This change in oil markets could be conducive to a more balanced European approach to the Israe-li-Palestinian conflict.

The Israelis must also do their part. As Dennis Ross rightly points out, there is also room for Israel to improve its attitude and be more helpful.[79] Even if the expansion of settlements is not as dramatic as it is reported to be, the settlement issue still paints Israel in a negative light and engenders loss of international support. If we also add the expropriation of Palestinian land for purposes of road construction and the obstacles Palestinians face when trying to purchase land in Area C, this negative image of Israel will only worsen. The same applies to the Israeli legalization of outposts as well as any other actions that may change facts on the ground. Likewise, Israel's security concerns have often forced the Israel Defense Forces to carry out military operations in Area A currently under the PA's full jurisdiction. Actions like these, even if they are justified, contribute to making the occupation even more offensive. Considering the fact that much of the international media and community tend to hold Israel responsible for the perpetuation of the conflict, these actions do not advance sympathy for Israel's cause and only help to absolve Palestinians and Arabs of any responsibility for the ongoing conflict in the region.

Likewise, it would be very important for the Israelis to ease some frustrations of Palestinians' daily lives by relieving the check-points, which were originally placed to control terrorism, avoid de-lays and allow Palestinians more freedom of movement. It is also imperative that Israel meaningfully responds to the Arab Peace Ini-tiative. Both the Arab Peace Initiative and the Trump plan could form the basis for negotiations that could allow all sides to move to a mid-point from which the Arabs may agree to abandon the de-mand for the Palestinian "right of return." Saudi Arabia supports the idea of two states based on the pre-1967 borders, mutual land swaps and a Palestinian capital in East Jerusalem. This position is no different from the position of Israel's Center and Center-left fac-tions. Based on these assurances, it seems reasonable that under the current situation where Arab-Israeli cooperation exists, the Saudis may become flexible on the issue of the "right of return." However, there is an additional important element to be added and this is Arab-Israeli engagement at the level of civil society.

Taking Advantage of the Arab Spring: People to People Relations

In a speech delivered in Jerusalem in March 2013, President Obama declared:

> This is precisely the time to respond to the wave of revolution with a resolve and commitment for peace. Because as more governments respond to popular will, the days when Israel could seek peace simply with a handful of autocratic leaders, those days are over. Peace will have to be made among peoples, not just governments.[80]

Retired Israeli General Michael Herzog, also the son of a former President of Israel, made the following remark about Israel and the Arab people:

> Israel is highly unpopular in the Arab street, there is a lot of hatred, resentment and so on. These people were educated that way for generations. So, there is a lot of hatred when the street speaks up. It's clearly an anti-Israel voice and we don't know how to communicate with these people.[81]

This quote reflects a common Israeli view of Arabs and results from the fact that the voice of the Arab people has never been heard. Besides the anti-Israel propaganda of Arab governments, the voice of the Islamists has drowned and largely suppressed the liberal voices.

In Chapter 3, we analyzed significant changes in the attitudes of certain Sunni Arab states towards Israel. The Arab Spring may not fully end animosity towards Israel but at least it has the potential to generate dissenting and competing voices that could challenge traditional Arab views of Israel. However, in order to take advantage of the consequences of the Arab Spring, it is imperative that civilians and non-government institutions be involved in promoting an environment of peace and reconciliation that parallels or complements the actions of their governments. This is what the broadcaster and author Joseph Braude has called "citizenship diplomacy." As Braude has pointed out, "[Citizen-diplomacy] is warranted because a climate conducive to Arab-Israeli partnership is a necessary condition for a future peace settlement as well as a lodestar for civil society in Arab lands."[82]

As we have seen in Chapter 4, there have been gatherings and contacts between Israelis and Iraqis as well as between Israelis and Libyans celebrating past co-existence between Arabs and Jews in these countries. Several Arab intellectuals have traveled to Israel and participated in conferences with Israelis.

These meetings could serve as good models for future citizenship diplomacy. Israeli and Arab intellectuals could work together to engage in dialogue. Dialogue can generate a new discourse that is favorable to peace and undo the environment of hostility created throughout the last seventy years. Such dialogues may help create mutual sympathy and understanding. If intellectuals and opinion leaders participate in and support these dialogues, they can help end or at least reduce Israel's demonization and vilification.[83] This point is extremely important.

Reversing anti-Israel hostility may not be an easy task. However, the fact that Arab governments are now changing some of their attitudes towards Israel can help this endeavor. We see a trend toward more tolerance at the level of the government itself. For example, in January 2020, an old synagogue was reopened in the Egyptian city of Alexandria with the participation of Egyptian officials, foreign ambassadors and others. Israeli representatives were not invited but they were invited to participate in a celebratory service a month later. There were also initiatives in Egypt to establish a museum of Egyptian Jewish history.[84]

In Abu Dhabi, a special site called "The Abrahamic Family House" is scheduled to open in 2022, and will include a mosque, a church, and a synagogue. In Dubai, there are active synagogues operating to serve foreign visitors. In Saudi Arabia, television series are broadcast that highlight Jewish life in Kuwait.

Since the conflict with Israel caused the flight of Jews from Arab lands and the spread of antisemitism, these gestures of recognition of the Jewish community may be small steps towards a general reconciliation with Israel. In fact, the UAE and Bahrein's agreements of normalization with Israel may prove this assumption right.

As Israeli scholars Yoel Guzansky and Ofer Winter have observed, "the discourse of tolerance contributes to strengthening the concept of the Jews as belonging to the regional fabric, and in the future, it may even help warm relations between the peoples and countries of the region and Israel."[85] Indeed, this type of action promoted by governments can further encourage citizenship diplomacy. An Arab-Jewish bridge may lead to an Arab-Israeli reconciliation.

The same can be done in other sectors of civil society, such as among business communities, trade unions, the arts, and others. The more civil partnerships take place between Arabs and Israelis, the more likely acrimony will be reduced. These are the kind of activities that were forbidden or repudiated in the aftermath of the Egyptian-Israeli and the Jordanian-Israeli peace agreements. People to people connections are crucial. Peace cannot be exclusively the work of governments. The efforts must involve civil society. So far, mutual perceptions at the Israeli and Arab grassroots have been the result of events and attitudes developed by their governments. People to people civic engagement could advance peace, especially if, such exchanges include Palestinians. This is significant precisely because the Palestinians are the most radicalized of all the groups in the Arab world. As Israeli-Arab rancor is reduced, Palestinian acrimony towards Israel will become more isolated. Signs of Palestinian isolation are already visible as the Arab League rejected Palestinian condemnation of normalization agreements between Israel and two Persian Gulf countries.

In the end, the Israeli-Palestinian conflict results from complex sociological, psychological, and political processes. Resolving this conflict will require a mutual understanding of such complexities.

Notes

Introduction

1   Asher Susser, "The Two-State Solution: Getting from Here to There," *Foreign Policy Research Institute*, October 2012, http://www.fpri.org/docs/media/Susser_-_Two_State_Solution.pdf .

2   Morris, Benny, *One State, Two States: Resolving the Israel-Palestine Conflict.* (New Haven: Yale University Press, 2009, 172-173.

3   Ibid., 124.

4   Adi Schwartz and Einat Wilf. *The War of Return: How Western Indulgence of the Palestinian Dream has Obstructed the Path to Peace* (New York, New York: All Points Books, 2020), 174-175.

5   Ibid., 3.

6   Ibid.

7   Yossi Alpher, "Israel-Palestine: From Oslo to the Slippery Slope." *Verdidebatt*, October 10, 2015. http://www.verdidebatt.no/debatt/cat1/subcat4/thread11602890/#post_11602890.

8   Seth Anziska, *Preventing Palestine: A Political History from Camp David to Oslo* (Princeton, NJ: Princeton University Press, 2018).

9   Yossi Beilin, "Looking Back on Oslo, 25 Years Later," *Al Monitor*, September 10, 2018. https:// www.al-monitor.com/pulse/originals/2018/09/israel-us-palestinians-oslo-yitzhak-rabin-shimonperes-abbas.html.

10   Ibid., 10-11.

11   Stein, Kenneth and Samuel Lewis, Making Peace Between Arabs and Israelis: Fifty Years of Negotiating Experiences, United States Institute of Peace, October 1991), 19-20.

12   Anti-Israel Incitement in the Palestinian Authority: An Analysis of its Roots and Aspects," *The Meir Amit Intelligence and Terrorism Information Center*, June 5, 2017, http://www.terrorism-info.org.il/en/21215/ .

13   Martin Indyk, Innocent *Abroad: An Intimate Account of American Peace Diplomacy in the Middle East* (New York, NY: Simon & Schuster, 2009), 324.

Chapter 1

1   Quoted in Fayez Sayegh, "The Camp David Agreement and the Palestine Problem," *Journal of Palestine Studies*, 8, No. 2 (1979): 43-44.

2   Avraham Selah, "The First Intifada: How the Arab-Israeli Conflict Was Transformed," *Haaretz*, 12/13/2012, https://www.haaretz.com/. premium-first-intifada-a-watershed-moment-1.5272288.

3   Dennis J. Deeb, *Israel, Palestine, & the Quest for Middle East Peace*, (University Press of America, Lanham, Maryland, 2013), 13.

4   Zeev Schiff, and Ehud Yaari, *Intifada* (New York, New York: Simon and Schuster, 1989), 79.

5   Ibid., 80.

6   James L. Gelvin, The *Israel- Palestinian Conflict: One Hundred Years of War* (New York, NY: Cambridge University Press, 2014), 221.

7   Ibid., 210.

8   "Agreement on Gaza Strip and Jericho Area", May 4, 1994, Israel's Ministry of Foreign Affairs. https://mfa.gov.il/mfa/foreignpolicy/ peace/guide/pages/agreement%20on%20gaza%20strip%20and%20 jericho%20area.aspx .

9   Itamar Rabinowitz, *Waging Peace: Israel and the Arabs 1948-2003* (Princeton, N.J.: Princeton University Press, 2004), 62-63.

10 Ibid.

11 Ralph Israeli, R., *The Oslo Idea: The Euphoria of Failure*, (London, Routledge, 2017), Chapter 2.

12 Eyal Levy interview with Prof. Shlomo Ben Ami Gives Up: Also, with a left-wing government we would not have reached peace," (*Maariv*, 09/22/2017 from Hebrew: פורפ. וב ימע סירה סיידי: גס סע תלשממ שמאל אל היה סולש).

13 Itamar Rabinowitz, *Waging* Peace, 66-68.

14 Israeli, *Oslo*, 64-65.

15 Ibid.

16 "The Beilin-Abu Mazen Document," *The Reut Institute*, 10/31/1995, http://reut-institute.org/ data/uploads/ExternaDocuments/20050328%20-%20The%20Beilin-Abu%20Mazen%20Document.pdf .

17 Rabinowitz, *Waging Peace*, 95.

18 Ibid., 87-88.

19 Ibid., 88.

20 Anshel Pfeffer, *Bibi: The Turbulent Life and Times of Benjamin Netanyahu*, (New York, New York: Basic Books, 2018), 246.

21 Ibid., 105.

22 Dennis Ross, *The Missing Peace: The Inside Story of the Fight for Middle East Peace*. (New York, NY: Farrar, Strauss and Giroux, 2004), 461.

23 Rabinowitz, *Waging Peace*, 91.
24 Pfeffer, *Bibi*, 267-269.
25 "The Sharm el-Sheikh Memorandum- Main Points", Israel' Ministry of Foreign Affairs, 09/04/1999, https://mfa.gov.il/mfa/foreignpolicy/peace/guide/pages/the%20sharm%20el-sheikh%20memorandum-%20main%20points.aspx .
26 Bill Clinton My *Life* (New York, New York: Alfred A. Knopf, 2004), 911.
27 Martin Indyk, Innocent *Abroad: An Intimate Account of American Peace Diplomacy in the Middle East* (New York, NY: Simon & Schuster, 2009), 143.
28 Ross, *Missing Peace*, 601-601.
29 Ibid., 600.
30 Ibid., 607.
31 Rabinowitz, *Waging Peace*, 152.
32 Indyk., *Innocent* Abroad, 312.
33 Ibid., 313.
34 Ibid., 314.
35 Ibid., 315.
36 Ibid., 324.
37 Ibid., 336.
38 Shlomi Eldar "Five Misassumptions about Second Intifada," *Al Monitor*, October 1, 2013, http://www.al-monitor.com/pulse/originals/2013/09/intifada-israel-palestine-abbas-netanyahu-negotiations.html 52 Indyk, *Innocent*, 366.
39 Ibid., 367
40 Aly Said; Monem Abdel, Shai Feldman, and Khalila Shikaki, Khalil, Arabs *and Israelis*, (New York, New York: Palgrave McMillian, 2013), 350.
41 Shlomo Ben- Ami, *Scars of War, Wounds of Peace: The Israeli-Arab Tragedy*, (Oxford, Oxford University Press, 2006), 275-276.
42 Indyk, Ibid., 376.
43 Abdel, Aly: Said: Monem: Shai Feldman: and Khalil Shikaki, *Arabs and Israelis*, 342-346.
44 Robert Malley and Agha Hussein, "Camp David: A Tragedy of Errors," *New York Review of Books*, New York, NY, August 9, 2001.
45 Aharon D Miller, *The Much Too Promised Land: America's Elusive Search for Arab-Israeli Peace*, (London: Bantam Press), 2008.
46 Gelvin, *The Israeli-Palestine Conflict*, 245.
47 Rashid Khalidi, *The Iron Cage: The Story of Palestinian Struggle for Statehood*, (Boston, MA: Beacon Press, 2007), 2nd Edition.

48 Speech by Emad El Faluji, December 5, 2000, https://www.youtube. com/watch?v=Qb5fIP-MfAc (retrieved on February 11, 2016).

49 "Suha Arafat Admits Husband Premeditated Intifada," *The Jerusalem Post*, December 29, 2012, http://www.jpost.com/Middle-East/Suha-Arafat-admits-husband-premeditated-Intifada (retrieved on February 11, 2016).

50 Sharm El-Sheikh Fact-Finding Committee Report, U.S State Department, April 30, 2001, see section under "What Happened? https://2001-2009.state.gov/p/nea/rls/rpt/3060.htm.

51 Grant Rumley, and Amir Tibon, *The Last Palestinian: The Rise and Reign of Mahmoud Abbas*, (Amherst, New York: Prometheus Books, 2017), 34.

52 Daniel Kurtzer and Scott Lasensky, *Negotiating Arab-Israeli Peace: American Leadership in the Middle East.* United States Institute of Peace, Washington, DC, 2008.

53 Ben-Ami, *Scars of War,* 265.

54 Jeremy Pressman, "The Second Intifada: Background and Causes of the Israeli /Palestinian Conflict", The *Journal of Conflict Studies*, The Gregg Centre for the Study of War and Society, 23, No. 2, (2003) https://journals.lib.unb.ca/index.php/JCS/article/view/220/378.

55 Amaney Jamal, *Barriers to Democracy: The Other Side of Social Capital in Palestine and the Arab World*, (Princeton, N.J: Princeton University Press, 2007), Chapter 2.

56 Wendy Perlman, "Spoiling Inside and Out: Internal Political Contestation and the Middle East Peace Process" in *Journal of International Security*, 33, No. 3, 2008/09, 79-109.

57 Mia M. Bloom "Palestinian Suicide Bombing: Public Support, Market Share, and Outbidding Author(s)", *Political Science Quarterly*, 119, No. 1 (2004), 61-88.

58 Wendy Pearlman, *Violence, Nonviolence, and the Palestinian National Movement*, (New York: Cambridge University Press, 2011).

59 Perlman, "Spoiling," Ibid. 79-109.

60 Robert Zelnick, *Israel's Unilateralism: Beyond Gaza.* (Stanford University Hoover Institute Press, 2006), 59.

61 Ibid., 87-88.

62 Yair Hirschfeld, *Track Two Diplomacy Towards an Israeli-Palestinian Solution 1978-2014*, (Baltimore: John Hopkins University Press, 2014), 303-304.

63 Ibid.

64 Zelnick, *Israel's Unilateralism,* 88.

65 Gal Luft, "The Karine-A Affair: A Strategic Watershed in the Middle East? " *Washington Institute for Near East Policy*, January 30, 2002,

http://www.washingtoninstitute.org/policy-analysis/view/the-kar-ine-a-affair-a-strategic-watershed-in-the-middle-east.

66 David Frum, *The Right Man: The Surprise presidency of George W. Bush* (New York: Random House, 2003), 256.

67 Elliot Abrams. *Tested by Zion: The Bush Administration and the Israe-li-Palestinian Conflict* (Cambridge, U.K.: Cambridge University Press, 2013), 24-27.

68 Ibid., 52.

69 "Sharon: "'Occupation' terrible for Israel, Palestinians" from Kelly Wallace, *CNN*, May 27, 2003. http://www.cnn.com/2003/WORLD/meast/05/26/mideast/.

70 Quoted in Abrams, 73.

71 Ibid., 72.

72 Ibid., 77-78.

73 Dennis Ross and David Makovsky, Myths, *Illusions and Peace* (New York, NY: Penguin Books, 2010), 140.

74 Henry Siegman, "Sharon and the Future of Palestine," *The New York Review of Books*, New York, NY, December 2, 2004. http://www.ny-books.com/articles/2004/12/02/sharon-and-the-future-of-palestine/-.

75 "Letter from President Bush to Prime Minister Sharon," The White House, April 14, 2004 http://georgewbush-whitehouse.archives.gov/news/releases/2004/04/20040414-3.htm .

76 Ibid.

77 Col. Uzi Buchbinder, head of civil defense in the IDF's Home Front Command, told the Knesset Interior Committee in January 2005 that the disengagement plan, if implemented, would expose 46 towns and cities in the Negev to Kassam rocket fire. Col. (res.) Mordechai Yoga also presented a report to the Knesset cautioning "the withdrawal of the IDF from the Gaza Strip and northern Samaria will bring numerous large population centers and communities within the range of Kassam rockets and mortar shells." Michael Freund, "Time for Gaza Apology," *The Jerusalem Post*, January 20, 2009.

78 Jonathan Schanzer, *State of Failure: Yasser Arafat, Mahmoud Abbas, and the Unmaking of the Palestinian State*. New York, NY: Palgrave McMil-lan, 2013), 126-127.

79 Ibid.,131.

80 Ibid.

81 Quoted in Clayton Swisher, *The Palestine Papers: The End of the Road?* (London: Hesperus Press Limited, 2011), 61.

82 "Salam Fayyad's new Palestinian emergency government and the beginning of its struggle against Ismail Haniya's Hamas government," Intelligence and Terrorism Information Center at the Israel Intelli-

gence Heritage and Commemoration Center (IICC), *The Meir Amit Intelligence and Terrorism Information Center* 06/28/2007, terroirism-info.org. il/en/19112/.

83   Ibid.
84   A good description of Abbas becoming protected by the West and the PA corruption is in Schanzer, Chapters 10-12. Schanzer describes the deep evolving crisis of legitimacy of the Palestinian Authority throughout most of his book.
85   Robert Danin, "Integrating the Top-Down with Bottom-Up Approach to Israeli -Palestinian Peace," in Kurtzer, 157-172.
86   Abrams, *Tested*, 276.
87   Ibid., 288-289.
88   Ibid., 290.
89   Indyk, *Innocent Abroad*, 310-311.
90   The Algiers Declaration, issued in November 1988, declares Palestinian Independence without specifying borders. The Declaration recognizes Resolution 242 as a basis for negotiations with Israel, which has been widely interpreted as recognition and acceptance of the legitimacy of the State of Israel. "Algiers Declaration (1988) Palestinian Declaration of Independence, Algiers, November 15, 1988" http://www.jmcc.org/Documentsandmaps.aspx?id=766 (Retrieved on June 8, June 8, 2016).
91   Ben Ami, Ibid., 320.
92   "Myths and Facts about the Peace Process," *The Geneva Initiative*, http://www.geneva-accord.org/mainmenu/myths-facts-about-the-peace-process .
93   Ian Black, Seumas Milne and Harriet Sherwood "Palestine papers are distortion of truth, say Palestinian officials," *The Guardian*, January 24, 2011, https://www.theguardian.com/world/2011/jan/24/palestine-papers-distortion-truth-reaction.
94   Ibid.
95   Rumley and Tibon, 204.
96   Ibid., 206.
97   Ibid.
98   Ibid.
99   Samir Awad, "The Impact of the Arab Revolutions on the Palestinian/ Israeli Conflict and Future Prospects," Birzeit University, West Bank, https://www.birzeit.edu/en/blogs/arab-spring-and-palestine
100 Tony Karon, "Despite Jewish Concerns, Obama Keeps Up Pressure on Israel," *Time Magazine*, July 14, 2009.
101 Michael B., Oren *Ally: My Journey across the American-Israeli Divide.* (New York, NY: Random House, 2015), 76.

102 Ibid., 79.
103 Cary Nelson, *Dream Deferred: A Concise Guide to the Israeli /Palestinian Conflict & The Movement to Boycott Israel* (Chicago and New York: MLA Members for Scholars Rights and Indiana University Press, 2016), 280-281.
104 Oren, 117.
105 "West Bank and the Settlement Blocs," *Peace Now*, http://peacenow.org.il/eng/content/west-bank-"settlement-blocs.
106 Isabel Kershner, "In West Bank, 99.7% of the Public Land Grants by Israel go to Settlers," *New York Times*, July 18, 2018.
107 On Netanyahu's Offer to Negotiate Settlement Blocs, see David A. Halperin, *Israel Policy Forum*, May 27, 2015, http://www.israelpolicyforum.org/blog/netanyahu's-offer-negotiate-settlement-blocs-.
108 David Makovsky, "Imagining the Border: Options for Resolving the Israeli-Palestinian Territorial Issue," *Washington Institute for Near East Policy*, January 2011, http://www.washingtoninstitute.org/policy-analysis/view/imagining-the-border-options-for-resolving-the-israeli-palestinian-territor .
109 Dennis Ross, *Doomed to Succeed: The U.S-Israel Relationship from Truman to Obama* (New York, NY: Farrar, Straus, and Giroux, 2015), 386-387.
110 Dennis Ross and David Makovsky, "If Trump Wants the Ultimate Deal, He Must Not Repeat These Mistakes", Washington Institute for Near East Policy, October 2, 2018, https://www.washingtoninstitute.org/policy-analysis/view/if-trump-wants-the-ultimate-deal-he-must-not-repeat-these-mistakes; and Amir Tibon, "Obama's Detailed Plans for Mideast Peace Revealed - and How Everything Fell Apart", *Haaretz*, June 8, 2017.
111 Rumley and Tibon, 190.
112 Dana Allin, and Steven Simon, *Our Separate Ways: The Struggle for the Future of the U.S-Israel Alliance* (New York, New York: Public Affairs, 2015), 117-118.
113 Ibid., 118.
114 "Mideast peace process futile while U.S. in charge, Lula says," *Fox News Latino*, December 20, 2010, http://latino.foxnews.com/latino/politics/2010/12/20/mideast-peace-process-futile-charge-lula-says/.
115 Aaron David Miller, "Are Settlements the Key to Middle East Peace," *The Atlantic*, October 2010.http://www.theatlantic.com/international/archive/2010/10/are-settlements-the-key-to-middle-east-peace-updated/64027 (retrieved on May 20, 2016).
116 Tamar Pileggi, "Labor approves Herzog's unilateral pullout plan", *The Times of Israel*, February 7, 2016. http://www.timesofisrael.com/labor-approves-herzogs-unilateral-pullout-plan/ .

117 Palestinian Center for Policy and Survey Research, Public Opinion Poll 63, March 26, 2017, http://www.pcpsr.org/en/node/688.
118 Palestinian Center for Policy and Survey Research, Public Opinion Poll 63, March 26, 2017, http://www.pcpsr.org/en/node/688.

Chapter 2

1   Ephraim, Lavy, "Hapalestinaim: Zehuyiot Kibutziot Mitharot Beheader Medina," (Hebrew) (The Palestinians: Competing Identities in Light of State Absence"), in *Lekidut Hamedinah Haarabit Bemivhan (The Unity of the Arab State Under Test)*, Tamar Ignas (ed.), Moshe Dayan Center for Middle East and African Studies, Tel Aviv University, 2006, 145-168.

2   Rashid Khalidi, *Palestinian Identity: The Construction of Modern National Consciousness*, (Columbia University Press, New York, New York, 1997), 182-183.

3   James Gelvin, *The Israel -Palestine Conflict, One Hundred Years of War*, 3rd ed. (Cambridge, U.K., Cambridge University Press, 2014), 95-96.

4   Barry Rubin, *Revolution until Victory? The Politics and History of the PLO*, (Harvard University Press, Cambridge, Massachusetts, 1994), 3.

5   Kenneth W. Stein, "Palestinians at the Negotiating Table: Past Meets Present? *in Focus*, Jewish Policy Center, Fall 2007, https://www.jewishpolicycenter.org/2007/08/31/palestinians-at-the-negotiating-table-past-meets/ (retrieved July 16, 2016).

6   Albert Hourani, *A History of the Arab Peoples*, (Warner Books, 1991), 401.

7   Ibid., 404- 405.

8   Ibid., 405.

9   Ibid., 201.

10   Mark Tessler, *A History of the Israeli-Palestinian Conflict*, (Indiana University Press, Bloomington and Indianapolis, 1994), 433.

11   *The Palestinian National Charter: Resolutions of the Palestine National Council July 1-17, 1968*, The Avalon Project, Yale Law School, Article 4, http://avalon.law.yale.edu/20th_century/plocov.asp (Retrieved on May 4, 2017).

12   Ibid.

13   Ibid., Article 7.

14   Ibid., Article 9.

15   Shaul Mishal, and Avraham Selah, Zman *Hahamas (The Hamas Wind)*, (Hebrew version) (Miskal- Yedihot Ahronoth and Chemed Books, Tel Aviv, 1999), 33.

16   Bernard Lewis *The Multiple Identities of the Middle East*, (Schoken Books, New York, NY, 1998), 103.

17   *The Palestinian National Charter*, Article 10.

18   Tessler. Ibid.

19   David Pryce Jones, *Closed Circle: An Interpretation of the Arabs*, (Ivan R, Dee, Chicago, 2002), 305-306.

20   Michael Makara, "From Concessions to Repression: Explaining regime survival strategies in Jordan during Black September", *The Journal of the Middle East and Africa,* 2016, Vol 7 (4), 387-403, 394

21   Georges Sorel, *Reflections on Violence*, (Cambridge University Press, Cambridge, 1999).

22   An analysis on Sorel's influence on Palestinians can be found in Luis Fleischman "Palestinian Rockets: A Tool of Mass Mobilization," *Palestinian Rocket Report,* Jewish Policy Center, September 17, 2008.

23   Pryce Jones, Ibid., 305-306.

24   "The Cairo Agreement", Palestine Refugee Research Net, http://prrn.mcgill.ca/research/papers/brynen2_09.htm (Retrieved June 21, 2017).

25   Robert Rabil, *Embattled Neighbors: Syria, Israel and Lebanon*, (Lynne Rienner Publishers, Boulder, CO, 2003), 47.

26   Andrew Gowers & Tony Walker, *Behind the Myth: Yasser Arafat and the Palestinian Revolution*, (Olive Branch Press, New York, 1992), 137-158.

27   Rabil, Ibid., 49.

28   Ibid., 55.

29   Howard Sachar, *A History of Israel: From the Rise of Zionism to Our Time*, (Alfred Knopf, New York, 2003), 826-828.

30   Khalidi, *Palestinian Identity*, 198.

31   Ibid.

32   Gilles Keppel, *Jihad: The Trail of Political Islam*, (The Belknap Press of Harvard University Press, Cambridge, Massachusetts, 2002), 158.

33   Meir Litvak "Hamas, Palestinian Identity, Islam and National Sovereignty" (Hebrew) in *Lekidut Hamedinah Haarabit Bemivhan" (The Unity of the Arab State Under Test)*, Tamar Ignas (ed.), Moshe Dayan Center for Middle East and African Studies, Tel Aviv University, 2006, 169-186.

34   *The Covenant of the Islamic Resistance Movement*, 18 August 1988, Article 1, http://avalon.law.yale.edu/20th_century/hamas.asp (retrieved on June 2, 2016).

35   Ibid.

36   Ibid., Article 2

37   Ibid., Article 2.

38   Ibid., Article 5.

39   Ibid., Article 9.

40   Ibid. Article 11.

41   Ibid., Article 12.

42   Ibid., Article 14.

43   Hazam Amin, "Al Qaeda Arrives to the West Bank and Gaza, As- piring to Take Over Hamas," published in *Al Hayat*, 4 April, 2006 from Spanish translation, "Al Qaeda Llega A Cisjordania y a La Franja De Gaza aspirando llegar al Puesto de Hamas" in Pedro Rojo Perez (ed) *El Mundo Visto por Los Arabes, Anuario de Prensa Árabe 2006*, (Icaria, Antrazyt, 2007), 229-240, 227.

44   Hamas Covenant, Article 13.

45   Ibid., Pre-Introduction.

46   Interview with Ismail Hanyeh, *Al Mushahid al Siyasi*, (international weekly) 24 December 2006, in Pedro Rojo Perez (ed.), 255-260.

47   Hamas argues in one of its leaflets, "the Jews are brothers of the mon- keys, murderers of the prophets, bloodsuckers, warmongers...Only Islam can break the Jews and destroy their dream," Mishal and Se- lah-Ibid, 82.

48   Ibid., Article 14.

49   Adi Schwartz and Einat Wilf. *The War of Return: How Western Indul- gence of the Palestinian Dream has Obstructed the Path to Peace* (New York, New York: All Points Books, 2020), chapter 5.

50   The United Nations Relief and Works Agency for Palestinian Ref- ugees (UNRWA), created in December 1949, provides aid for relief and human development to Palestinian refugees from the 1948 and the 1967 wars and their descendants. Currently 5 million refugees are registered. UNRWA, which is very active in refugee camps, is often held responsible for the perpetuation of the refugee status of the Pal- estinians.

51   Howard Sachar, *A History of Israel: From the Rise of Zionism to Our Time*, (Alfred Knopf, New York, 2003), 443.

52   Robert Rabil, *Salafism in Lebanon: From Apoliticism to Transnational Ji- hadism*, (Georgetown University Press, Washington, DC, 2014), 133- 134.

53   Ibid., 134.

54   Ibid., 136.

55   Ibid., 141.

56   Hazam Amin, Ibid, 227.

57   Khaled Abu Tomhe, "The Palestinians: Refugee Camps or Terror- ist Bases?" *The Gatestone Institute*, July 21, 2016 https://www.gate- stoneinstitute.org/8511/palestinians-refugee-camps (Retrieved on June 21, 2017).

58   This statement was made by Dr. Munif Samara, a leading figure in the Salafi jihadist movement, quoted from Speckhard, Anne, "The Jihad in Jordan: Drivers of Radicalization into Violent Extremism in Jordan," *International Center for the Study of Violent Extremism*, March 25, 2017 (Retrieved on June 23, 2017).

59   Ibid.

60   Aron Magid, "Jordan monarch's comments on Palestinians raise tensions in the Kingdom," *Al Monitor*, May 16, 2017. http://www.al-monitor.com/pulse/originals/2017/05/jordan-king-palestinians-terrorism.html#ixzz4kyaY8Y81 (Retrieved on June 20, 2017).

61   Sami Moubayed, S. "Hamas powerless as ISIS gains ground in Palestine," *Asian Times*, January 11, 2017. http://www.atimes.com/article/hamas-powerless-isis-gains-ground-palestine/ (Retrieved June 25, 2017).

62   Rebecca Collard, "Palestinians Have Created a United Force to Keep ISIS Out of Their Camps," *Time Magazine*, April 21, 2015.

63   David Rosen, *Armies of the Young: Child Soldiers in War and Terrorism*, (Rutgers University Press, New Jersey, 2005), 92.

64   Ibid.

65   Ibid., 96.

66   Ibid.

67   Rosen, Ibid., 93.

68   Khalidi- Palestinian Identity, xxxiv.

69   Justus Reid Weiner, "Palestinian Children and the New Cult of Martyrdom," *Harvard Israel Review*, Issue 3, Summer 2003. http://www.hcs.harvard.edu/~hireview/content.php?type=article&issue=summer03/&name=martyrdom. (retrieved July 2, 2016).

70   Edward Said, "The Morning After," *London Review of Books*, October 21, 1993.

71   Fouad Ajami, *The Dream Palace of the Arabs: A Generation's Odyssey*, (Vintage Books, New York, New York, 1998), 253-263.

72   Ibid., 266.

73   James Gelvin, Ibid., 58.

74   Ibid.,157.

75   Edward Said, "The One State Solution," *New York Times*, January 10, 1999.

76   Itamar Marcus, "Palestinian Authority Antisemitism Overview of 2015," Palestinian Media Watch, January 12, 2016. http://www.palwatch.org/STORAGE/special%20reports/summary%20report%20on%20PA%20antisemitism%20in%202015.pdf.

77   Itamar Marcus, "The Unique Nature of Palestinian Antisemitism: A Foundation of Palestinian National Identity" in Charles Asher Small

(ed.) *Global Antisemitism: A Crisis of Modernity,* Volume 5, Institute for the Study of Global Antisemitism and Policy, 2013, 115-122.

78   Itamar Marcus, Nana Jacques Zilberdick, "PA kids' education: "To war that will... destroy the Zionist's soul", Palestinian Media Watch, April 17, 2013 http://palwatch.org/main.aspx?fi=157&doc_id=8804 (retrieved on April, 3, 2017).

79   "Gazan Child Recites Violent Nakba Poem", *Jerusalem Post,* May 22, 2014. http://www.jpost.com/middle-east/watch-gazan-child-sings-about-nakba-353062. (Retrieved April 6, 2017).

80   Itamar Marcus and Nana Jacques Zilberdik, *Deception: Betraying the Peace Process,* Palestinian Media Watch, Jerusalem, 2011, 5-6.

81   Marcus and Zilberdik, *Deception,* Ibid., 147-148.

82   To see more examples of glorification of terrorists by the PA see Appendix 2 in Marcus and Zilberdik, *Deception,* 257-262.

83   Bernard Avishai, "What Provoked Palestinian Knife Attacks in Israel," *The New Yorker,* October 23, 2015.

84   Marcus and Zilbernick, Ibid., 8.

85   Anne Speckhard, *Talking to Terrorists: Understanding the Psychosocial Motivations of Militant Jihadi Terrorists, Mass Hostage Takers, Suicide Bombers and Martyrs,* (Advance Press, McLean VA, 2012), Chapter 2.

86   Ibid., Chapter 8.

87   Quoted in Gershon Shafir, *A Half Century of Occupation: Israel, Palestine, and the Most Intractable Conflict,* (University of California Press, Oakland, California, 2017), 46-47.

88   Ibid., 227.

89   Ibid., 228.

90   Mali Soibelman, "Palestinian Suicide Bombers", *Journal of Investigative Psychology and Offender Profiling,* 1: 175-190, 2004,

91   "Inside the Mind of Suicide Bombers", Documentary, Directed by Tom Roberts 2003, https://www.youtube.com/watch?v=UpY0zJ-tu8Ts

92   Martha Crenshaw, "The Subjective Reality of the Terrorist: Ideological and Psychological Factors in Terrorism," *Current Perspectives in international terrorism,* ed. Slater and Stohl, (Hampshire: Macmillan, 1988), 12-13.

93   Ibid., 13.

94   Charles Tilly & Sidney Tarrow, *Contentious Politics,* (Oxford University Press, Incorporated, 2015), 236.

95   Ibid.

96   Jerusalem Post staff, "Barghouti leaves violence option open", The Jerusalem Post, November 25, 2009 https://www.jpost.com/Middle-East/Barghouti-leaves-violence-option-open (Retrieved on June 14, 2020).

97   Ibid.

98   Khalidi, *The Iron Cage*, 178.

99   ש"ערורטלוןיעידומלעדימהזכרמ" הינייפאאמוהישרוש :תיניטסלפהתושרבלארשידגנהתסהה"
      תימעריאמ, 06/05/2017", (Incitement Against Israel in the Palestinian Authority, Meir Amit Intelligence Terrorism Information Center, June 5, 2017, 1.

100   Marcus and Zilberdik, Ibid., 83.

101   Ibid.

102   Robert Danin, "Integrating the Top-down with the Bottom-up Approach to Israeli-Palestinian-Peace" in Kurtzer, Daniel (ed.) *Pathways to Peace: America and the Arab-Israeli Conflict*, (Palgrave-Macmillan, New York, New York), 2012, 157-172.

103   Ibid., 9.

104   David Pollock, "New Palestine Poll Shows Hardline Views but Some Pragmatism Too," *Washington Institute for Near East Policy*, June 25, 2014.   http://www.washingtoninstitute.org/policy-analysis/view/new-palestinian-poll-shows-hardline-views-but-some-pragmatism-too.
      Ibid.

237   "The ADL Global 100: An Index of Anti-Semitism," May 2014 http://global100.adl.org/.

238   Jacques Ellul, *Propaganda: The Formation of Men's Attitudes*, Trans. Konrad Kellen & Jean Lerner, (Vintage Books, New York, 1973), 25.

239   Nico Voigtlander & Joachim Voth, "Nazi Indoctrination and anti-Semitic beliefs in Germany," Proceeding of the National Academy of Sciences, Vol. 112, No. 26, June 20, 2015, http://www.pnas.org/content/112/26.toc (retrieved on July 1, 2016).

240   Ibid.

241   Jacques Semelin, "Analysis of Mass Crime: Ethnic Cleansing in the Former Yugoslavia 1991-1999," in Gellately, Robert and Kiernan, Ben (Ed) *The Specter of Genocide: Mass Murder in Historical Perspective*, (Cambridge University Press, New York, N.Y, 2003), 353-372.

242   Robert Melson, "Modern Genocide in Rwanda: Ideology, Revolution, War and Mass Murder in an African State," in Gellatelly and Kiernan, Ibid., 325-338.

243   "A Rising Tide Lifts Mood in the Developing World" Pew Research, Center, July 24, 2007 http://www.pewglobal.org/2007/07/24/a-rising-tide-lifts-mood-in-the-developing-world/ (Retrieved on 06/20/2017).

244   Richard Wike, "Widespread concerns about extremism in Muslim nations, and little support for it," *PEW Research Center*, February 5, 2015 http://www.pewresearch.org/fact-tank/2015/02/05/extremism-in-muslim-nations/ (Retrieved on 06/20/2017).
245   Marcus and Zilberik, 82.
246   Miriam Berger, & David Halbfinger, "For Palestinian Families, No Light at the End of the Tunnel," *The New York Times*, April 21, 2019.
247   Ibid.

Chapter 3

1   Michael Herzog, "The Kerry Legacy": Inside the Black Box of Israeli-Palestinian Talks," *The American Interest*, 02/27/2017, https://www.the-american-interest.com/2017/02/27/inside-the-black-box-of-israeli-palestinian-talks/ (retrieved on January 15, 2020).
2   Dalia Dassa Kaye, *Beyond the Handshake: Multilateral Cooperation in the Arab-Israeli Peace Process 1991-1996*, (Columbia University Press, New York, New York, 2001), xiii-xiv.
3   Shimon Peres & Aryeh Naor, *The New Middle East*, (New York: Henry Holt and Company, 1993).
4   David Dalin, & John Rothman, *Icon of Evil: Hitler's Mufti and the Rise of Radical Islam*, (Random House, New York, 2008), 12.
5   The World Islamic Congress was convened in Jerusalem in December 1931 by initiative of al-Husseini to create opposition to the Jewish community in Palestine. The conference was attended by 130 delegates from 22 Muslim countries.
6   Dallin and Rothman, 35.
7   Ibid., 35- 37.
8   Iraqi delegate quoted in Alexander Yakobson & Amnon Rubinstein, *Israel and the Family of Nations*, (Routledge, London, 2010), 44.
9   Ibid.
10   Address by Albert Hourani (representing Arab office) to the Final Session of the Anglo-American Committee of Inquiry, March 25, 1947, in Gavison, Ruth (ed.), *The Two State Solution: The UN Partition Resolution of Mandatory Palestine*, (Bloomsbury, New York, 2003), 102-122.
11   Hourani, 104.
12   Ibid., 105.
13   Yakobson and Rubenstein, 44.
14   Ibid., 44-45.
15   Full text of "Address by President Gamal Abdel Nasser at the Meet-

ing of the National Assembly's Ordinary Session," Cairo, Egypt, 26, March 1964. Section 32, https://archive.org/stream/Nasser2_201401/Nasser2_djvu.txt.

16   Michael Oren, *Six Days of War: June 1967 and the Making of the Modern Middle East*, (Oxford University Press, Oxford, 2002), 19.

17   Oren. Ibid., 20.

18   Ibid., 21.

19   "Israel's Road to the June 1967 War-Timeline, *Center for Israel Education*, https://israeled.org/israels-road-war-victory-1967/, June 1, 2017 (retrieved on May 15, 2020).

20   Ibid.

21   "Saudi Bid's Arabs Destroy Israel: New Ruler Would Sacrifice 10,000,000 if Necessary to 'Liberate' Palestine", *New York* Times, 01/10/1954   https://www.nytimes.com/1954/01/10/archives/saud-bids-arabs-destroy-israel-new-ruler-would-sacrifice-10000000.html (retrieved on February 21, 2018).

22   The Six Days War: *Speech by President Nasser to Egyptian National Assembly*, May 29, 1967. http://www.mideastweb.org/nasser29may67.htm (retrieved on July 8, 2016).

23   David Pryce Jones, *Closed Circle: An Interpretation of the Arabs*, (Ivan R, Dee, Chicago, 2002), chapter 2.

24   Ibid.

25   Aly Said, Monem Abdel, Shai Feldman and Khalil Shikaki, *Arabs and Israelis*, (Palgrave, Mc Millan, New York, New York, 2013), 129.

26   Ibid., 139.

27   Raphael Patai, *The Arab Mind*, (Hatherleigh Press, New York, New York, 2002), 96.

28   Ibid.,100.

29   Ibid., 334-335.

30   Ibid., 336.

31   Ibid., 336.

32   Ajami, Fouhad *The Dream Palace of the Arabs: A Generation's Odys*sey, (Vintage Books, New York, New York, 1999), 285.

33   Adam Rasgon-"Trump ties and Iran fears: Why US' Arab allies opting not to rebuke peace plan," *The Times of Israel*, January 30, 2020, http://www.timesofisrael.com/keen-on-ties-most-of-us-arab-allies-choose-not-to-directly-rebuke-peace-plan/ (retrieved on January 30, 2020).

34   Ehud Yaari, "Israeli-Egyptian peace: Forty Years After the 1973 War and Holding," *Washington Institute for Near East Policy*, October 2, 2013,   http://www.washingtoninstitute.org/policy-analysis/view/israeli-egyptian-peace-forty-years-after-the-1973-war-and-holding (retrieved on July 10, 2016).

35   Hassanein Haisam "Egypt and Israel's Growing Economic Cooperation", *The Washington Institute for Near East Policy*, November 2, 2016   https://www.washingtoninstitute.org/policy-analysis/view/egypt-and-israels-growing-economic-cooperation (Retrieved on July 8, 2020).

36   Jacob Abadi (2006) Egypt›s Policy towards Israel: The Impact of Foreign and Domestic Constraints, *Israel Affairs*, 12:1, 159-176.

37   Itamar Rabinowitz. *Waging Peace: Israel and the Arabs, 1948-2003*, (Princeton University Press, Princeton, NJ, 2004), 62.

38   Uri Savir, "Europe and the Multilateral Negotiations" in *The Arab-Israeli Negotiations: Political Positions and Conceptual Frameworks*, 116-121.

39   Tasheen Basheer, "The Background to the Multilateral Talks: An Egyptian Perspective," in *The Arab-Israeli Negotiations: Political Positions and Conceptual Framework*, 104-107.

40   Said, Abdel, Feldman, and Shikaki, Ibid., 284.

41   Ibid., 288.

42   Ibid., 282.

43   Ibid., 287.

44   Ibid., 291.

45   Ajami, 276.

46   Ibid.

47   Kristian Coates Ulrichsen, "Israel and the Arab Gulf States: Drivers and Direction of Change," *James A. Baker III Institute for Public Policy*, Rice University, 2016, 3-4.

48   Indyk. 128.

49   Ibid., 324.

50   Shlomo Ben Ami- *Scars of War, Wounds of Peace: The Israeli-Arab Tragedy*, (Oxford University Press, Oxford, 2006), 329.

51   Dennis Ross, *The Missing Peace: The Inside Story of the Fight for Middle East Peace* (Farrar, Strauss and Giroux, New York, NY. 2004), 773.

52   Gilles Keppel, *Jihad: The Trail of Political Islam*, (The Belknap Press of Harvard University Press, Cambridge, Massachusetts, 2002), 85.

53   Ibid., 278-279.

54   Ibid., 279.

55   Ibid., 281.

56   Ibid., 282.

57   Ibid.

58   Ibid.

59   Robert Wistrich, *Antisemitism*, (Pantheon Books, New York, New York, 1991), 225-226.

60   Ibid., 285.

61   Ibid.
62   Ibid.
63   Kenneth W. Stein,, "Los Acuerdos de Camp David de 1978: una nue-va mirada de como Egipto e Israel pasaron de la Guerra a la paz," Center for Israel Education, September 26, 2018, https://israeled.org/los-acuerdos-de-camp-david-de-1978/ (retrieved on May 15, 2020).
64   Mohamed Abdelaziz, "Egyptian Newspapers: On Jews and Israel," April 22, 2016, http://www.washingtoninstitute.org/policy-analysis/view/egyptian-newspapers-on-jews-and-israel (retrieved August 2, 20016).
65   Israel Kasnett, "Israeli and Jordanian experts downplay significance of peace-treaty changes", *Jewish News Syndicate*, October 23, 2018, https://www.jns.org/israeli-and-jordanian-experts-downplay-signif-icance-of-peace-treaty-changes/ (retrieved on February 16, 2019).
66   Yitzhak Gal, "Fruit of Israeli-Jordanian peace still on the tree," *Ynet News*, March 30, 2018, https://www.ynetnews.com/arti-cles/0,7340,L-5209464,00.html (retrieved on June 30, 2018).
67   Author interview with Dr. Abdullah Swalha, April 23, 2018.
68   Michael Sharnoff, "The Pervasiveness of Antisemitism in Jordanian Media and Prospects for Change", *Foreign Policy Research Institute*, September 20, 2017, https://www.fpri.org/article/2017/09/pervasive-ness-anti-semitism-jordan-change/ (Retrieved on June 30, 2018).
69   Wasfi Kailani, "The Breakdown of Arab-Israeli Peace: Research from remote, Reciprocal Stereotypes and Anti-Normalization- The Case of Jordan," in Maoz, Moshe (ed.) *Muslim Attitudes to Jews and Israel: The Ambivalences of Rejection, Antagonism, Tolerance and Cooperation*, (Sussex Academic Press, Toronto, 2011), 69-89.
70   Ibid., 84.
71   Ibid., 85.
72   Bernard Lewis, *The Crisis of Islam: Holy War and Unholy Terror*, (The Modern Library, New York, NY, 2003), 130.
73   Ibid., 133.
74   A puritanical and rigid form of Islam
75   Simon Henderson, "Wahhabism and Terrorism: Is Saudi Arabia the Arsonist or the Fireman?" *The Washington Institute for Near East Policy*", June 7, 2017 https://www.washingtoninstitute.org/policy-anal-ysis/view/wahhabism-and-terrorism-is-saudi-arabia-the-arsonist-or-the-fireman (retrieved on June 7, 2016).
76   Farah Pandith, *How We Win: How Cutting –Edge Entrepreneurs, Political Visionaries, Enlightened Business Leaders, and Social Media Mavens Can Defeat the Extremist   Threat*, (Custom House, New York, New York, 2019), 114

77   Ibid., 123-124.
78   Ibid., 115.
79   John Bradley, "Al Qaeda and the House of Saud: Eternal Enemies or Secret Bedfellows?" *Washington Quarterly*, Autumn 2005, Vol. 28 Issue 4, 139-152.
80   Joseph Sassoon, *Anatomy of Authoritarianism in the Arab Republics*, (Cambridge University Press, United Kingdom, 2016), 49.
81   Ibid.
82   Ibid., 84.
83   Steven Heydemann, "War, Institutions, and Social Change in the Middle East," in Heydemann, Steven (ed), *War, Institutions, and Social Change in the Middle East*, (University of California Press, Berkley, 2000), 1-32.
84   Volker Perthes, "State Building, National Security and War Preparation in Syria," in Heydemann, Steven (ed), (*War, Institutions, and Social Change in the Middle East*, University of California Press, Berkley, 2000). 149-173.
85   Ibid., 151.
86   Ibid., 153.
87   Ibid., 154.
88   Ibid
89   Ibid., 159.
90   Ibid., 168.
91   Ephraim Karsh, Ephraim, *The Oslo Disaster Revisited: How It Happened*, The Begin-Sadat Center for Strategic Studies, Bar-Ilan University, *Mideast Security and Policy Studies*, No. 154, Ramat Gan, Israel, 2018.
92   "The Arab Peace Initiative," the Council of Arab States at the Summit level at its 14th ordinary session, Official Translation of the full text of Saudi Inspired peace plan adopted by the Arab Summit, Beirut, 2002. www.al-bab.com/arab/docs/league/peace02.htm.
93   Ibid.
94   Bruce Maddy Weitzman, "Arabs and the Abdullah Plan," in *Middle East Quarterly*, Summer 2010, 3-12, 4.
95   Ibid.
96   Ibid., 6.
97   Ibid., 9.
98   "Iran Nuclear Deal: Key Details", BBC, June 11, 2019, https://www.bbc.com/news/world-middle-east-33521655 (Retrieved on July 28, 2020).
99   "The Obama Doctrine:" The Atlantic's Exclusive Report on the U.S. President's Hardest Foreign Policy Decisions," Jeffrey Goldberg interviews Barack Obama, *The Atlantic*, March 10, 2016.

100 Ibid.
101 Phillip Smyth, *The Shiite Jihad in Syria and Its Regional Effects*, The *Washington Institute for Near East Policy*, Washington DC, 2015.
102 Prince Turki Al Faisal, "Mr. Obama, we are not Free Riders," *Arab News*, March 14, 2016 http://www.arabnews.com/columns/news/894826#.VubddRYBwbU.twitter (Retrieved, on 08/16/2017).
103 The discussion between General Yaacov Amidror and Prince Turki Al Faisal can be watched in https://www.youtube.com/watch?v=Ro-5FODlYj3c.
104 Ibid.
105 Ibid.
106 Simon Henderson, "Riyadh's Diplomatic Dance with Israel," *The Washington Institute for Near East Policy*, July 25, 2016, http://www.washingtoninstitute.org/policy-analysis/view/riyadhs-diplomatic-dance-with-israel (Retrieved on May 30, 2016).
107 "Israel, Saudi Arabia said to discuss open economic ties," *The Times of Israel*, June 17, 2017. http://www.timesofisrael.com/israel-saudi-arabi-said-to-discuss-open-economic-ties/ (retrieved on June 31, 2017).
108 Ibid.
109 Jeffrey Goldberg "Saudi Crown Prince: Iran's Supreme Leader 'Makes Hitler Look Good', *The Atlantic*, April 2, 2018 https://www.theatlantic.com/international/archive/2018/04/mohammed-bin-salman-iran-israel/557036/ (retrieved on May 8, 2018).
110 Ibid.
111 "Palestinians must make peace or shut up, Saudi crown prince said to tell US Jews", *The Times of Israel*, April 29, 2018, https://www.timesofisrael.com/palestinians-must-make-peace-or-shut-up-saudi-crown-prince-said-to-tell-us-jews/ (retrieved on May 8, 2018).
112 Lally Weymouth, "Egyptian President Abdel Fatah al-Sisi, who talks to Netanyahu 'a lot,' says his country is in danger of collapse," interview with Egyptian President Abdel Fatah al-Sisi *Washington Post*, March 12, 2015
113 Raymond Ibrahim, "Egypt's Sisi: Islamic "Thinking" Is "Antagonizing the Entire World," 01/01/ 2015 by, http://www.raymondibrahim.com/2015/01/01/egypts-sisi-islamic-thinking-is-antagonizing-the-entire-world/hinking.
114 Ibid.
115 Ibid.
116 Ahmad Hafez, "Al-Azhar's education move a blow to extremism", *The Arab Weekly*, September 30, 2018.
117 Ibid.

118 Ibrahim-ibid.

119 Ibid.

120 Eric Trager, "Egypt Two Years After Morsi: Part I," *The Washington Institute for Near East Policy*, Testimony submitted to the House Committee on Foreign Affairs, May 20, 2015. http://docs.house.gov/meetings/FA/FA13/20150520/103497/HHRG-114-FA13-Wstate-TragerE-20150520.pdf.

121 Eric Trager, Ibid.

122 Weymouth, Ibid.

123 "Under El-Sisi, chapter on Camp David Accords added to Egyptian schoolbook," *Jewish News Service*, February 16, 2016. http://www.jns.org/news-briefs/2016/2/17/under-el-sissi-chapter-on-camp-david-added-to-egypt-schoolbooks#.V1xlCnM2qvp= (retrieved on January 23, 2018).

124 Ibid.

125 "60 Minutes," interview with Egyptian President Abdel Fatah al-Sisi, CBS, January 6, 2019.

126 "Egyptian army in Sinai Peninsula doubles in a year, with Israel's blessing", *The Times of Israel*, March 1, 2018 https://www.timesofisrael.com/egyptian-army-in-sinai-peninsula-doubles-in-a-year-with-israels-blessing/ (Retrieved on January 16, 2019).

127 David Wainer, & Yaacov Benmeleh, "Israel-Egypt $15 Billion Gas Deal Boosts Energy Hub Prospects", *Bloomberg News*, February 19, 2018 https://www.bloomberg.com/news/articles/2018-02-19/noble-delek-sign-15-billion-deal-to-export-israel-gas-to-egypt (retrieved on January 16, 2019).

128 Mirette Magdy, "Talks Underway to Build New Gas Pipeline to Egypt, Israel Says", *Bloomberg News*, January 15, 2019, https://www.bloomberg.com/news/articles/2019-01-15/talks-underway-to-build-new-gas-pipeline-to-egypt-israel-says.

129 "Arab states issue 13 demands to end Qatar-Gulf crisis," *Al Jazeera*, July 12, 2017. http://www.aljazeera.com/news/2017/06/arab-states-issue-list-demands-qatar-crisis-170623022133024.html (Retrieved on June 31 2017).

130 Israel Kasnett, "Does Bahrain expect returns on its now-public association with Israel?" Israel Hayom, July 30, 2019 https://www.israelhayom.com/2019/07/30/does-bahrain-expect-returns-on-its-now-public-association-with-israel/ (retrieved on August 6, 2019).

131 David D. Kirkpatrick "Tapes Reveal Egyptian Leaders' Tacit Acceptance of Jerusalem Move," *The New York Times,* January 6, 2018.

132 "The New Arab Summit is Old", *Al-Arabiya al-Jadeed*, London, April 3, 2019, reproduced in *Jerusalem Post* on April 11, 201 https://www.jpost.com/Magazine/Voices-From-The-Arab-Press-THE-NEW-ARAB-SUMMIT-IS-OLD-586487 (retrieved on April 11, 2019).

Chapter 4

1 Tarek Heggy, *The Arab Mind Bound*, (Vallentine Mitchell, Portland, Oregon, 2011).
2 Mark Lynch, *The New Arab Wars, Uprising and Anarchy in the Middle East*, (Public Affairs, New York, New York, 2016).
3 Steve A. Cook, *False Dawn: Protest, Democracy and Violence in the New Middle East*, (Oxford University Press, 2017).
4 Shmuel Sandler, "The Arab Spring and the Linkage between Israeli Domestic and Foreign Policies," in Inbar, Efraim, (ed), *The Arab Spring, Democracy and Security: Domestic and International Ramifications*, (Routledge, New York, 2014), 130.
5 Excerpts from PM Netanyahu's statement at the Knesset, Israel Foreign Ministry, November 23, 2011. https://mfa.gov.il/MFA/PressRoom/2011/Pages/PM_Netanyahu_statement_Knesset_23-Nov-2011.aspx. Retrieved May 11, 2019.
6 Byman, Daniel, "Israel's Pessimistic View of the Arab Spring," *The Washington Quarterly*, Volume 34, 2011, 125.
7 Ibid.
8 Noah Feldman, *The Arab Winter*, (Princeton University Press, Princeton N.J, 2020), 42.
9 Ibrahim, Saad Eddin, "Hosni Mubarak All Out War against Democracy", *The Forward*, April 8, 2005.
10 Offer Winter, "El Sissi's First Year as President," in *Strategic Assessment*, Volume 18, No. 2, July 2015, 11.
11 Eric Trager, *Arab Fall: How the Muslim Brotherhood Won and Lost Egypt in 891 Days*, (Georgetown University Press, Washington DC, 2016), 167-168.
12 Ibid., 169.
13 Ibid., 175.
14 Ibid., 177.
15 Ibid., 179.
16 Ibid., 181-182.
17 Ibid., 189.
18 Ibid., 190-191.
19 "Egypt's Shura Council and constitution panel 'invalid'", BBC, June 2, 2013 https://www.bbc.com/news/world-middle-east-22745568 (retrieved on July 6, 2017.
20 Ibid., 193.
21 Ibid., 205.
22 Salwha, Abdullah, (President of the Center for Israel Studies, Amman), interview with author, April 23, 2018.

23   Noah Feldman, *The Arab Winter*, (Princeton Univ. Press, Princeton: NJ, 2020), 59.

24   Shadi Hamid, *Temptations of Power: Islamists and Illiberal Democracy in a New Middle East*, (Oxford University Press, New York, New York, 2014), 50.

25   Adeed Dawisha, *The Second Arab Awakening Revolution, Democracy, and the Islamist Challenge from Tunis to Damascus*, (W.W Norton & Company, New York, New York, 2013). 114.

26   Racheed Ghanhouchi, "From Political Islam to Muslim Democracy," *Foreign Affairs*, September/October 2016, Volume 95, Number 5, 58-68.

27   Ibid., 64.

28   Duncan Pickard, "Prospects for Implementing Democracy in Tunisia", in *Mediterranean Politics*, 2014, Vol. 19, No. 2, 259-264.

29   Ibid., 261.

30   Ibid.

31   Ibid., 44-45.

32   Ibid., 46-47.

33   Ghannouchi, 59-60.

34   Ibid.. 64.

35   Marks. Ibid.

36   Dawisha. 250-253.

37   Ibid. 161-162.

38   Meir Litvak, "Radical Islamism and the Arab Upheaval" in Small Charles (ed), *The ISGAP Papers: Antisemitism in Comparative Perspective*, Volume II, Institute for the Study of Global Antisemitism and Policy (ISGAP), 2016, 75-90,

39   Deborah Amos, "The Flood of Syrian Refugees Puts ISIS on The Defensive," September 22, 2015. https://www.npr.org/sections/parallels/2015/09/22/442520787/the-flood-of-syrian-refugees-puts-isis-on-the-defensive (retrieved August 4, 2019).

40   "The Raqqa Diaries: Life under ISIS Rule," *The Guardian*, February 26, 2017, https://www.theguardian.com/books/2017/feb/26/the-raqqa-diaries-life-under-isis-rule-samer-mike-thomson-syria (retrieved on November 6, 2017).

41   Ibid.

42   Leila Fadel & Karen Yong "Aysd Allawi's Bloc Wins most Seats in Iraq's parliamentarian election," *The Washington Post*, March 27, 2010.

43   Emma Sky, "Mission Still not Accomplished: Why the United States Should Not Leave," *Foreign Affairs*, Volume 96, Number 6, November/December 2017, 9-15.

44   Ibid.

45 "How Nouri al-Maliki fell out of favor with the US", *The Guardian,* June 19, 2014, https://www.theguardian.com/world/2014/jun/19/ how-nouri-al-maliki-fell-out-favour-with-us-iraq (retrieved on July 14, 2018). 425

46 O'Driscoll, Dylan, "Autonomy Impaired: Centralization, Authoritarianism and the Failing Iraqi State," in *Ethnopolitics,* Routledge, 2017, Vol. 16, No. 4, 315–332.

47 Sky, Ibid.

48 Mustafa Saadoun, "If Iran has its way, Abadi won't see a second term in Iraq", Al Monitor, April 21, 2017 http://www.al-monitor.com/ pulse/ru/originals/2017/07/iran-iraq-prime-minister-abadi-khamenei-pmu-shiite-militias.html#ixzz4yv0DAyve (Retrieved on November 19, 2017).

49 Sky, 11.

50 Emile Simpon, "Iraq's Dangerous Moment: Nationalists and Iran sympathizers vie for power in Baghdad," *National Review,* Vol. 69, Issue 21, November 13, 2017.

51 Ibid.

52 Elliot Abrams, Realism *and Democracy: American Foreign Policy after the Arab Spring,* Cambridge University Press, New York, N.Y, 2017, 123.

53 Oliver Roy, "The Transformation of the Arab World" in *Journal of Democracy,* Volume 23, Number 3, July 2012, 5-18, 7.

54 Dawisha. Ibid.

55 Marwan Muasher, *The Second Arab Awakening and the Battle for Pluralism.* Yale University Press, 2014, 85.

56 Elliot Abrams, *Realism and Democracy,* 109-110.

57 Ibid., 108.

58 Cook, *False Down,* 156.

59 Interview with Prince Mohamed Bin Salman, "I will return Saudi Arabia to moderate Islam, says crown prince", *The Guardian,* October 24, 2017, https://www.theguardian.com/world/2017/oct/24/i-will-return-saudi-arabia-moderate-islam-crown-prince (retrieved on May 4, 2018).

60 Ibid.

61 Interview with Muhammad bin Salman, *The Economist,* January 6, 2016, http://www.economist.com/saudi_interview (retrieved on April 3, 2018).

62 Ibid., 12.

63 Ibid.

64 "Is Sissi losing his Grip on Egypt", Al Jazeera, April 28, 2016, http://www.aljazeera.com/news/2016/04/sisi-losing-grip-egypt-160426080703098.html, (retrieved on December 17, 2016).

65   Mohammed Al Anaary, Mahmoud Farouk, and Ahmed Rizk, "Between a Rock and a Hard Place: How Egypt's Constitutional Amendments Erode Judicial Independence," Project on Middle East Democracy, April 18, 2019. https://pomed.org/qa-between-a-rock-and-a-hard-place-how-egypts-constitutional-amendments-erode-judicial-independence/ (retrieved on May 22, 2019).

66   Al-Masry Al Youm, "Egyptians continue voting on constitutional amendments for the second day", *Egyptian Independent*, April 21, 2019 https://www.egyptindependent.com/egyptians-continue-voting-on-constitutional-amendments-for-the-second-day/ (retrieved, May 23, 2019).

67   Ibid.

68   Ibid.

69   "Egypt blocks petition against Sisi's constitutional amendments hours after launch", Middle East Eye, April 9, 2019. https://www.middleeasteye.net/news/egypt-blocks-petition-against-sisis-constitutional-amendments-hours-after-launch, (retrieved on May 22, 2019).

70   "Egypt opposition urges voters to reject constitutional amendments" *Al Jazeera*, April 18, 2019. https://www.aljazeera.com/news/2019/04/egypt-opposition-urges-voters-reject-constitutional-amendments-190418160131914.html (Retrieved on May 223, 2019).

71   Al Youm, Ibid.

72   Position Paper – "The Constitutional Amendments Do Not Establish A Democracy that Supports Women in Politics," Nazra for Feminist Studies, March 7, 2019 https://nazra.org/en/2019/03/constitutional-amendments-do-not-establish-democracy-supports-women-politics (retrieved on June 20, 2019).

73   Emily Crane Linn, "Egypt's Sisi is not Mubarak", *Middle East Eye*, February 5, 2016, http://www.middleeasteye.net/columns/egypts-sisi-not-mubarak-1332297997 (retrieved on December 10, 2016).

74   Gianni Del Panta, "From Mubarak to al-Sisi: What has changed in Egypt's Political Structure?" Reset Dialogues on Civilizations, March 3, 2020 https://www.resetdoc.org/story/from-mubarak-to-al-sisi-what-has-changed-in-egypt-political-structure/ (Retrieved on July 8, 2020).

75   Sky, 11.

76   "Analyst: Iraq protests have 'overcome sectarianism'", *Al Jazeera*, November 4, 2019 https://www.aljazeera.com/news/2019/11/analyst-iraq-protests-overcome-sectarianism-191104190411464.html (retrieved on January 16, 2019).

77   Ibid.

78   Sune Haugbolle, "Lebanon has Suffered from Sectarianism for Too Long", *Foreign Policy*, November 1, 2019   https://foreignpolicy.com/2019/11/01/lebanon-has-suffered-from-sectarianism-for-too-long/_ (retrieved on January 5, 2020).

79   Abby Sewell, "Families of victims reflect on tragedy one month after Beirut port explosion", *Al Arabiya English*, September 5, 2020 https://english.alarabiya.net/en/News/middle-east/2020/09/05/Families-of-victims-reflect-on-tragedy-one-month-after-Beirut-port-explosion#:~:text=At%20least%20191%20people%20died%20in%20the%20blast,wall%20on%20the%20side%20of%20the%20road%20 (Retrieved on September 5, 2020).

80   Maha Yahya, "The Middle East's Lost Decades," in *Foreign Affairs*, Volume 98, Number 6, November- December 2019, 48-55.

81   Tocqueville, Alexis, *The Ancient Regime and the French Revolution*, Jon Elster (ed), (Cambridge University Press, New York, 2011), 157.

82   Jurgen Habermas, "Further Reflections on the Public Sphere" in Calhoun, Craig (ed), (*Habermas and the Public Sphere*, The MIT press, Cambridge, Massachusetts), 1996, 421-461, 423.

83   Ibid

84   Ibid.

85   Jurgen Habermas, *The Structural Transformation of the Public Sphere*, (M.I.T. Press, Cambridge, 1992), 30-31.

86   Nahrain Al Mousawi, "Literature after the Arab Spring", Middle East Institute, February 5, 2016 http://www.mei.edu/content/article/literature-after-arab-spring (retrieved, February 23, 2017).

87   Lin Noueihed & Alex Warren, *The Battle for the Arab Spring: Revolution, Counterrevolution and the Making of a New Era*, (Yale University Press, New Haven, 2012), 48.

88   Ibid., 50-51.

89   Ibid. , 53-54.

90   Rachel Aspden, *Generation Revolution: On the Front Line between Tradition and Change in the Middle East*, (Other Press, New York, New York, 2016), 64.

91   Kevin Wagner &. & Jason Gainous, Digital Uprising: The Internet Revolution in the Middle East, Journal of Information Technology & Politics, 2013, 10:3, 261-275, DOI: 10.1080/19331681.2013.778802, 263

92   Ibid., 264-265.

93   Ibid.

94   "Egypt's Cybercrime Law and Media Regulation Bill violate right to freedom of expression", Association for Freedom of Thought and Expression, September 6, 2018 , https://ifex.org/egypts-cybercrime-law-and-media-regulation-bill-violate-right-to-freedom-of-expression/ (Retrieved on July 7, 2020)

95   "The Slippery Slope of Internet Censorship in Egypt", *Internet Monitor*, October 17, 2017, https://thenetmonitor.org/bulletins/the-slippery-slope-of-internet-censorship-in-egypt (retrieved on May 24, 2019).

96   "A Dangerous Deterioration: Egypt Under al-Sisi A Conversation with Dr. Ashraf El Sherif," Project on Middle East Democracy, June 2017, https://pomed.org/wp-content/uploads/2017/06/Ashraf_QA_FINAL.pdf (retrieved June 1, 2018).

97   Sara Saif, interview with author, July 10, 2019.

98   Bessma Momani, B. *Arab Dawn: Arab Youth and the Demographic Dividend They Will Bring,* (University of Toronto Press, Scholarly Publishing Division, 2015), Chapter 4.

99   Ibid- Chapter 3.

100   *Arab Human Development Report 2016: Youth and the Prospects for Human Development in a Changing Reality,* United Nations Development Program, 2016.

101   Ibid. Page 7.

102   *Arab Development Challenges Report 2011: Towards the Developmental State in the Arab Region,* United Nations Development Program, Cairo, 2011, 3.

103   Ibid., 5.

104   *Arab Human Development Report 2016,* 17.

105   Ibid., 19.

106   Ibid., 20-21.

107   Ibid., 26.

108   Ibid., 27.

109   Ibid., 39.

110   Sara Saif, interview with author, ibid.

111   Ibid.

112   Ibid.

113   Ibid.

114   Ibid.

115   Esther Webman, , "The Image of the Jew/Zionist/Israeli in the Arab World" in in Maoz, Moshe (ed) *Muslim Attitudes to Jews and Israel: The Ambivalences of Rejection, Antagonism, Tolerance and Cooperation,* (Sussex Academic Press, Brighton), England, 2011, 48-68, 48.

116   Ibid., 49.

117   Ibid., 52.

118   Ibid., 53.

119   Ibid., 56.

120   Roy, Olivier, "The Transformation of the Arab World," 16.

121   "Arab Youth Survey 2015: 23% Palestinian-Israeli conflict biggest ob-

stacle facing the Middle East," Independent Media Review Analysis, May 1, 2015. http://www.imra.org.il/story.php3?id=67146 (retrieved on December 18, 2016).

122 Khaldoon Bakhail, interview with author, May 12, 2018
123 The Houthis are a Zadi sect of Islam in Yemen that represent one side of the civil war in the country and is supported by Iran).
124 Ibid.
125 Ibid.
126 Mohammed Al Samawi, M, *The Fox Hunt: A Refugee Memoir of Coming to America*, (Harper Collins Publishers, 2018), 106.
127 Ibid.
128 Sara Saif interview with author, Ibid.
129 Author Interview with a Young Palestinian/Egyptian woman via mediators.
130 The author organized this event as part of his role at the Jewish Federation of Palm Beach County. The event took place on July 22, 2013 in West Palm Beach, Florida, see Glaser, Nina, "A Briefing on Syria," TC Palm, 07/31/2013 http://archive.tcpalm.com/news/a-briefing-on-syria-hosted-by-jewish-federation-of-palm-beach-county-ep-379391408-342453641.html (retrieved Mary 22, 2016).
131 The article appeared originally in *The Jerusalem Post* on July 31, 2018. https://www.meforum.org/articles/2018/syrian-activists-ahed-tamimi-lucky-not-to-be-imp (retrieved on August 11, 2018)._
132 "Shehadi: "Lebanon Never Developed A Strong 20th Century State, And That's Good for The Future," interview with Suzette Grillot and Annie Davenport, KGOU Radio (Oklahoma), February 17, 2017, https://www.kgou.org/post/shehadi-lebanon-never-developed-strong-20th-century-state-and-thats-good-future (retrieved on February 3, 2019).
133 Joshua Davidovich, "Iranians target Tehran's support for Palestinians amid massive protests *The Times of Israel*, December 31, 2017 https://www.timesofisrael.com/iranians-target-tehrans-support-for-palestinians-amid-massive-protests/ (retrieved on April 22, 2019).
134 This is according to Nathan Sales, under-secretary for civilian security, democracy and human rights, Department of State, presentation made at Washington Institute for Near East Policy on November 13, 2018 https://www.state.gov/countering-irans-global-terrorism/ (retrieved on July 14, 2019).
135 "Iran students refuse to walk over US and Israeli flags," BBC, January 12, 2020, https://www.bbc.com/news/av/world-middle-east-51084619/iran-students-refuse-to-walk-over-us-and-israeli-flags (Retrieved on January 18, 2020).

136 Ibid.
137 Avi Melamed, *Inside the Middle East: Making Sense of the Most Complicated and Dangerous Region on Earth*, (Skyhorse Publishing, New York, N.Y., 2016), 3.
138 Ibid.
139 Ibid., 5.
140 Ibid.
141 The Sykes-Picot agreements (1916) were secret agreement dividing the lands of the collapsed Ottoman Empire in the Middle East between Great Britain and France in the aftermath of WWI.
142 Melamed, 7.
143 Ibid., 18.
144 Nadim Shehadi, interview with author, February 21, 2019.
145 Salman Masalha, "The Massacre of Arab Nationalism", *Haaretz*, April 9, 2018 https://www.haaretz.com/opinion/.premium-the-massacre-of-arab-nationalism-1.5979184 (retrieved on March 15, 2019).
146 Ofra Bengio, "Babylon vs Zion: Changing Iraqi Perceptions of Israel," in Maoz, Moshe (ed) *Muslim Attitudes to Jews and Israel: The Ambivalences of Rejection, Antagonism, Tolerance and Cooperation*, (Sussex Academic Press, Brighton, England, 2011), 142-158.
147 Ibid., 144.
148 Ibid., 148-149.
149 "Three Iraqi delegations said to make unprecedented Israel visits, meet officials", *The Times of Israel*, January 6, 2019, https://www.timesofisrael.com/three-iraqi-delegations-said-to-make-unprecedented-israel-visits-meet-officials (retrieved on February 7, 2019).
150 https://www.facebook.com/IsraelinIraqi/
151 https://www.facebook.com/IsraelArabic/posts/2039694549401276
152 Ibid.
153 Ibid.
154 Joseph Braude, *Reclamation: A Cultural Policy for Arab-Israeli Partnership*, (The Washington Institute for Near East Policy, 2019), 55.
155 "Young Iraqis risk prison to reconnect with Israelis", Jewish Refugees BlogSpot, September 24, 2018, http://jewishrefugees.blogspot.com/2018/09/young-iraqis-risk-prison-to-reconnect.html (retrieved on February 5, February 5, 2019).
156 Bendedeta Berti, "Israel and the Arab Spring: Understanding Attitudes and Responses to the "New Middle East" in Vidino, Lorenzo (ed), *The West and the Muslim Brotherhood After the Arab Spring*, e-book, Foreign Policy Research, Philadelphia, 2013, 130-146, 138.
157 Samuel Ghiles-Meilhac, "Tunisia's relations with Israel in a comparative approach," *Bulletin du Centre de recherche français à Jérusalem* [Online], 2014, http://bcrfj.revues.org/7352.

158 Ambassador Shalom Cohen, interview with author, August 21, 2019

159 Chhaibi Abdelrrahim. interview with author, January 4, 2019

160 The Berbers are part of an ethnic group resident of North Africa that descended from pre-Arab indigenous inhabitants of the region.

161 Bruce Maddy-Weitzmann, "Morocco's Berbers and Israel," *Middle East Quarterly*, Winter 2011, 79-85.

162 Ibid., 80.

163 Abdelrrahim. Interview with author, ibid.

164 Braude. 47.

165 Ibid., 55.

166 Ibid., 55-56.

167 Ibid., 58.

168 David Halbfinger, "Arab thinkers Call to Abandon Boycotts and Engage with Israel," *The New York Times*, November 20, 2019.

169 Braude, Ibid., 113.

170 Ethan Bronner, "Mideast Din Drowns Out Palestinians," *New York Times*, March 7, 2012.

Chapter 5

1   *Peace to Prosperity*, The White House, January 2020, 19- https://www.whitehouse.gov/wp-content/uploads/2020/01/Peace-to-Prosperity-0120.pdf (retrieved on May 10, 2020).

2   Felicia Schwartz, "Trump Middle East Peace Plan Calls for $50 Billion in Investment", Market Screener, June 22, 2019 https://www.marketscreener.com/news/Trump-Middle-East-Peace-Plan-Calls-for-50-Billion-in-Investment-Update--28799216/ (retrieved on June 25, 2019).

3   *Peace to Prosperity*, 19.

4   Ibid., 20.

5   Robert Danin, "Integrating the Top- Down with Bottom -Up Approach to Israeli -Palestinian Peace" in Kurtzer, Daniel (ed.) *Pathways to Peace: America and the Arab-Israeli Conflict*, (Palgrave MC Millan, New York, NY, 2012), 157-172, 164.

6   Ibid.

7   Jon Donnison, "What next as Palestinian PM Salam Fayyad resigns?" *BBC News*, April 16, 2013. https://www.bbc.com/news/world-middle-east-22154759 (Retrieved on July 2, 2019).

8   Danin, Ibid.

9   See Raja Khalidi & Sobhi Samour, "Neoliberalism as Liberation: The Statehood Program and the Remaking of the Palestinian Na-

tional Movement," *Journal of Palestine Studies*, Vol. 40 No. 2, Winter 2011: 6-25.

10   Ahmed Charad, "Kushner's Middle East Plan Wins Its First Round", *The National Interest*, June 29, 2019.

11   *Peace to Prosperity*, 12.

12   "Trump plan would see Palestinian state on up to 70% of West Bank, reports say", *The Times of Israel*, January 26, 2020, https://www.timesofisrael.com/trump-plan-would-see-palestinian-state-on-up-to-70-of-west-bank-reports-say/ (retrieved on January 28, 2020).

13   *Peace to Prosperity*, 9.

14   Ibid., 12.

15   Ibid., 9.

16   Jacob Magid, "Borders, security, Jerusalem, settlements, refugees: Key elements of Trump plan", *The Times of Israel*, January 29, 2020, https://www.timesofisrael.com/borders-security-jerusalem-settlements-refugees-key-elements-of-trump-plan/ (retrieved on January 29, 2020).

17   Arwa Ibrahim, "'A new Balfour': Palestinians reject Trump's Middle East plan," Al Jazeera, January 28, 2020 https://www.aljazeera.com/news/2020/01/balfour-palestinians-angered-trump-middle-east-plan-200128194613728.html (retrieved on June 11, 2020).

18   "Hamas to join Palestinian leadership meeting against Trump plan – officials", Times of Israel, January 28, 2020, https://www.timesofisrael.com/hamas-to-join-palestinian-leadership-meeting-against-trump-plan-officials/ (Retrieved on June 11, 2020).

19   Omri Nhamias, "Saudi Arabia, Egypt, Qatar, UAE welcome Trump peace plan," *The Jerusalem Post*, January 29, 2020, https://www.jpost.com/Middle-East/Saudi-Arabia-Egypt-Qatar-UAE-welcome-Trump-peace-plan-615752?utm_source=Jeeng (retrieved on January 19, 2020).

20   Ibid.

21   Dion Nissenbaum, "Arab Leaders' Support for Mideast Peace Plan Marks a Regional Shift," *The Wall Street Journal*, January 30, 2020.

22   Dore Gold, "Israel Comes Full Circle with Sudan", The Jerusalem Center for Public Affairs, February 4, 2020 https://jcpa.org/israel-comes-full-circle-with-sudan-analysis/ (retrieved on February 4, 2020).

23   Ibid.

24   "Arab League rejects Trump's Middle East plan," *Al Jazeera*, February 1, 2020, https://www.aljazeera.com/news/2020/02/arab-league-holds-emergency-meeting-trump-plan-200201105251740.html (retrieved on February 1, 2020).

25   "Arab League foreign ministers reject Trump peace plan," *Axios*, February 1, 2020, https://www.axios.com/arab-league-foreign-ministers-reject-trump-peace-plan-612f8cde-c8cc-4955-8504-7b6e6142c103.html (retrieved on 02/01/2020).

26   Khaled Abu Toameh "Arab League Rejects Palestinian Demand to Condemn Israel-UAE Deal," *The Jerusalem Post*, September 9, 2020.

27   Sudaran Raghava, and Steve Hendrix, "Arab governments denounce Israel's plans to annex the West Bank, warning it will imperil regional security and peace building. But will Israel listen?" *The Washington Post*, June 27, 2020.

28   Yossi Beilin, "The Two-State Solution Can Be Achieved through a Confederation", *The Jerusalem Post*, September 9, 2019, https://www.jpost.com/Israel-News/The-two-state-solution-can-be-achieved-through-a-confederation-60 (retrieved on September 10, 2019).

29   Ibid.

30   Ibid.

31   Hirsch Goodman, and Alan Baker, "The Dangers of a Unilateral Israeli Withdrawal from the West Bank and Eastern Jerusalem", Jerusalem Center for Public Affairs," Jerusalem, March 2017, http://jcpa.org/the-dangers-of-a-unilateral-israeli-withdrawal-from-the-west-bank-and-east-jerusalem/ (retrieved on July 10, 2019).

32   Mark Tessler, *A History of the Israeli-Palestinian Conflict*, (Indiana University Press, Bloomington and Indianapolis, 1994), 655.

33   Ibid.

34   Ibid., 657.

35   Caroline Glick, "Statecraft in the Absence of Statesmen," *Jerusalem Post*, May 25, 2007, http://www.jpost.com/Opinion/Columnists/Column-One-Statecraft-in-the-absence-of-statesmen (retrieved 10/12/2016).

36   Osama Al Sharif, "Why confederation with Palestine is suddenly a hot issue in Amman", *Al Monitor Pulse*, May 31, 2016, http://www.al-monitor.com/pulse/originals/2016/05/palestine-jordan-confederation-abbas-dahlan-israel.html (retrieved on 09/06/2016).

37   Khaled Abu Toameh, "Palestinians and Jordan: Will a Confederation Work?" Gateston Institute, May 25, 2016, https://www.gatestoneinstitute.org/8112/palestinians-jordan-confederation (retrieved on 09/05/2016).

38   Al Sharif. Ibid.

39   Yotam Berger and Amir Tivon, "Abbas: Trump's Team Offered Me to Establish a Jordanian-Palestinian Confederation", *Haaretz*, March 9, 2018, https://www.haaretz.com/israel-news/.premium-abbas-trump-s-team-offered-jordanian-palestinian-confederation-1.6435791 (retrieved on April 21, 2019).

40   Adam Abu Amer, "A Palestine-Jordan Confederation is becoming a very real possibility", *The Middle East Monitor*", February 18, 2019 https://www.middleeast-monitor.com/20190218-a-palestine-jordan-confederation-is-becoming-a-very-re-al-possibility/ (retrieved on July 16, 2020).

41   Ibid.

42   C. Jacob , "Idea Of Jordanian-Palestinian Confederation Resurfac-es, Only To Be Rejected By Both Sides", The Middle East Media Re-search Institute, October 2, 2016, https://www.memri.org/reports/idea-jordanian-palestinian-confederation-resurfaces-only-be-reject-ed-both-sides (retrieved on July 15, 2019).

43   Abu Toameh. Ibid.

44   Asher Susser, "Israel, Jordan, and Palestine: One State, Two States or Three?" in *The Yale Papers: Antisemitism in Comparative Perspective*, Charles Asher Small (ed), (*Institute for the Study of Global Antisemitism and Policy*, New York, 2015), 485-496, 486.

45   Ibid., 494.

46   Benny Morris, *One State, Two States*: *Resolving the Israel-Palestine Con-flict*, (Yale University   Press, New Haven, 2009), 199-200.

47   Osama Al Sharif, "Jordan fears long-term threat to its national secu-rity following Trump's peace plan", Al-Monitor, January 30, 2020, https://www.al-monitor.com/pulse/originals/2020/01/jordan-re-acts-trump-peace-plan-palestinians-israel-threat.html (retrieved on January 31, 2020).

48   Neville Teller, "Israel-Palestinian Peace: The 'Regional Umbrella' Ap-proach", *The Eurasia Review News and Analysis,* March 31, 2017 https://www.eurasiareview.com/31032017-israel-palestinian-peace-the-re-gional-umbrella-approach-oped/ (retrieved on July 13, 2020).

49   Morris, 200.

50   Morris, Ibid.

51   Daniel Pipes, "Give Gaza to Egypt", *The Jerusalem Post*, January 30, 2008, http://www.danielpipes.org/5426/give-gaza-to-egypt (re-trieved on November 13, 2019).

52   Anna Ahronheim, "Egypt destroys 37 tunnels which infiltrated from Gaza in 2018", *The Jerusalem Post* May 1, 2019 https://www.jpost.com/arab-israeli-conflict/egypt-destroys-37-tunnels-which-infiltrated-from-gaza-in-2018-576410 (retrieved on 01/05/2019) On Hamas-Isis tensions see Abuheweila, Iyad and Kershner, Isabel "ISIS Declares War on Hamas, and Gaza Families Disown Sons in Sinai," *The New York Times, January 11, 2018.*

53   Yasmine Saleh, "Exclusive: With Muslim Brotherhood crushed, Egypt sets sights on Hamas," Reuters, 01/14/2014 https://www.reu-ters.com/article/us-egypt-gaza/exclusive-with-muslim-brotherhood-

crushed-egypt-sets-sights-on-hamas-idUSBREA0D09D20140114 (retrieved on July 13, 2020).

54   Yousuf Selman, "Hamas distances itself from Muslim Brotherhood, seeks new role in region", Daily Sabah, Mideast, February 17, 2017. https://www.dailysabah.com/mideast/2017/02/25/hamas-distances-itself-from-muslim-brotherhood-seeks-new-role-in-region (retrieved on Mary 20, 2018).

55   Grace Wermenbol, "Disrupting a Delicate Status Quo: The Hamas Crackdown on Salafi Jihadists", Middle East Institute, October 22, 2019 https://www.mei.edu/publications/disrupting-delicate-status-quo-hamas-crackdown-salafi-jihadists (retrieved on November 2, 2019).

56   Foundation for Middle East Peace "Clinton Proposal on Israeli-Palestinian Peace", Meeting with President Clinton, White House, December 23, 2000 https://fmep.org/resource/clinton-parameters/ (retrieved on September 11, 2020).

57   Asem Khalil, "Palestinians to Citizens", *Middle East Law and Governance*, 2014-12, Vol.6 (3), 204-224, 217.

58   Ibid.

59   Ibid., 212.

60   Ibid., 216.

61   Ibid., 218.

62   Ibid., 219.

63   Howard Sachar, *A History of Israel: From the Rise of Zionism to Our Time*, (Alfred Knopf, New York, 2003), 443.

64   Arnold Toynbee and Jacob. L. Talmon, "The Argument between Arabs and Jews," in Laqueur Walter (ed.), *The Israel Arab Reader*, (The Citadel Press, New York, New York, 1968), 260-272, 267.

65   Farah Pandith, *How We Win: How Cutting –Edge Entrepreneurs, Political Visionaries, Enlightened Business Leaders, and Social Media Mavens Can Defeat the Extremist Threat*, (Custom House, New York, New York, 2019), 420.

66   Adam Rasgon, "Trump ties and Iran fears: Why US's Arab allies opting not to rebuke peace plan", *The Times of Israel*, January 30, 2020, https://www.timesofisrael.com/keen-on-ties-most-of-uss-arab-allies-choose-not-to-directly-rebuke-peace-plan/ (retrieved on January 30, 2020).

67   "Saudi king tells Trump he wants a fair and permanent solution for Palestinians", Reuters, September 6, 2020 https://www.theguardian.com/world/2020/sep/07/saudi-king-tells-trump-he-wont-normalise-israeli-ties-without-palestinian-statehood (Retrieved on September 7, 2020).

68   "The Unfulfilled Potential of Israel's relations with Arab countries,"
      Conference, organized by Mitvim, The Israeli Institute for Regional
      Foreign Policies, June 2018, http://www.mitvim.org.il/images/Con-
      ference_summary_-_The_unfulfilled_potential_of_Israels_relations_
      with_Arab_countries_-_June_2018.pdf (retrieved on April 21, 2019).
69   Dr. Nimrod Goren in "The Unfulfilled Potential of Israel's relations
      with Arab countries," Ibid.
70   Dennis Ross, & David Makovsky, *Myths, Illusions and Peace,* (Penguin
      Books, New York, New York, 2010), 129-130.
71   David Harris, President and CEO of the American Jewish Committee,
      quoted from Alex Traiman, "58 Jewish groups gather in New York to
      mobilize against anti-Semitism," Jewish News Syndicate, August 2,
      2019. https://www.jns.org/58-jewish-groups-gather-in-new-york-to-
      mobilize-against-anti-semitism/ (Retrieved on October 23, 2019).
72   Pipes, Daniel, "A New Strategy for Israeli Victory", *Commentary Mag-
      azine,* January 2017, 13-18.
73   Ethan Bronner, and Isabel Kershner, "Head of U.N. Panel Regrets
      Saying Israel Intentionally Killed Gazans," *New York Times, April 2,*
      2011.
74   Luis Fleischman, "Europe Stands Israel is a Stand against Itself,"
      Newsmax, April 4, 2016, http://www.newsmax.com/LuisFleischman/
      South-Africa/2016/04/04/id/722123/. (Retrieved on October 24, 2019)
75   Joshua Muravchik, *Making David into Goliath: How the World Turned
      Against Israel,* (Encounter Books, New York, NY, 2015), 92-93.
76   Javier Blas, "US ends its reliance on foreign oil for the first time in
      75 years," *Bloomberg News,* December 7, 2018. https://www.msn.com/
      en-us/money/markets/us-ends-its-reliance-on-foreign-oil-for-the-
      first-time-in-75-years/ar-BBQAM92 (retrieved on July 15, 2019).
77   "Joint U.S.-EU Statement following President Juncker's visit to the
      White House," July 25, 2018 http://europa.eu/rapid/press-release_
      STATEMENT-18-4687_en.htm (retrieved on July 14, 2019).
78   Jillian Carr and Shila Khara, "US crude oil exports to Europe increasing
      on wider Brent/WTI spread", Standard and Poor, April 9, 2018 https://www.
      spglobal.com/platts/en/market-insights/latest-news/oil/040918-us-crude-oil-
      exports-to-europe-increasing-on-wider-brentwti-spread (retrieved on July
      15, 2019).
79   Dennis Ross, Ibid., xii.
80   "Remarks of President Barack Obama to the People of Israel", The
      White House, March 21, 2013 https://obamawhitehouse.archives.gov/
      the-press-office/2013/03/21/remarks-president-barack-obama-peo-
      ple-israel (Retrieved on July 8, 2019).
81   Paul Danahar, *The New Middle East: The World after the Arab Spring,*
      (Bloomsbury Paperbacks, 2015, New York, New York), 10.

82 Braude. Ibid., 137.
83 Ibid., 140-141.
84 Guzansky, Yoel; Winter, Ofer, "Apolitical Normalization: A New Approach to Jews in Arab States," June 8, 2020, The Institute for National Security Studies, Tel Aviv University, https://www.inss.org.il/publication/judaism-in-the-arabworld/?utm_source=activetrail&utm_medium=email&utm_campaign=INSS%20Insight%20No.%201332
85 Guzansky and Winter. Ibid.

Bibliography

Abdelaziz, Mohamed, "Egyptian Newspapers: On Jews and Israel," *The Washington Institute, Improving the Quality of US Middle East Policy*, April 22, 2016, http://www.washingtoninstitute.org/policy-analysis/view/egyptian-newspapers-on-jews-and-israel

Abderrhaim, Chhaibi, interview with author, January 4, 2019.

Abrams, Elliot. *Tested by Zion: The Bush Administration and the Israeli-Palestinian Conflict*. Cambridge University Press, 2013.

Abrams, Elliot, *Realism and Democracy: American Foreign Policy after the Arab Spring*, (New York: Cambridge University Press, 2017).

Abu Amer, Adnan "A Palestine-Jordan Confederation is becoming a very real possibility", *The Middle East Monitor*", February 18, 2019, https://www.middleeastmonitor.com/20190218-a-palestine-jordan-confederation-is-becoming-a-very-real-possibility/

Abuheweila, Iyad and Kershner, Isabel "ISIS Declares War on Hamas, and Gaza Families Disown Sons in Sinai," *The New York Times*, January 11, 2018.

Abu Toameh, Khaled, "The Palestinians: Refugee Camps or Terrorist Bases?" *The Gatestone Institute*, July 21, 2016, https://www.gatestoneinstitute.org/8511/palestinians-refugee-camps.

Abu Toameh, Khaled, "Arab League Rejects Palestinian Demand to Condemn Israel-UAE Deal", *The Jerusalem Post*, September 9, 2020.

"Agreement on Gaza Strip and Jericho Area," May 4, 1994, Israel's Ministry of Foreign Affairs, https://mfa.gov.il/mfa/foreignpolicy/peace/guide/pages/agreement%20on%20gaza%20strip%20and%20jericho%20area.aspx .

Ahronheim, Anna, "Egypt destroys 37 tunnels which infiltrated from Gaza in 2018," *The Jerusalem Post*, January 5, 2019, https://www.jpost.com/arab-israeli-conflict/egypt-destroys-37-tunnels-which-infiltrated-from-gaza-in-2018-576410 last modified June 1, 2019.

Ajami, Fouad, *The Dream Palace of the Arabs*, Vintage Books, New York, New York, 1998.

Algiers Declaration (1988) Palestinian Declaration of Independence, Algiers, November 15, 1988" http://www.jmcc.org/Documentsandmaps.aspx?id=766.

Al Youm, Al-Masry, "Egyptians continue voting on constitutional amendments for the second day," *Egyptian Independent*, April 21, 2019 https://www.egyptindependent.com/egyptians-continue-voting-on-constitutional-amendments-for-the-second-day/.

Allin, Dana & Simon, Steven *Our Separate Ways: The Struggle for the Future of the U.S-Israel Alliance* (New York: Public Affairs, 2015).

Alpher, Yossi, "Israel-Palestine: From Oslo to the Slippery Slope," *Verdidebatt,*http://www.verdidebatt.no/debatt/cat1/subcat4/thread11602890/#post_11602890.

Amin, Hazam, "Al Qaeda Arrives to the West Bank and Gaza, Aspiring to Take Over Hamas," published in *Al Hayat*, 4 April, 2006 from Spanish translation, "Al Qaeda Llega A Cisjordania y a La Franja De Gaza aspirando llegar al Puesto de Hamas" in Pedro Rojo Perez ed., *El Mundo Visto por Los Arabes, Anuario de Prensa Arabe 2006*, Icaria, Antrazyt, 2007.

Anziska, Seth, Preventing Palestine: A Political History from Camp David to Oslo (Princeton: Princeton University Press, 2018).

Al Anaary, Mohammed, Farouk, Mahmoud, and Rizk, Ahmed, "Between a Rock and a Hard Place: How Egypt's Constitutional Amendments Erode Judicial Independence", *Project on Middle East Democracy*, April 18, 2018, https://pomed.org/qa-between-a-rock-and-a-hard-place-how-egypts-constitutional-amendments-erode-judicial-independence/ .

Al Mousawi, Nahrain, "Literature after the Arab Spring", *Middle East Institute*, February 5, 2016 http://www.mei.edu/content/article/literature-after-arab-spring.

Al Samawi, Mohammed, *The Fox Hunt: A Refugee Memoir of Coming to America*, Harper Collins Publishers, 2018.

Al Sharif, Osama, "Jordan fears long-term threat to its national security following Trump's peace plan," *Al Monitor*, 01/30/2020, https://www.al-monitor.com/pulse/originals/2020/01/jordan-reactions-trump-peace-plan-palestinians-israel-threat.html.

Al Sharif, Osama "Why confederation with Palestine is suddenly a hot issue in Amman", *Al Monitor Pulse*, May 31, 2016, http://www.al-monitor.com/pulse/originals/2016/05/palestine-jordan-confederation-abbas-dahlan-israel.html .

"Analysis: Iraq protests have 'overcome sectarianism," *Al Jazeera*, November 4, 2019, https://www.aljazeera.com/news/2019/11/analyst-iraq-protests-overcome-sectarianism-1911041900411464.html.

"Anti-Israel Incitement in the Palestinian Authority: An Analysis of its Roots and Aspects," *The Meir Amit Intelligence and Terrorism Information Center*, June 5, 2017, http://www.terrorism-info.org.il/en/21215/.

Anonymous young Palestinian who resides in Egypt, interview with author, January 2019.

Arab Development Challenges Report: Towards the Developmental State in the Arab Region, United Nations Development Program, Cairo, 2011.

Arab Human Development Report 2016: Youth and the Prospects for Human Development in a Changing Reality, United Nations Development Program, 2016.

"Arab League Foreign Ministers Reject Trump Peace plan," *Axios*, February 1, 2020, https://www.axios.com/arab-league-foreign-ministers-reject-trump-peace-plan-612f8cde-c8cc-4955-8504-7b6e6142c103.html.

"Arab League Rejects Trump's Middle East Plan," *Al Jazeera*, February 2, 2020, https://www.aljazeera.com/news/2020/arab-league-holds-emergency-meeting-trump-plan-200201105251740.html.

"Arab States Issue 13 Demands to end Qatar-Gulf crisis," *Al Jazeera*, July 12, 2017, http://www.aljazeera.com/news/2017/06/arab-states-issue-list-demands-qatar-crisis-170623022133024.html.

"Arab Youth Survey 2015: 23% Palestinian-Israeli Conflict Biggest Obstacle Facing the Middle East," *Middle East Eye*, April 9, 2019, https://www.middleeasteye.net/news/egypt-blocks-petition-against-sisi-constitutional-amendments-hours-after-launch.

Aspden, Rachel, *Generation Revolution: On the Front Line between Tradition and Change in the Middle East* (New York: Other Press, 2016).

Avishai, Bernard, "What Provoked Palestinian Knife Attacks in Israel", *The New Yorker*, October 23, 2015.

Awad, Samir, "The Impact of the Arab Revolutions on the Palestinian/Israeli Conflict and Future Prospects," (blog) undated, https://www.birzeit.edu/en/blogs/arab-spring-and-palestine.

Bakhail, Khaldoon, interviewed with author, May 12, 2018.

Basheer, Tasheen, "The Background to the Multilateral Talks: An Egyptian Perspective," in Hermann, Robin and Tamar Hermann, *The Arab-Israeli Negotiations: Political Positions and Conceptual Framework* (Tel Aviv: Papyrus Publishing House, 1993), 104-107.

Becker, Tal, "The Claim for Recognition of Israel as a Jewish State: A Reassessment," *Washington Institute for Near East Policy*, Policy Paper 108, (2011).

Beilin, Yossi, "Looking Back on Oslo, 25 years later," *Al Monitor*, September 10, 2018. https://www.al-monitor.com/pulse/originals/2018/09/israel-us-palestinians-oslo-yitzhak-rabin-shimonperes-abbas.html.

Beilin, Yossi, "The Two-State Solution Can be Achieved through a Confederation," *The Jerusalem Post*, September 9, 2019, https://www.jpost.com/israel-news/the-two-state-solution-can-be-achieved-through-a-confederation-601058.

Ben-Ami, Shlomo, *Scars of War, Wounds of Peace: The Israeli-Arab Tragedy,* (Oxford University Press: Oxford, 2006),

Bengio, Ofra, "Babylon vs Zion: Changing Iraqi Perceptions of Israel," in Maoz, Moshe ed., *Muslim Attitudes to Jews and Israel: The Ambivalences of Rejection, Antagonism, Tolerance and Cooperation,* (Brighton: Sussex Academic Press, 2011), 142-158.

Berger, Miriam and Halbfinger, David, "For Palestinian Families, No Light at the End of the Tunnel," *The New York Times,* April 21, 2019.

Berger, Yotam and Tivon, Amir "Abbas: Trump's Team Offered Me to Establish a Jordanian-Palestinian Confederation", *Haaretz,* March 9, 2018, https://www.haaretz.com/israel-news/.premium-abbas-trump-s-team-offered-jordanian-palestinian-confederation-1.6435791.

Berman, Sheri, "Against the Technocrats", *Dissent,* Winter (2018), https://www.dissentmagazine.org/article/against-technocrats-liberal-democracy-history.

Berti, Benedeta, "Israel and the Arab Spring: Understanding Attitudes and Responses to the 'New Middle East'" ed. Lorenzo Vidino, *The West and the Muslim Brotherhood after the Arab Spring,* e-book, (Foreign Policy Research, Philadelphia, 2013), 130-146.

Bin Salman, Muhammed, interview, *The Economist,* January 6, 2016, http://www.economist.com /saudi_interview.

Bin Salman, Muhammed, "I will return Saudi Arabia to Moderate Islam, says the Crown Prince," interview in *The Guardian,* October 24, 2017, https://www.theguardian.com/world/2017/oct/24/i-will-return-saudi-arabia-moderate-islam-crown-prince.

Blas, Javier "US ends its reliance on foreign oil for the first time in 75 years", *Bloomberg News,* December 7, 2018, https://www.msn.com/en-us/money/markets/us-ends-its-reliance-on-foreign-oil-for-the-first-time-in-75-years/ar-BBQAM92.

Bloom, Mia M, "Palestinian Suicide Bombing: Public Support, Market Share, and Outbidding Author(s)," in *Political Science Quarterly,* Vol. 119, No. 1, (Spring, 2004): 61-88.

Bradley, John, "Al Qaeda and the House of Saud: Eternal Enemies or Secret   Bedfellows?" *Washington Quarterly,* Vol. 28, Issue 4 (Autumn 2005): 139-152.

Braude, Joseph, "Reclamation: A Cultural Policy for Arab-Israeli Partnership," *The Washington Institute for Near East Policy,* 2019.

Bronner, Ethan, "Mideast Din Drowns Out Palestinians," *New York Times,* March 7, 2012.

Bronner, Ethan, Kershner, Isabel, "Head of U.N. Panel Regrets Saying Israel Intentionally Killed Gazans," *New York Times,* April 3, 2011.

Byman, Daniel, "Israel's Pessimistic View of the Arab Spring," *The Washington Quarterly*, Volume 34, (2011).

Carr, Jillian, Khara, Ahila "US crude oil exports to Europe increasing on wider Brent/WTI spread", Standard and Poor, April 9, 2018, https://www.spglobal.com/platts/en/market-insights/latest-news/oil/040918-us-crude-oil-exports-to-europe-increasing-on-wider-brentwti-spread.

Chachko, Elena, "Israel's Settlement Regularization Law: The Attorney General's Extraordinary Brief and What it Means for Israel's Legal Stance on Illegal Settlements," *Lawfare*, December 18, 2017, https://www.lawfareblog.com/israels-settlement-regularization-law-attorney-generals-extraordinary-brief-and-what-it-means.

Charad, Ahmed, "Kushner's Middle East Plan Wins Its First Round," *The National Interest*, June 29, 2019.

Center for Israel Education, "Israel's Road to the June 1967 War – Timeline," June 2020, https://israeled.org/israels-road-war-victory-1967/

Cohen, Shalom (Ambassador), interview with author, August 21, 2019.

Coffman Wittes, Tamara (Convener) *Politics, Governance and State –Society Relations: A Working Report of the Middle East Strategy Task Force*, Brookings Institution/Atlantic Council, November 2016.

Cohen, Gilad, "International Holocaust Remembrance Day almost didn't happen," *The Times of Israel*, January 20, 2020, https://blogs.timesofisrael.com/international-holocaust-remembrance-day-almost-didnt-happen.

Collard, Rebecca, "Palestinians Have Created a United Force to Keep ISIS Out of Their Camps," *Time Magazine*, April 21, 2015.

Dalin, David G. and Rothman John F., *Icon of Evil: Hitler's Mufti and the Rise of Radical Islam*, (New York: Random House, 2008).

Danahar, Paul *The New Middle East: The World After the Arab Spring*, (New York: Bloomsbury Paperbacks, 2015).

Danin, Robert "Integrating the Top-down with the Bottom-up Approach to Israeli-Palestinian-Peace" in *Pathways to Peace: America and the Arab-Israeli Conflict* ed. Daniel Kurtzer, (New York: Palgrave-Macmillan, 2012), 157-172.

Danin, Robert, "A Third Way to Palestine", *Foreign Affairs*, Vol 90 Issue 1, (Jan/Feb 2011): 94-109.

Dassa Kaye, Dalia, *Beyond the Handshake: Multilateral Cooperation in the Arab-Israeli Peace Process 1991-1996*, (New York: Columbia University Press, 2001), xiii-xiv.

Davidovich, Joshua, "Iranians Target Tehran's Support for Palestinians Amid Massive Protest," *The Times of Israel*, December 31, 2017, https://www.timesofisrael.com/iranians-target-tehrans-support-for-palestinians-amid-massive-protests/.

Dawisha, Adeed, *The Second Arab Awakening: Revolution, Democracy, and the Islamist Challenge from Tunis to Damascus*, (New York: W.W Norton & Company, 2013).

Deeb, Dennis J, Israel, *Palestine, & the Quest for Middle East Peace*, (Lanham, Maryland: University Press of America, 2013).

Donnison, Jon "What next as Palestinian PM Salam Fayyad resigns?" *BBC News*, April 16, 2013, https://www.bbc.com/news/world-middle-east-22154759.

Downs, Ray," "As secretary of state, Kerry blamed Israel for Lack of Peace with Palestine": United Press International (UPI), November 8, 2017, https://www.upi.com/Top_News/World-News/2017/11/08/As-secretary-of-state-Kerry-blamed-Israel-for-lack-of-peace-with-Palestine-reports/6561510200223/.

"Egyptian army in Sinai Peninsula doubles in a year, with Israel's blessing," *The Times of Israel*, March 1, 2018, https://www.timesofisrael.com/egyptian-army-in-sinai-peninsula-doubles-in-a-year-with-israels-blessing/.

"Egypt opposition urges voters to reject constitutional amendments," *Al Jazeera*, April 18, 2019. https://www.aljazeera.com/news/2019/04/egypt-opposition-urges-voters-reject-constitutional-amendments-190418160131914.html

Eldar, Shlomi. "Five Misassumptions about Second Intifada," *Al Monitor*, October 1, 2013, http://www.al-monitor.com/pulse/originals/2013/09/intifada-israel-palestine-abbas-netanyahu-negotiations.html .

Ellul, Jacques, *Propaganda: The Formation of Men's Attitudes*, Trans. Konrad Kellen & Jean Lerner, (New York: Vintage Books, 1973).

Erekat, Saeb, remarks to *Al Arabyia*, "PLO opposes Kurdish Self-Determination," *Jerusalem on Line*, September 10, 2015, http://www.jerusalemonline.com/news/middle-east/the-arab-world/plo-opposes-kurdish-self-determination-15814 .

Excerpts from PM Netanyahu's statement at the Knesset, Israel Foreign Ministry, November 23, 2011, https://mfa.gov.il/MFA/PressRoom/2011/Pages/PM_ Netanyahu_statement_ Knesset_23-Nov-2011.aspx

Fadel, Leila and Yong, Karen, "Aysd Allawi's Bloc Wins most Seats in Iraq's parliamentarian   election," *The Washington Post*, March 27, 2010.

Feund, Michael, "Time for Gaza Apology," *The Jerusalem Post*, January 20, 2009.

Feldman, Noah, *The Arab Winter*, (Princeton: Princeton University Press, 2020).

Fleischman, Luis "Europe Stands Israel is a Stand against Itself", *Newsmax*,

April 4, 2016 http://www.newsmax.com/LuisFleischman/South-Africa/2016/04/04/id/722123/ .

Fleischman, Luis, "Palestinian Rockets: A Tool of Mass Mobilization," Palestinian Rocket Report, *Jewish Policy Center*, 09/17/2008.

Foundation for Middle East Peace "Clinton Proposal on Israeli-Palestinian Peace", Meeting with President Clinton, White House, December 23, 2000, https://fmep.org/resource/clinton-parameters/

Gal, Yitzhak, "Fruit of Israeli-Jordanian peace still on the tree," *Ynet News*, 03/30/2018, https://www.ynetnews.com/articles/0,7340,L-5209464,00. html, last modified June 30 2018.

Garreton, Manuel Antonio, "Political Processes in an Authoritarian Regime: The Dynamics of Institutionalization and Opposition in Chile, 1973-1980," in *Military Rule in Chile: Dictatorships and Oppositions*, Samuel Valenzuela ed. (Baltimore: the John Hopkins University Press, Baltimore, 1986).

"Gazan Child Recites Violent Nakba Poem," *Jerusalem Post*, May 22, 2014, http://www.jpost.com/middle-east/watch-gazan-child-sings-about-nakba-353062.

Gelvin, James L., *The Israel -Palestine Conflict, One Hundred Years of War*, (Cambridge: Cambridge University Press, 2014).

Ghanhouchi, Racheed, "From Political Islam to Muslim Democracy," *Foreign Affairs* 95, (2016): 58-68.

Ghiles-Meilhac, Samuel, "Tunisia's relations with Israel in a comparative approach", *Bulletin du Centre de recherche français à Jérusalem* accessed 2014, http://bcrfj.revues.org/7352.

Glaser, Nina, "A Briefing on Syria", TC Palm, July 31, 2013 http://archive. tcpalm.com/news/a-briefing-on-syria-hosted-by-jewish-federation-of-palm-beach-county-ep-379391408-342453641.html

Glick, Caroline, "Statecraft in the Absence of Statesmen," *Jerusalem Post*, May 25, 2007, http://www.jpost.com/Opinion/Columnists/Column-One-Statecraft-in-the-absence-of-statesmen, last modified October 12, 2016.

Goldberg, Jeffery, "The Obama Doctrine:" The Atlantic's Exclusive Report on the U.S. President's Hardest Foreign Policy Decisions," interview with Barack Obama, *The Atlantic*, March 10, 2016.

Goldberg, Jeffrey, "Saudi Crown Prince: Iran's Supreme Leader 'Makes Hitler Look Good', *The Atlantic*, April 2, 2018, https://www.theatlantic. com/international/ archive /2018/04 /mohammed-bin-salman-iran-israel/557036/.

Gold, Dore, "Israel comes full circle with Sudan," *The Jerusalem Center for Public Affairs*, February 4, 2020, https://www.jcpa.org/israel-comes-full-circle-with-sudan-analysis/.

Goodman, Hirsch, Baker, Alan, "The Dangers of a Unilateral Israeli With-drawal from the West Bank and Eastern Jerusalem," *Jerusalem Center for Public Affairs*," Jerusalem, March 2017, http://jcpa.org/the-dangers-of-a-unilateral-israeli-withdrawal-from-the-west-bank-and-east-jeru-salem/ .

Goren, Nimrod, "The Unfulfilled Potential of Israel's relations with Arab countries," Conference Summary, The Israeli Institute for Regional Foreign Policies and the Leonard Davis Institute for International Re-lations at the Hebrew University of Jerusalem, 2018.

Guzansky, Yoel and Winter, Ofer, "Apolitical Normalization: A New Ap-proach to Jews in Arab States", (Tel Aviv University: The Institute for National Security Studies, 2020), https://www.inss.org.il/publication/judaism-in-the-arab-world/?utm_source=activetrail&utm_medi-um=email&utm_campaign=INSS%20Insight%20No.%201332 .

Habermas, Jürgen, "Further Reflections on the Public Sphere" in *Habermas and the Public Sphere*, Craig Calhoun, ed. (Cambridge: The MIT press, 1996).

Habermas, Jürgen, *The Structural Transformation of the Public Sphere*, (Cam-bridge: The MIT press, 1992).

Hafez, Ahmad, "Al-Azhar's education move a blow to extremism", *The Arab Weekly*, September 30, 2018.

Halperin, David A, On Netanyahu's Offer to Negotiate Settlement Blocs, *Israel Policy Forum*,   May 27, 2015, http://www.israelpolicyforum.org/blog/netanyahu's-offer-negotiate-settlement-blocs-.

Halbfinger, David, "Arab thinkers call to abandon boycotts and engage with Israel," *The New York Times*, November 20, 2019.

Halbfinger, David and Hubbard Ben, "Arab Envoy Warns Israelis That Annexation Threatens Warming Ties", *The New York Times, June 12, 2020.*

"Hamas Violently Disperse Demonstrators on 3rd Day of Internal Pro-tests," *The Times of Israel*, March 16, 2019.

Hamid, Shadi, *Temptations of Power: Islamists and Illiberal Democracy in a New Middle East*, (New York: Oxford University Press, 2014).

Hanyeh, Ismail, Interview in *Al Mushahid al Siyasi*, December 24, 2006, in Pedro Rojo, *El Mundo Visto por los Arabes*, (Madrid: Icaria Editorial: 2006), 255-260.

Harris, David, "58 Jewish groups gather in New York to mobilize against anti-Semitism," Alex Traiman, *Jewish News Syndicate*, August 2, 2019.

Haugbolle, Sune, "Lebanon has suffered from Sectarianism for too long," *Foreign Policy*, November 1, 2019, https://foreignpolicy.com/2019/11/01/lebanon-has-suffered-from-sectarianism-for-too-long/.

Hawthone, Amy and Ashraf El Sherif, A Dangerous Deterioration: Egypt Under al-Sisi, *Project on Middle East Democracy*, June 2017, https://pomed.org/a-dangerous-deterioration-egypt-under-al-sisi-a-conversation-with-dr-ashraf-el-sherif/.

Henderson, Simon, "Riyadh's Diplomatic Dance with Israel," *The Washington Institute for Near East Policy*, July 25, 2016, http://www.washingtoninstitute.org/policy-analysis/view/riyadhs-diplomatic-dance-with-israel.

Henderson, Simon, "Wahhabism and Terrorism: Is Saudi Arabia the Arsonist or the Fireman?" *The Washington Institute for Near East Policy*, June 7, 2017, https://www.washingtoninstitute.org/policy-analysis/view/wahhabism-and-terrorism-is-saudi-arabia-the-arsonist-or-the-fireman.

Herez, Roger "How Palestinians Came to Reject Kurdish Demands for Homeland", *The New Arab*, September 25, 2017, https://www.alaraby.co.uk/english/Comment/2017/9/25/ How-Palestinians-came-to-reject-Kurdish-demands-for-homeland.

Hertzog, Michael, "The Kerry Legacy": Inside the Black Box of Israeli-Palestinian Talks," *The American Interest*, February 27, 2017, https://www.the-american-interest.com /2017/02/27/inside-the-black-box-of-israeli-palestinian-talks/.

Heydemann, Steven, "War, Institutions, and Social Change in the Middle East," in *War, Institutions, and Social Change in the Middle East*, Steven Heydemann ed., (Berkeley: University of California Press, 2000), 1-32.

Hirschfeld, Yair, *Track Two Diplomacy towards an Israeli-Palestinian Solution 1978-2014*, (Baltimore: John Hopkins University Press, 2014).

Hourani, Albert, *A History of the Arab Peoples*, (New York: Warner Books, 1991.

Hourani, Albert, Address to the Final Session of the Anglo-American Committee of Inquiry, March 25, 1946, in *The Two State Solution: The UN Partition Resolution of Mandatory Palestine*, Ruth Gavison ed., (New York: Bloomsbury, 2003).

Hussein, Abdel Rahman "Egypt defence chief Tantawi ousted in surprise shakeup," *The Guardian*, August 13, 2012, https://www.theguardian.com/world/2012/aug/12/egyptian-defence-chief-ousted-shakeup._

Ibrahim, Arwa, "'A new Balfour': Palestinians reject Trump's Middle East plan", *Al Jazeera*, January 28, 2020, https://www.aljazeera.com/news/2020/01/balfour-palestinians-angered-trump-middle-east-plan-200128194613728.html.

Ibrahim, Raymond, "Egypt's Sisi: Islamic "Thinking" Is "Antagonizing the Entire World," January 1, 2015, http://www.raymondibrahim.com/2015/01/01/egypts-sisi-islamic-thinking-is-antagonizing-the-entire-world/thinking.

"Incitement against Israel in the Palestinian Authority," (לארשי דגן התסהה)
(תימע ריאמ ש"ע רורטלו ויעידומל עדימה זכרמ "היניפאמו הישרוש :תיניטסלפה תושרב),
Meir Amit Intelligence Terrorism Information Center, June 5, 2017,
https://www.terrorism-info.org.il/he/21215/.

Indyk, Martin, *Innocent Abroad: An Intimate Account of American Peace Di-plomacy in   the Middle East* (New York: Simon & Schuster, 2009).

"Iran Nuclear Deal: Key Details," *BBC News*, June 11, 2019, https://www.bbc.com/news/world-middle-east-33521655.

"Iran Students Refuse to Walk over US and Israeli flags," *BBC News*, January 12, 2020, https://www.bbc.com/news/av/world-middle-east-51085619/iran-students-refuse-to-walk-over-us-and-israeli-flags.

"Iranians Target Teheran Support for Palestinians amid Massive Protests" *The Times of Israel*, December 31, 2017, https://www.timesofisrael.com/iranians-target-tehrans-support-for-palestinians-amid-massive-pro-tests/

Israel's Foreign Ministry Facebook Page in Arabic https://www.facebook.com/IsraelArabic/posts/2039694549401276

Israel's Foreign Ministry Israel in Iraq Facebook page https://www.facebook.com/IsraelinIraqi/

"Is Sissi Losing His Grip on Egypt," *Al Jazeera*, April 28, 2016, http://www.aljazeera.com /news/2016/04/sisi-losing-grip-egypt-160426080703098.html.

"Israel, Saudi Arabia Said to Discuss Open Economic ties," *The Times of Israel*, June 17, 2017, http://www.timesofisrael.com/israel-saudi-arabi-said-to-discuss-open-economic-ties/.

Israeli, Rafael, *The Oslo Idea: The Euphoria of Failure*, (London: Routledge, 2017).

Jacob C., "Idea of Jordanian-Palestinian Confederation Resurfaces, Only To Be Rejected By Both Sides", *The Middle East Media Research Institute*, October 2, 2016, https://www.memri.org/reports/idea-jordanian-pal-estinian-confederation-resurfaces-only-be-rejected-both-sides.

Jamal, Amaney, *Barriers to Democracy: The Other Side of Social Capital in Pal-estine and the Arab World*, (Princeton: Princeton University Press, 2007).

"Joint U.S.-EU Statement following President Juncker's visit to the White House," July 25, 2018, http://europa.eu/rapid/press-release_STATE-MENT-18-4687_en.htm.

Kailani, Wasfi, "The Breakdown of Arab-Israeli Peace: Research from re-mote, Reciprocal Stereotypes and Anti-Normalization- The Case of Jordan," in *Muslim Attitudes to Jews and Israel: The Ambivalences of Rejec-tion, Antagonism, Tolerance and Cooperation*, Moshe Maoz ed., (Toronto: Sussex Academic Press, 2011).

Karsh, Ephraim, "Arafat's Grand Strategy," *Middle East Quarterly*, (Spring 2004): 3-11.

Kasnett, Israel, "Israeli and Jordanian experts downplay significance of peace-treaty changes", *Jewish News Syndicate*, October 23, 2018, https://www.jns.org/israeli-and-jordanian-experts-downplay-significance-of-peace-treaty-changes/.

Keinon, Herb "Jabari: Palestinians who Follow Peace Path with Israelis will be Harassed", *Jerusalem Post*, July 1, 2019.

Keppel, Gilles, *Jihad: The Trail of Political Islam*, (Cambridge: The Belknap Press of Harvard University Press, 2002).

Kershner, Isabel, "In West Bank, 99.7% of the Public Land Grants by Israel go to Settlers," *The New York Times*, July 18, 2018.

Khalidi, Raja & Samour, Sobhi "Neoliberalism as Liberation: The Statehood Program and the Remaking of the Palestinian National Movement," *Journal of Palestine Studies*, Vol. 40 No. 2, (Winter 2011): 6-25.

Khalidi, Rhashid, *The Iron Cage: The Story of Palestinian Struggle for Statehood*, (Boston: Beacon Press, 2nd edition, 2007).

Khalidi, Rashid, *Palestinian Identity: The Construction of Modern National Consciousness*, (New York: Columbia University Press, 1997).

Khalil, Asem, "Palestinians to Citizens", *Middle East Law and Governance*, Vol.6 (3), (2014): 204-224.

Kirpatrick, David D., "Tapes Reveal Egyptian Leaders' Tacit Acceptance of Jerusalem Move," *The New York Times*, January 6, 2018.

Kurtzer, Daniel, and Scott Lasensky, *Negotiating Arab-Israeli Peace: American Leadership in the Middle East* (Washington, DC: United States Institute of Peace, 2008).

Laqueur, Walter, "Is Peace in the Middle East Possible?" in *The Israel Arab Reader*, Walter Laqueur ed., (New York: The Citadel Press, 1968).

Lavy, Ephraim, "Hapalestinaim: Zehuyiot Kibutziot Mitharot Beheader Medina," (The Palestinians: Competing Identities in Light of State Absence,) in *Lekidut Hamedinah Haarabit Bemivhan*, *(The Unity of the Arab State under Test)*, Ignas Tamar ed., (Tel Aviv University, Moshe Dayan Center for Middle East and African Studies, 2006), 145-168.

Letter from President Bush to Prime Minister Sharon, The White House, April 14, 2004 http://georgewbush-whitehouse.archives.gov/news/releases/2004/04/20040414-3.htm.

Levi Eyal, "Shlomo Ben Ami Gives Up: Also with a left-wing government we would not have reached peace," *Maariv*, September 22, 2017 (from Hebrew ומלש ןב עמי םירמ סירדי :גס עס תלשממ שמאל אל היה שלוס).

Lewis, Bernard, *The Crisis of Islam: Holy War and Unholy Terror*, (New York: The Modern Library, 2003).

Lewis, Bernard, *The Multiple Identities of the Middle East*, (New York: Schoken Books, 1998).

Litvak, Meir, "Hamas, Palestinian Identity, Islam and National Sovereignty" (Hebrew) in *Lekidut Hamedinah Haarabit Bemivhan"* *(The Unity of the Arab State under Test)*, Ignas Tamar ed., (Tel Aviv University, Moshe Dayan Center for Middle East and African Studies, 2006), 169-186.

Litvak, Meir, "Radical Islamism and the Arab Upheaval," in Small Charles (ed), *The ISGAP Papers: Antisemitism in Comparative Perspective*, Volume II, Institute for the Study of Global Antisemitism and Policy (IS-GAP), (2016): 75-90.

Luft, Gal, "The Karine-A Affair: A Strategic Watershed in the Middle East?" *Washington Institute for Near East Policy*, January 30, 2002, http://www.washingtoninstitute.org /policy-analysis/view/the-karine-a-affair-a-strategic-watershed-in-the-middle-east .

Lynch, Mark, *The New Arab Wars, Uprising and Anarchy in the Middle East*, (New York: *Public Affairs*, 2016).

Maddy-Weitzmann, Bruce, "Morocco's Berbers and Israel," *Middle East Quarterly*, (Winter   2011): 79-85.

Magdy, Mirette, "Talks Underway to Build New Gas Pipeline to Egypt, Israel Says", Bloomberg News, January 15, 2019, https://www.bloomberg.com/news/articles/2019-01-15/talks-underway-to-build-new-gas-pipeline-to-egypt-israel-says.

Magid, Aron, "Jordan monarch's comments on Palestinians raise tensions in kingdom," *Al Monitor*, May 16, 2017 http://www.al-monitor.com/pulse/originals/2017/05/jordan-king- palestinians-terrorism.html#ixzz4kyaY8Y81.

Magid, Jacob, "Borders, Security, Jerusalem, settlements, refugees: Key elements of Trump plan," *The Times of Israel,* January 29, 2020, https://www.timesofisrael.com/borders-security-jerusalem-settlements-refugees-key-elements-of-trump-plan/.

Makovsky, David. "Imagining the Border: Options for Resolving the Israeli-Palestinian Territorial Issue," *Washington Institute for Near East Policy*, January   2011,   http://www.washingtoninstitute.org/policy-analysis/view/imagining-the-border-options- for-resolving-the-israeli-palestinian-territor.

Malley, Robert and Hussein Agha, "Camp David: A Tragedy of Errors", *New York Review of Books*, August 9, 2001.

Marcus, Itamar and Nan Jacques Zilberdik, "Deception: Betraying the Peace Process," *Palestinian Media Watch*, Jerusalem, 2011.

Marcus, Itamar, "Palestinian Authority Antisemitism Overview of 2015," Palestinian Media Watch, January 12, 2016, http://www.palwatch.org/STORAGE/special% 20reports /summary%20report%20on%20PA%20antisemitism%20in%202015.pdf.

Marcus, Itamar, "The Unique Nature of Palestinian Antisemitism: A Foundation of Palestinian National Identity" in *Global Antisemitism: A Crisis of Modernity*, Charles Small ed., Vol. 5, Institute for the Study of Global Antisemitism and Policy, (2013): 115-122.

Marcus, Itamar and Nana Jacques Zilberdick, "PA kids' Education: "To war that will... destroy the Zionist's soul", *Palestinian Media Watch*, April 17, 2013 http://palwatch.org /main.aspx?fi=157&doc_id=8804.

Marks, Monica, "Tunisia" in Hamid, Shadi and McCants, William, *Rethinking Political Islam*, (New York, Oxford University press, 2017).

Martinez, Javier, "Fear of the State, Fear of Society," in Corradi, Juan E., Weiss Fagen, Patricia and Garretón, and Manuel Antonio (eds.), *Fear of the Edge: State Terror and Resistance in Latin America*, (Berkley, University of California Press, 1992), 142-161.

Masalha, Salman, "The Massacre of Arab Nationalism", *Haaretz*, April 9, 2018, https://www.haaretz.com/opinion/.premium-the-massacre-of-arab-nationalism-1.5979184.

Melson, Robert, "Modern Genocide in Rwanda: Ideology, Revolution, War and Mass Murder in an African State," in Gellatelly and Kiernan, (eds.), *The Specter of Genocide: Mass Murder in Historical Perspective*, (New York: Cambridge University Press, 2003).

"Mideast Peace Process Futile While U.S. in Charge, Lula says," *Fox News Latino*, December 20, 2010, http://latino.foxnews.com/latino/politics/2010/12/20/mideast-peace-process-futile-charge-lula-says/.

Miller, Aaron David. Interview with Jeffrey Goldberg, "Are Settlements the Key to Middle East Peace," *The Atlantic*, October 2010, https://www.theatlantic. com/international/ archive/2010/10/are-settlements-the-key-to-middle-east-peace-updated/64027/ .

Miller, Aharon D. *The Much Too Promised Land: America's Elusive Search for Arab-Israeli Peace*, (New York: Bantam, 2008).

Mishal, Shaul and Selah, Avraham, *Zman Hahamas (The Hamas Wind)*, (Hebrew version) Miskal-Yedihot Ahronoth and Chemed Books, Tel Aviv, 1999.

Mitchel, George J and Sachar, Alon, *A Path to Peace: A Brief History Israeli-Palestinian Negotiations and a Way Forward in the Middle East*, (New York: Simon and Schuster, 2016).

Momani, Bessma, *Arab Dawn: Arab Youth and the Dividend they will Bring*, (Toronto: University of Toronto Press, 2015).

Morris, Benny, *One State, Two States: Resolving the Israel-Palestine Conflict*, (New Haven: Yale University Press, 2009).

Moubayed, Sami, "Hamas powerless as ISIS gains ground in Palestine," *Asian Times*, January 11, 2017, http://www.atimes.com/article/hamas-powerless-isis-gains-ground-palestine/.

Muasher, Marwan. *The Second Arab Awakening and the Battle for Pluralism*, (New Haven: Yale University Press, 2014).

Muñoz, Carlos, "Russia calls for cultural autonomy' for ethnic Kurds in postwar Syria", *The Washington Times,* February 2, 2017.

Muravchik, Joshua, Making David into Goliath: How the World Turned Against Israel, (New York: Encounter Books, 2015).

"Myths and Facts about the Peace Process," *The Geneva Initiative,* http://www.geneva-accord.org/mainmenu/myths-facts-about-the-peace-process.

Nasser, Gamal Abdel, "Address by President Gamal Abdel Nasser at the Meeting of the National Assembly's Ordinary Session," Cairo, Egypt, 26, March 1964. Section 32, https://archive.org/stream/Nasser2_201401/Nasser2_djvu.txt

Nelson, Cary. *Dream Deferred A Concise Guide to the Israeli /Palestinian Conflict & The Movement to Boycott Israel,* (Chicago and New York MLA Members for Scholars Rights and Indiana University Press, 2016).

Nhamias, Omri, "Saudi Arabia, Egypt, Qatar, UAE welcome Trump peace plan," *The Jerusalem Post,* January 29, 2020, https://www.jpost.com/Middle-East/Saudi-Arabia-Egypt-Qatar-UAE-welcome-Trump-peace-plan-615752?utm_source=Jeeng.

Nissenbaum, Dion, "Arab Leaders' Support for Mideast Peace Plan Marks a Regional Shift," *The Wall Street Journal,* January 30, 2020.

Noueihed, Lin & Warren, Alex, *The Battle for the Arab Spring: Revolution, Counterrevolution and the Making of a New Era,* (New Haven: Yale University Press, 2012).

O'Driscoll, Dylan "Autonomy Impaired: Centralisation, Authoritarianism and the Failing Iraqi State," *Ethnopolitics,* 16:4, (2017): 315-332, DOI: 10.1080/17449057.2015.1086126 .

Oren, Michael B., *Ally: My Journey across the American-Israeli Divide* (New York: Random House, 2015).

Oren, Michael, *Six Days of War: June 1967 and the Making of the Modern Middle East,* (Oxford: Oxford University Press, 2002).

Pandith, Farah, *How We Win: How Cutting –Edge Entrepreneurs, Political Visionaries, Enlightened Business Leaders, and Social Media Mavens Can Defeat the Extremist Threat,* (New York: Custom House, 2019).

"Palestinians Must Make Peace or Shut up, Saudi Crown Prince said to tell US Jews," *The Times of Israel,* April 29,2016, https://www.timesofisrael.com/palestinians-must-make-peace-or-shut-up-saudi-crown-prince-said-to-tell-us-jews/.

Patai, Raphael, *The Arab Mind,* (New York: Hatherleigh Press, 2002).

Peace to Prosperity: A Vision to Improve the Lives of the Palestinian and Israeli People, The White House, January 2020.

Pearlman, Wendy, "Spoiling Inside and Out: Internal Political Contestation and the Middle East Peace Process" in *Journal of International Security,* Vol. 33, No. 3, (Winter 2008/09): 79-109.

Pearlman, Wendy *Violence, Nonviolence, and the Palestinian National Movement*, (New York: Cambridge University Press, 2011).

Peres, Shimon, with Aryeh Naor, *The New Middle East*, (New York: Henry Holt and Company. 1993).

Perthes, Volker, "State Building, National Security and War Preparation in Syria," in *War, Institutions, and Social Change in the Middle East*, Steven Heydemann ed., (Berkeley: University of California Press, 2000), 149-173.

Pickard, Duncan, "Prospects for Implementing Democracy in Tunisia", in *Mediterranean Politics*, Vol. 19, No. 2, (2014): 259-264, http://dx.doi.org/10.1080/13629395. 2014.917796.

Pileggi, Tamar, "Labor approves Herzog's unilateral pullout plan", *The Times of Israel*, February 7, 2016, http://www.timesofisrael.com/labor-approves-herzogs-unilateral-pullout-plan/.

Pipes, Daniel, "A New Strategy for Israeli Victory", *Commentary Magazine*, January 2017: 13-18.

Pipes, Daniel "Give Gaza to Egypt", *The Jerusalem Post*, January 30, 2018, http://www.daniel pipes.org/5426/give-gaza-to-egypt.

Pfeffer, Anshel, *Bibi: The Turbulent Life and Times of Benjamin Netanyahu*, (New York: Basic Books, 2018).

Pollack, Kenneth M., "Learning from Israel's Political Assassination Program," a review of Ronen Bergman, *Rise and Kill First: The Secret History of Israel's targeted Assassinations*, *The New York Times*, March 7, 2018.

Pollock, David, "New Palestine Poll Shows Hardline Views but Some Pragmatism Too," *Washington Institute for Near East Policy*, June 25, 2014, http://www.washington institute.org/policy-analysis/view/new-palestinian-poll-shows-hardline-views-but-some-pragmatism-too.

Pressman, Jeremy, "The Second Intifada: Background and Causes of the Israeli /Palestinian Conflict", The *Journal of Conflict Studies*, The Gregg Centre for the Study of War and Society, 23, No. 2, (2003).

Prince Turki Al Faisal, "Mr. Obama, we are not Free Riders," *Arab News*, March 14, 2016, http://www.arabnews.com/columns/news/894826#.VubddRYBwbU.twitter.

Pryce Jones, David, *Closed Circle: An Interpretation of the Arabs*, (Chicago: Ivan R, Dee, 2002).

Public Opinion Poll 63, Palestinian Center for Policy and Survey Research, March 26, 2017, http://www.pcpsr.org/en/node/688.

Rabil, Robert, *Embattled Neighbors: Syria, Israel and Lebanon*, (Boulder, CO: Lynne Rienner Publishers, 2003).

Rabil, Robert, *Salafism in Lebanon: From Apoliticism to Transnational Jihadism*, (Washington, DC: Georgetown University Press, 2014).

Rabinowitz, Itamar, *Waging Peace: Israel and the Arabs, 1948-2003*, (Princeton: Princeton University Press, 2004).

Raghava, Sudaran and Hendrix, Steve, "Arab governments denounce Israel's plans to annex the West Bank, warning it will imperil regional security and peace building. But will Israel listen?" *The Washington Post*, June 27, 2020.

Rasgon, Adam, "Trump ties and Iran fears: Why US' Arab allies opting not to rebuke peace plan," *The Times of Israel*, January 30, 2020, http://www.timesofisrael.com/keen-on-ties-most-   of-us-arab-allies-choose-not-to-directly-rebuke-peace-plan/.

"Remarks of President Barack Obama To the People of Israel", The White House, March 12, 2013, https://obamawhitehouse.archives.gov/the-press-office/2013/03/21/remarks-president-barack-obama-people-israel.

Rhymond, Jonathan, *The Failure of the Oslo Process: Inherently Flawed or Flawed Implementation?* The Begin-Sadar Center for Strategic Studies, Bar-Ilan University, Mideast Security and Policy Studies, No. 76, (March 2008).

"A Rising Tide Lifts Mood in the Developing World", Pew Research Center, July 24, 2007, http://www.pewglobal.org/2007/07/24/a-rising-tide-lifts-mood-in-the-developing-world/.

Robbins, Michael and Jamal, Amaney, "The State of Social Justice in the Arab World: The Arab Uprisings of 2011 and Beyond" in *Contemporary Readings in Law and Social Justice* Vol. 8, 1, (2016): 127–157.

Rosen, David, *Armies of the Young: Child Soldiers in War and Terrorism*, (New Jersey: Rutgers University Press, 2005).

Ross, Dennis and David Makovsky, *Myths, Illusions and Peace*, (New York: Penguin Books, 2010).

Ross, Dennis and Makovsky, David "If Trump Wants the Ultimate Deal, He Must Not Repeat These Mistakes," Washington Institute for Near East Policy, October 2, 2018, https://www.washingtoninstitute.org/policy-analysis/view/if-trump-wants-the-ultimate-deal-he-must-not-repeat-these-mistakes,

Ross, Dennis, *Doomed to Succeed The U.S-Israel Relationship from Truman to Obama*, (New York: Farrar, Straus and Giroux, 2015).

Ross, Dennis. *The Missing Peace: The Inside Story of the Fight for Middle East Peace*, (New York: Farrar, Strauss and Giroux, 2004).

Roy, Oliver "The Transformation of the Arab World" in *Journal of Democracy*, Vol. 23, Number 3, (July 2012): 5-18.

Rubin, Barry, *Revolution until Victory? The Politics and History of the PLO*, (Cambridge: Harvard University, 1994).

Rumley, Grant and Tibon, Amir, *The Last Palestinian: The Rise and Reign of Mahmoud Abbas*, (New York: Prometheus Books, 2017).

"Russia-drafted new Constitution Promises Greater Autonomy to Kurds",

The New Arab, January 26, 2017, https://www.alaraby.co.uk/english/news/2017/1/26/russia-drafted-new-constitution-for-syria-promises-kurds-greater-autonomy.

Saadoun, Mustafa, "If Iran has its way, Abadi won't see a second term in Iraq", Al Monitor, April 21, 2017, http://www.al-monitor.com/pulse/ru/originals/2017/07/iran-iraq-prime-minister-abadi-khamenei-pmu-shiite-militias.html#ixzz4yv0DAyve.

Sachar, Howard, *A History of Israel: From the Rise of Zionism to Our Time,* (New York: Alfred Knopf, 2003).

Said, Aly, Abdel Monem, Feldman, Shai and Shikaki, Khalil, *Arabs and Israelis: Conflict and Peacemaking in the Middle East,* (New York: Palgrave, Mc Millan, 2013).

Said, Edward, "The Morning After," *London Review of Books,* October 21, 1993.

Said, Edward, "The One State Solution," *New York Times,* January 10, 1999.

Saif, Sara, interview with author, July 10, 2019.

Saleh, Yasmine, "Exclusive: With Muslim Brotherhood crushed, Egypt sets sights on Hamas", Reuters, January 14, 2014, https://www.reuters.com/article/us-egypt-gaza/exclusive-with-muslim-brotherhood-crushed-egypt-sets-sights-on-hamas-idUSBREA0D09D20140114.

Salwha, Abdullah, (President of the Center for Israel Studies, Amman), interview with author, April 23, 2018.

Samara, Munif, in Speckhard, Anne, "The Jihad in Jordan: Drivers of Radicalization into Violent Extremism in Jordan," *International Center for the Study of Violent Extremism,* March 25, 2017.

Sandler, Shmuel, "The Arab Spring and the Linkage between Israeli Domestic and Foreign Policies," in *The Arab Spring, Democracy and Security: Domestic and International Ramifications,* Ebraim Inbar, ed., (New York: Routledge, 2013).

Sasson, Joseph, *Anatomy of Authoritarianism in the Arab Republics,* (Cambridge: Cambridge University Press, 2016).

"Saudi king tells Trump he wants a fair and permanent solution for Palestinians", *Reuters,* September 6, 2020 https://www.theguardian.com/world/2020/sep/07/saudi-king-tells-trump-he-wont-normalise-israeli-ties-without-palestinian-statehood.

"Saudi Bid's Arabs Destroy Israel: New Ruler Would Sacrifice 10,000,000 if Necessary to 'Liberate' Palestine," *New York* Times, January 10, 1954, https://www.nytimes.com/1954/01/10/archives/saud-bids-arabs-destroy-israel-new-ruler-would-sacrifice-10000000.html.

Savir, Uri, "Europe and the Multilateral Negotiations" in Robin, and Tamar Hermann. *The Arab-Israeli Negotiations: Political Positions and Conceptual Framework* (Tel Aviv Publishing House: Papyrus, 1993), 116-121.

Savir, Uri, *Scars of War, Wounds of Peace: The Israeli-Arab Tragedy,* (Oxford: Oxford University Press, 2006).

Sayegh, Fayez, "The Camp David Agreement and the Palestine Problem," *Journal of Palestine Studies,* Vol. 8, No. 2 (Winter, 1979): 3-40.

Schanzer, Jonathan. *State of Failure: Yasser Arafat, Mahmoud Abbas, and the Unmaking of the Palestinian State,* (New York: Palgrave McMillan, 2013).

Schiff, Zeev and Yaari, Ehud, *Intifada,* (New York: Simon and Schuster, 1989).

Schwartz, Adi & Wilf, Einat, *The War of Return: How Western Indulgence of the Palestinian Dream has obstructed the Path to Peace* (New York: All Points Books, 2020).

Schwartz, Felicia "Trump Middle East Peace Plan Calls for $50 Billion in Investment", Market Screener, June 22, 2019, https://www.market-screener.com/news/Trump-Middle-East-Peace-Plan-Calls-for-50-Billion-in-Investment-Update--28799216/.

"Scores Wounded as Lebanon's Anti-gov't Protests Turn Violent," *Al Jazeera,* January 18, 2020. https://www.aljazeera.com/news/2020/01/lebanon-anti-government-protests-turn-violent-beirut-200118160101017.html.

Selah, Avraham" The First Intifada: How the Arab-Israeli Conflict Was Transformed', *Haaretz,* December 13, 2012, https://www.haaretz.com/.premium-first-intifada-a-watershed-moment-1.5272288.

Selman, Yousuf, "Hamas distances itself from Muslim Brotherhood, seeks new role in region", Daily Sabah, Mideast, February 17, 2017, https://www.dailysabah.com/mideast/2017/02/25/hamas-distances-itself-from-muslim-brotherhood-seeks-new-role-in-region.

Semelin, Jacques, "Analysis of Mass Crime: Ethnic Cleansing in the Former Yugoslavia 1991-1999," in Gellately, Robert and Kiernan, Ben, *The Specter of Genocide: Mass Murder in Historical Perspective,* (New York: Cambridge University Press, 2003).

Sewell, Abby, "Families of victims reflect on tragedy one month after Beirut port explosion", *Al Arabiya English,* September 5, 2020, https://english.alarabiya.net/en/News/middle-east/2020/09/05/Families-of-victims-reflect-on-tragedy-one-month-after-Beirut-port-explosion#:~:text=At%20least%20191%20people%20died%20in%20the%20blast,wall%20on%20the%20side%20of%20the%20road%20

Shafir, Gershon, *A Half Century of Occupation: Israel, Palestine, and the World Most Intractable Conflict,* (Oakland: University of California Press, 2017).

Sharm El-Sheikh, Fact-Finding Committee Report, U.S State Department, April 30, 2001, see "What Happened?" https://2001-2009.state.gov/p/nea/rls/rpt/3060.htm.

Sharnoff, Michael, "The Pervasiveness of Antisemitism in Jordanian Media and Prospects for Change," Foreign Policy Research Institute, September 20, 2017, https://www.fpri.org/ article /2017/09/ pervasiveness-anti-semitism-jordan-change/.

Shehadi: "Lebanon Never Developed A Strong 20th Century State, And That's Good for The Future", interview with Suzette Grillot and Annie Davenport, KGOU Radio (Oklahoma), 02/17/2017, https://www.kgou. org/post/shehadi-lebanon-never-developed-strong-20th-century-state-and-thats-good-future.

Shehadi, Nadim, interview with author, February 21, 2019.

Shlaim, Avi, The Iron Wall: Israel and the Arab World, (New York: W.W. Norton & Company, 2014).

Siegman, Henry. "Sharon and the Future of Palestine," The New York Review of Books, December 2, 2004, http://www.nybooks.com/articles/2004/12/02/sharon-and-the-future-of-palestine/-.

Simpson, Emile, "Iraq's Dangerous Moment: Nationalists and Iran sympathizers vie for power in Baghdad," National Review, Vol. 69, 21, (December 2017).

Sky, Emma, "Mission Still not Accomplished: Why the United States Should Not Leave," Foreign Affairs, Vol. 6, 6, (November/December 2017): 9-15.

Smyth, Phillip, The Shiite Jihad in Syria and Its Regional Effects, (Washington DC: The Washington Institute for Near East Policy, 2015).

Sorel, Georges, Reflections on Violence, (Cambridge: Cambridge University Press, 1999).

Speckhard, Anne, Talking to Terrorists: Understanding the Psychosocial Motivations of Militant Jihadi Terrorists, Mass Hostage Takers, Suicide Bombers and Martyrs, (McLean VA: Advance Press, 2012).

Stein, Kenneth W., "Los Acuerdos de Camp David de 1978: una nueva mirada de como Egipto e Israel pasaron de la Guerra a la paz," Center for Israel Education, September 26, 2018, https://israeled.org/los-acuerdos-de-camp-david-de-1978/.

Stein, Kenneth W., "Palestinians at the Negotiating Table: Past Meets Present? in Focus, Jewish Policy Center, Fall 2007, https://www. jewishpolicycenter.org/200708/31/palestinians-at-the-negotiating-table-past-meets/.

Stein, Kenneth and Samuel Lewis, Making Peace between Arabs and Israelis: Fifty Years of Negotiating Experiences, United States Institute of Peace, October 1991.

Suchkov, Maxim "How Russia sees Kurdish quest for autonomy," Al Monitor, May 6, 2016, http://www.al-monitor.com/pulse/originals/2016/05/russia-syria-iraq-kurds-quest-autonomy.html.

Susser, Asher, "Israel, Jordan, and Palestine: One State, Two States or Three?" in *The Yale Papers: Antisemitism in Comparative Perspective*, Charles Asher Small ed., *Institute for the Study of Global Antisemitism and Policy*, (New York: 2015), 485-496.

Susser, Asher, "The Two-State Solution: Getting from Here to There," *Foreign Policy Research Institute*, October 2012, http://www.fpri.org/docs/media/Susser_-Two_State_Solution.pdf.

Swisher, Clayton, *The Palestine Papers: The End of the Road*, (United Kingdom: Hesperus Press Limited, 2011).

Shehadi, Nadim, interview with author, February 21, 2019.

Shehadi, Nadim, 'Lebanon Never Developed A Strong 20th Century State, and that's Good for the Future'," interview with Suzette Grillot and Annie Davenport, KGOU Radio (Oklahoma), February 17, 2017.

"Suha Arafat Admits Husband Premeditated Intifada," *The Jerusalem Post*, December 29, 2012, http://www.jpost.com/Middle-East/Suha-Arafat-admits-husband-premeditated-Intifada.

Teller, Neville "Israel-Palestinian Peace: The 'Regional Umbrella' Approach", *The Eurasia Review News and Analysis*, March 31, 2017, https://www.eurasiareview.com/31032017-israel-palestinian-peace-the-regional-umbrella-approach-oped/.

"The ADL Global 100: An Index of Anti-Semitism," May 2014, http://global100.adl.org/.

"The Arab Peace Initiative," the Council of Arab States at the Summit level at its 14th Ordinary Session, Official Translation of the full text of Saudi Inspired peace plan adopted by the Arab Summit, Beirut, 2002, www.al-bab.com/arab/docs/league/peace02.htm.

"The Cairo Agreement", Palestine Refugee Research Net, http://prrn.mcgill.ca/ research/papers /brynen2_09.htm.

"The Constitutional Amendments Do Not Establish A Democracy that Supports Women in Politics," Position Paper, *Nazra for Feminist Studies*, February 17, 2019.

The Covenant of the Islamic Resistance Movement, Avalon Project, Yale University, August 1988, http://avalon.law.yale.edu/20th_century/hamas.asp

"The Raqqa Diaries: Life under ISIS Rule," *The Guardian*, February 26, 2017, https://www.theguardian.com/books/2017/feb/26/the-raqqa-diaries-life-under-isis-rule-samer-mike-thomson-syria.

"The Slippery Slope of Internet Censorship in Egypt", *Internet Monitor*, October 17, 2017, https://thenetmonitor.org/bulletins/the-slippery-slope-of-internet-censorship-in-egypt.

"Three Iraqi Delegations said to Make Unprecedented Israel Visits, Meet Officials," *The Times of Israel*, January 6, 2019, https://www.timesofisrael.com/three-iraqi-delegations-said-to-make-unprecedented-israel-visits-meet-officials.

Telhami, Shibley, *The World through Arab Eyes: Arab Public Opinion and the Reshaping of the Middle East,* (New York Basic Books, 2013).

Tessler, Mark *A History of the Israeli-Palestinian Conflict,* (Bloomington and Indianapolis: Indiana University Press, 1994).

TheBeilin-AbuMazenDocumentO,October31,1995,*TheReutInstitute,*http:// reut-institute.org/data/uploads/ExternaDocuments/20050328%20 -%20The%20Beilin-Abu%20Mazen%20Document.pdf.

The Covenant of the Islamic Resistance Movement, 18 August 1988, Article 1 http://avalon.law.yale.edu/20th_century/hamas.asp.

The Palestinian National Charter: Resolutions of the Palestine National Council July 1-17, 1968, The Avalon Project, Yale Law School, Article 4, http:// avalon.law .yale.edu/20th_century/plocov.asp.

"The Six Days War": *Speech by President Nasser to Egyptian National Assembly,* May 29, 1967. http://www.mideastweb.org/nasser29may67.htm.

"They Say, We Say: "The term 'settlement bloc' merely describes an objective reality on the ground." Americans for Peace Now, https://peacenow.org/page.php?name=settlement-bloc-objct-reality#. XxG-Ui2ZPow

Tibon, Amir, "Obama's Detailed Plans for Mideast Peace Revealed - and How Everything Fell Apart," *Haaretz,* June 8, 2017.

Tilly, Charles and Sidney Tarrow, *Contentious Politics,* (Oxford University Press, Inc., 2015).

Times of Israel Staff "Hamas to join Palestinian leadership meeting against Trump plan – officials", *Times of Israel,* January 28, 2020, https://www. timesofisrael.com/hamas-to-join-palestinian-leadership-meeting-against-trump-plan-officials/ .

Tocqueville, Alexis de, *The Ancien Regime and the French Revolution,* Elster, Jon (ed.), (New York: Cambridge University Press, 2011).

Toynbee, Arnold and J. L Talmon, "The Argument between Arabs and Jews" in *The Israel Arab Reader,* Walter Laqueur ed. (New York: The Citadel Press, 1968), 260-267.

Trager, Eric, *Arab Fall: How the Muslim Brotherhood Won and Lost Egypt in 891 Days,*   (Washington DC: Georgetown University Press, 2016).

Trager, Eric, "Egypt Two Years After Morsi: Part I," Testimony submitted to the House Committee on Foreign Affairs *The Washington Institute for Near East Policy,* May 20, 2015, http://docs.house.gov/meetings/FA/ FA13/20150520/103497/HHRG-114-FA13-Wstate-TragerE-20150520. pdf.

"Trump plan would see Palestinian state on up to 70% of West Bank, reports say," *The Times of Israel,* January 26, 2020, https://www.timesofisreal.com/trump-plan-would-see-palestinian-state-on-up-to-70-of-west-bank-reports-say/.

"Under El-Sisi, chapter on Camp David Accords added to Egyptian Schoolbook," *Jewish News Service*, February 16, 2016, http://www.jns. org/news-briefs/2016/2/17/under-el-sissi-chapter-on-camp-david-added-to-egypt-schoolbooks#.V1xlCnM2qvp=.

"Voices from the Arab World: The New Arab Summit is Old," *The Jerusalem Post*, April 11, 2019.

Voigtlander, Nico and Voth, Joachim, "Nazi Indoctrination and anti-Semitic beliefs in Germany," Proceeding of the National Academy of Sciences, Vol. 112, 26, (June, 20, 2015), http://www.pnas.org/content/112/26.toc.

Wagner, Kevin M. and Gainous, Jaison, "Digital Uprising: The Internet Revolution in the Middle East," *Journal of Information Technology & Politics*, 10:3, (2013): 261-275.

Wainer, David and Benmeleh, Yaacov, "Israel-Egypt $15 Billion Gas Deal Boosts Energy Hub Prospects," Bloomberg News, February 19, 2018, https://www.bloomberg.com/news/articles/2018-02-19/noble-delek-sign-15-billion-deal-to-export-israel-gas-to-egypt .

Wallace, Kelly, "Sharon: "'Occupation' terrible for Israel, Palestinians" *CNN*, May 27, 2003. http://www.cnn.com/2003/WORLD/meast/05/26/mideast/.

Webman, Esther, "The Image of the Jew/Zionist/Isralei in the Arab World" in *Muslim Attitudes to Jews and Israel: The Ambivalences of Rejection, Antagonism, Tolerance and Cooperation* Moshe Mao ed., (Brighton, England: Sussex Academic Press, 2011), 48-68.

Weiner, Justus Reid, "Palestinian Children and the New Cult of Martyrdom," *Harvard Israel Review*, Issue 3, (Summer 2003).

Weitzman, Bruce Maddy, "Arabs and the Abdullah Plan," in *Middle East Quarterly*, (Summer 2010), 3-12.

Wermenbol Grace, "Disrupting a delicate status quo: The Hamas crackdown on Salafi-jihadists," October 22, 2019, https://www.mei.edu /publications/disrupting-delicate-status-quo-hamas-crackdown-salafi-jihadists

Weymouth, Lally, "Egyptian President Abdel Fatah al-Sisi, who talks to Netanyahu 'a lot,' says his country is in danger of collapse," interview with Egyptian President Abdel Fatah al-Sisi *Washington Post*, March 12, 2015.

Wike, Richard, "Widespread concerns about extremism in Muslim nations, and little support for it," *PEW Research Center*, February 5, 2015, http://www.pewresearch.org/fact-tank/2015/02/05/extremism-in-muslim-nations/.

Winter, Offer, "El Sissi's First Year as President," in *Strategic Assessment*, Vol. 18, No. 2,(July 2015).

Wistrich, Robert *Antisemitism*, (New York: Pantheon Books, 1991.

Wright, Robin, *Dreams and Shadows: The Future of the Middle East*, (New York: The Penguin Group, 2008).

Yaari, Ehud, "Israeli-Egyptian peace: Forty Years After the 1973 War and Holding," *Washington Institute for Near East Policy*, October 2, 2013, http://www.washingtoninstitute.org/policy-analysis/view/israeli-egyptian-peace-forty-years-after-the-1973-war-and-holding.

Yahya, Maha, "The Middle East's Lost Decades," *Foreign Affairs*, Vol. 98, No. 6, (November/December 2019).

Yakobson, Alexander and Rubinstein, Amnon *Israel and the Family of Nations*, (London: Routledge, 2010).

Yerkes, Sarah, "What Egypt under Sissi is really like for Christian Coptics," Brookings Institute   June 20, 2016, https://www.brookings.edu/blog/markaz/2016/06/20/what-egypt-under-   sissi-is-really-like-for-coptic-christians/ .

"Young Iraqis Risk Prison to Reconnect with Israelis," *Jewish Refugees Blogspot*, September 24, 2018, http://jewishrefugees.blogspot.com/2018/09/young-iraqis-risk-prison-to-reconnect.html .

Zelnick, Robert. *Israel's Unilateralism: Beyond Gaza*. (Stanford: Hoover Institute Press, 2006).

Index

A

Abadi, Haider Al, 129, 134

Abbas, Mahmoud, 6, 10, 11, 17, 24, 30, 35–37, 41–46, 49–51, 72, 73, 76, 159, 164

Abderrhaim, Chhaibi, 150–51

Abu Ala, 26, 43

Abu Dis, 18, 21–22, 158

Abu Mazen (See Mahmud Abbas)

Abu Qatada, 68

Abu Salma, 72

Afghanistan, 63, 68

Aflaq, Michel, 55

Agha, Hussein, 27

Ahed Tamimi, 146

Ahmadinejad, Mahmoud, 115

Al-Ahram, 99

AIPAC (American Israel Public Affairs Committee), 47, 100

Ajami, Fouhad, 99

Al Ahram, 123

Al Alusi, Mithal, 149

Al Aqsa Brigades, 32, 158

Al Attiya, Ghassan, 135

Al Azhar University, 114

Al Bashir, Omar, 159

Al Bijar, Salah Al din, 92

Al Jazeera, 44, 117, 137–38

Al Kalifa, Khalid Bin Ahmed, 117

Al Nusra, 68

Al Qaeda, 35, 66, 80, 84, 103, 128, 130, 170

Al Samawi, Mohammed, 145

Al Zarqawi, Abu Musab, 68

Alexandria, 177

Algiers Declaration, 43

Allawi, Iyad, 128, 134

Alpher, Yossi, 5–6

Alusi, Mithal, 149

Aly, Said , 95

Anan, Sami, 123

Aniska, Seth, 6

Annapolis Conference, 3

annexation, 14, 23, 39, 48, 93, 158, 160–162, 167

Anti-Christian, 123

Anti-Defamation League, 78

anti-imperialism, 56

anti-Israel, 9–10, 18–19, 62, 72, 76–77, 80, 98–100, 118, 120–21, 137, 150–52, 154, 155, 173, 176–77

Anti-Israel propaganda, 9, 18–19

anti-monarchism, 56

Anti-semitism, 78–79, 101, 143, 148, 174,

anti-Zionism, 4, 56, 87, 143

Anziska, Seth, 6,

Arab: intellectuals, 152, 177; Israeli Relations, 109; public opinion, 121, 144, 153; states and societies, 11; Youth, 140

Arab governments, 131, 135

Arab Higher Committee, 87

Arab Human Development Report, 140

Arab lands, 171, 177–78

Arab League, 56, 90, 92, 107, 160, 170
Arab Peace Initiative, 107–9, 113, 160, 171–72, 175
Arab Spring, 9–10, 12, 44–45, 100, 118–23, 125–53, 160, 176–77
Arab states, civil society, 12
Arab Sunni states, 111
Arab-Israeli cooperation, 85
Arafat: Suha, 29; Yasser, 4, 5, 10–11, 15–27, 29–37, 43–44, 61-63, 70–72, 83, 95–97, 168, 172
Arafat-Hussein agreement, 163
Araj, Bader, 74–75
area a, 15–16, 35, 175
area b, 15–16, 19, 61
area c, 3, 16, 39, 48, 175
armistice lines of 1949, 38
Armon, Hanatziv, 47
Asharq Al Awsat, 148
Aspden, Rachel, 138
Assa, Hafiz, 106
Assad, 104–5, 107, 110–11, 145; Bashar, 68, 111, 145; Hafez , 104, 106
Assad regime, 84, 104, 106, 128, 145–46
Atallah, Samir, 147
authoritarian state (s), 45, 103, 104, 108, 137, 144
autonomy, 6, 13, 70, 81
Ayn Al Helweh, 67
Aziz, Basma Abdel , 137
Azzam, Abdallah, 68

B
Baath Party (Iraq), 55, 148
Bab Al-Mandab Strait, 115
Baghdad Pact, 56
Bahai, 123
Bahrain, xi, 110, 116–19, 144, 156, 159, 161, 172

Bahrain Conference, 157
Bakhail, Khaldoon, 144
Balfour Declaration, 159
Barak, Ehud, 2, 20–23, 25, 27–28, 44, 46
Barghouti, Marwan, 76
Basheer, Tahseen, 94
Batel, 133
Begin: Benny, 20; Menachem, 5–6
Beilin, Yossi, 6–7, 162
Beilin-Abu Mazen Agreement, 18, 36
Bekah Valley, 105
Belaya, Chokri, 126
Belhaj Abd Al Hakim, 127
Ben Ali, Zine El Abidine, 96
Bengio, Ofra, 148
Benny Morris, 166
Berbers, friendship, 151
Bethlehem, 19, 36, 68
Bilateral negotiations, engagement, 3, 7, 9, 11, 81, 92–93, 100, 118, 164, 172
Bin Laden, Osama, 68, 103, 130
Bin Salman, Mohammed, 112, 131–32 (*see also* Prince Salman or Crown Prince)
Bloggers, 138
Bloom, Mia, 32
Blue and White Party, 159
Bourguiba, Habib, 150
Braude, Joseph, 151–52, 177
British Mandate, 57, 85
bureaucracy, 31, 157
Bush, George W., 3, 26–27, 34- 39, 47-48, 97, 103, 108,
Byman, Daniel, 121

C
Cairo, 92, 115, 120, 169; agreements, 61
Camp David Agreement between

Israel and Egypt, 6, 13, 22, 92-93, 99
Camp David Conference between Israel and Palestinians, 1-2, 4, 11, 18, 20–22, 25, 27–30, 44, 70, 172
Carter Administration, 13
Casablanca Protocol, 56, 169
censorship, 138–39
China, 54
Christian Arabs, 55
Christians, 41, 61, 149
citizenship diplomacy, 177–78
Civil society, 10, 12, 14, 28, 45, 51, 99–100, 104, 119–22, 130, 132–33, 135–37, 142, 144, 152–53, 155, 176-178
civil society, Egypt, 133
civil war, 61, 80, 84, 88, 107, 110, 119–20, 124, 128–29, 133, 135
Clinton, Bill, 2, 11, 21, 23, 24–27, 83, 96–97, 108,
Clinton Parameters, 2, 25–26, 28, 49, 95, 169
Cohen, Shalom, 150
Constituency; Islamic Constituency, 44, 97
constitution, constitutional, 64, 114, 122–23, 127, 133, 146, 150
Cook, Steven , 120
Coptic Christians, 114, 133
corruption, 29, 31, 41–42, 45, 135, 141
Custodianship, 23

D
Danin, Robert, 77
Darwish, Mahmoud, 71
Dawisha, Adeed , 130
De Pianta, Gianni, 134
Declaration of Principles (DOP), 7
democracy, 36, 45, 108, 119–20, 122, 125-127, 130–37, 167

Democratic Party of the Iraqi nation, 149
disengagement policy, 38–40, 162
Druze, 61
dual power, 41

E
East Jerusalem, 23–25, 41, 47, 49, 158, 160, 175
Egypt, 54–55, 84–85, 91–96, 98–99, 107, 112–17, 119–20, 122–27, 132, 138–40, 167–69; abandonment of multilateral negotiations, 85; economy, 169; intellectuals, 92; judiciary, 123; National Assembly, 88, 193; political parties, 124; Supreme Court, 124
Egyptian Air, 98
Egyptian/Israeli agreement, 13
Egyptian/Israeli Camp David Accords, 6

El-Dessouki, Mustafa, 152
Elections, 7–8, 20–22, 26, 40, 44, 46, 51, 95, 97, 110–11, 122, 124–25, 127–29
Ellul, Jacques, 78
El Sherif, Ashraf , 139
El Sisi, 113–16, 125, 132–34, 169
Ennahda, 125–26, 150
Erekat, Saeb, 40, 42, 50
Eshki, Anwar, 112
Europe, 68, 95, 137, 143, 171, 174–75
European, countries, 173–74
European Union, 95, 174

F
Fatah, 8-9, 25, 28, 31–34, 36, 40–41, 45, 58, 67, 70, 76, 157, 164
Fatahland, 61
Fatwa, 101, 130

Fayyad, Salam; Fayyadism, 41, 156–57
Fedayeen, 61
Feldman: Noah , 124, 199–200; Shai , 95
final status agreement, 15–16, 21, 27, 35, 38, 42
First Gulf War, 148
Force 17, 32
France, 174
Free Syrian Army (FSA), 128
freedom of expression, 103, 122, 203
French initiative, 174

G
Gaddafi, Muammar, 56
Gainous, Jason, 138
Gamaa al-Islamiyah, 123
Gaza, 2, 4–5, 14–16, 33–34, 36–43, 45–46, 60, 63, 71–72, 78, 114–15, 147, 156–58, 161–64, 166–69, 174
Gaza Strip, 2, 15, 38, 41, 158, 167
Gelvin, James, 14, 28–29, 54, 56
Geneva Accords, 48
Geneva Initiative, 18, 43, 81
Germany, 78, 126
Ghannouchi, Rachid, 125–27, 130
Gilo, 47–48
Golan Heights, 93, 105–6, 117
Goldberg, Jeffrey, 109
Goldstein, Baruch, 17
Goldstone Report, 174
Google Drive, 139
governance, 8, 140, 153
government, 19–21, 34–35, 39, 41, 55–56, 98–100, 110–11, 122–27, 129–30, 132–33, 135–37, 139–42, 155–56, 161, 176–78
Gramsci, Antonio, 79
Greater Israel, 38, 161
Gulf Cooperation Council (GCC), 113, 144

Gulf States, 94–96, 110, 120
Guzansky, Yoel, 178

H
Habermas, Jurgen, 136–37
Haddara, Waleed, 132
Hamas , 5, 8–10, 14, 17, 25, 28, 30–33, 36, 39–41, 44–46, 50, 63–66, 68–71, 73, 75–76, 81, 107, 113, 114–15, 121–22, 144, 148, 150–151, 155, 157, 159, 162, 164, 166, 167–69, 173, 174
Hamas, takeover of Gaza, 40–41, 167
Hamas Charter, 64–65
Hamid, Shadi, 125
Haniye, Ismail, 66, 150
Har Homa, 19
Haram Al Sharif , 23–25
Hashemite, 56, 96, 163
Haydemann, Steve, 104
Hebron, 17, 19–20, 72, 77; agreements, 19, 77
hegemony, 59, 66, 87–88, 95, 97, 112, 151
Heggy, Tarek, 119
Herzog, Michael, 83, 176
Hezbollah, 30–31, 34, 42, 101, 109, 111, 147, 159
Hidji, Ahmed, 151
Holy Sites, 2, 5, 24, 42, 158
honor, 89–93, 96, 101, 104, 116 (*see also* "shame")
Hourani, Albert, 86
Houthi, 109–10, 115
human rights, 41, 126, 132, 139
Hussein, Saddam , 148–49
Al-Husseini, Amin, 85–86

I
International Crisis Group (ICG), 66

ideology, 21–22, 75, 101, 103–4, 116
IDF (Israel Defense Forces), 33, 35, 58, 162, 175
Idris, Yusef , 92
imperialism, 88, 143, 148
incitement, 4, 18, 60, 70, 73, 77, 154
indoctrination, 70, 78–80, 155
Indyk, Martin, 23, 26, 43
International community, 46, 157, 166, 171, 173–74
International Crisis Group (ICG), 66
internet, use of, 137–40, 142 (see also social media)
Intifada, 14, 29, 75
Intifada First, 8, 14–17, 31–32, 63, 69, 93
Iran, 12, 66, 84, 109–16, 120–21, 125, 129, 135, 146–47, 153, 159–60; government, 147
Iraq, 67–68, 84, 89, 93, 104, 108–11, 128–29, 134–35, 144, 149, 162, 168
Iraqi parliament, 149
Iraqi Shiite, 109–10, 129
IRGC (Islamic Revolutionary Guard Corps), 110, 116
ISIS, 12, 68–69, 84, 113, 128–30, 134, 159, 168 (see also Islamic State)
Islam, 55, 63–66, 68, 85, 99, 125, 127, 149–50
Islamic Revolutionary Guard Corps (IRGC), 110, 116
Islamic State, 12, 67–68, 84, 129 (see also ISIS)
Islamism, xii, 66, 68–70, 102, 122, 125, 128
Islamist parties, 127, 130
Israel, x–xii, 2–20, 22–27, 29–30, 32–43, 46–51, 53–56, 66–77, 83–96, 98–108, 111–13, 115–23, 142–56, 158–66, 170–78;

borders, 5;
control, 14, 23;
occupation, 45, 51, 81, 161 (see also occupation); population, 8, 19–20, 121;
security, 7, 46, 72;
security establishment, 94;
settlements, 6, 15–16, 23, 29, 47, 93, 111;
tourism, 92;
war in Lebanon, 93;
withdrawal, x, 2, 7, 16–17, 20–21, 27, 34, 36, 38–40, 42, 161–62, 164;
Zionist Left, 30
Israel Defense Forces. See IDF
Israel-Gaza disengagement, 40
Israeli Defense Forces, 162
Israeli Foreign Ministry, 149–50
Israeli Prime Minister Benjamin Netanyahu, 109, 120
Israeli Prime Minister Ehud Olmert, 2, 42
Israeli settlement construction, 165
Israeli-Arab conflict, 13, 153
Israeli-Palestinian conflict, 10–13, 35, 37, 111–12, 144, 146–47, 150, 152–55, 158, 160–61, 172, 175, 178
Israeli-Palestinian negotiations, bilateral, 9, 164
Israeli-Palestinian peace process, 11, 84, 93, 172
Israeli-Syrian negotiations, 106
Israel-United Arab Emirates agreement, 160

J
JCPOA (Joint Comprehensive Plan of Action), 109, (see also nuclear deal)
Jericho, 15

Jerusalem, 2, 15–16, 18–19, 21–24, 27, 43–44, 47, 49, 85, 96–97, 158, 162, 164
Jewish settlements, 3, 16, 158 (*see also* Israeli settlements)
Jews, 23–24, 72–73, 80–81, 87, 96, 99, 101, 143, 145, 149, 151, 171, 177–78
jihad, 17, 63, 68, 70, 144
Al-Jisr, Basim, 147
Joint Comprehensive Plan of Action (JCPOA), 109
Jordan, 34, 54, 56, 58–60, 62, 68, 88, 91, 94–96, 100–101, 108, 163–67, 169–70; Media, 100–101; River, 23, 57, 161, 165; Valley, 23, 43, 158
Jordanian-Israeli peace agreement, 178
Jordanian/Palestinian Confederation, 163, 165
J-Street, 47
Judgement Day, 65

K
Kach movement, 17
Kailani, Wasfi , 101
Karameh, 58–59
Karsh, Ephraim, 5,
Keppel, Gilles, 63
Kerry, John, 49–50,
Khalidi, Rashid, 29, 76
King Abdullah, 68, 96, 100
King Salman, Mohamed, 110, 172
Knesset, 19, 21–22, 44
Koran, 64, 86 (*see also* Quran)
Kosovo, 79
Kurds, 129
Kushner, Jared, 157
Kuwait, 92, 144, 168, 177

L
Labor Party, x, 14, 20, 38, 50
Labor unions, 126
land swaps, 2, 18, 42, 49, 158
League of Nations, 57, 85
Lebanese government, 60–61, 68
Lebanon, 60–63, 67–68, 74, 84, 89, 93, 101, 105, 135, 144, 147, 168–70
legitimacy, 8, 51, 77, 97, 102, 104, 106, 118, 130, 132, 134; crisis of, 8, 40, 45, 51, 83, 97, 104, 125
Libya, 56, 84, 119–20, 124, 127–29, 144
Likud Party, 6, 20, 38–39
Livni, Tzipi, 50
Lynch, Mark, x, 120

M
Madrid Conference, 14, 93
Maha Yahyah, 135
Al-Mahalla Al Kobra, 138
Mahfuz, Naguib, 71
Mahmood Abbas, 17–18, 36
Majali, Abdelsalam, 163
Makovsky, David, 49
Maliki, Nouri Al, 110, 129, 134
Malley, Robert, 27
Marks, Monica, 127
Martha Crenshaw, 75
Meshal, Khaleed, 151
Middle East, 131, 138, 140, 144, 148, 172–74
Middle East Riddle, 2–166, 170, 172, 174, 176, 178
Miller, Aaron David, 28
Mishal, Shaul, 57
Mitchell, George, 30, 47
mobilization, 58, 62, 66, 68, 70, 104, 155
Momani, Besma, 140
Monem, Abdel , 95

monopoly of the means of violence, 8, 34, 50, 83, 96, 125, 130, 163, 166

Morocco, 95, 127, 131, 144, 147, 150–51, 160

Morris, Benny, 4, 167

Morsi, Mohamed, 115, 122–24, 132

Mosque and state , 127

mosques, 102–3, 114, 125, 127, 177

Muasher, Marwan , 130

Mubarak, Hosni, 92, 95, 96–99, 101, 113–15, 116, 120–22, 124-25, 132, 134, 146

Mughrabi, Dalal, 73

multilateral, talks, negotiations, xi, 11, 85, 93–96, 156

Muslim Brotherhood (MB), 14, 63–66, 85–86, 97–99, 103, 113–16, 120, 122–25, 132, 134, 140, 143–44, 168

N

Nablus, 24, 36, 45, 68

Nakbah, 74, 88

Nasser, Gamal Abdel, 55–56, 87–91, 133

National Constituent Assembly, 127

National Forces Alliance, 127

National Security Council, 49, 77, 111

nationalism, 53, 55, 65–66, 95, 99, 116, 148

nation-state, 4, 112

natural growth, 19, 47

negotiations, 2–4, 7–8, 10–11, 15–16, 18, 23–24, 26–30, 42–44, 47–48, 50, 83–84, 106–7, 163, 165, 174–75

nepotism, 141

Netanyahu, Benjamin, 3, 7, 18–21, 46–47, 77, 115, 120

New Middle East, 85, 95

Non-Proliferation Treaty (NPT), 94

non-violence, 76–77

normalization ; Israel, Bahrain and UAE, 178; Israel and Saudi Arabia, 172; Israel and Arab states, 92, 99–101, 153, 160–61;Israel and Tunisia, 150 see also Palestinian (life) normalization

North Africa, 126

nuclear deal, 109 (*see also* JCPOA)

Nusseibeh, Sari, 165

O

Obama, Barack, 46–50, 103, 109–11, 176

Occupation (*see also* Israeli occupation), 7, 14, 23, 36–37, 39–40, 112, 159, 164, 175

Occupied territories, 60, 63, 106, 162–63

October War, 91–92 (*see also* Yom Kippur War)

oil, 101–2, 105, 174–75

Olmert, Ehud, 6, 42, 44, 46

Olmert proposal, 2

Oman, 96, 117, 144, 159–60

one-state solution, 72, 161–62

Operation Defensive Shield, 35, 107, 174

opposition parties: in Egypt, 126; in Tunisia, 126

Oren, Michael , 89, 193

Oslo, 4, 6–8, 10, 13–51, 63, 71–72; agreements, x, 7, 16–17, 34, 48, 94; negotiations, 6, 10, 77; peace process, x–xi, 4, 6, 12–13, 47, 63, 71, 103

Oslo Accords, 13–17, 48, 72, 84, 95

Ottoman Empire, 54, 86

P

PA (Palestinian Authority), 6, 8–10, 17–19, 30–31, 33–36, 40–45, 50–51, 53, 69–73, 77–78, 81, 83, 155–57, 163–64, 166

Palestine Papers, 44

Palestinian: autonomy, 6, 93; economy, 156–57; identity, 57, 64, 67, 169; militias, 61, 67; organizations, 32, 59; Police, x, 15; population, x, 3, 16, 100; refugees, 2, 4, 15–16, 18, 25, 43, 54, 60–61, 88, 108, 169–71; revolution, 61, 66; rights, 7, 55, 62

Palestinian boycotts and anti-Israeli incitement, 118

Palestinian businesspeople, 157

Palestinian leadership, 8–10, 14, 18, 31, 44–46, 51, 153, 155, 157, 159–60, 165, 168

Palestinian Liberation Organization (also see PLO), 4, 6, 8, 14–16, 31–32, 34, 44, 56–63, 67–68, 76, 93, 105, 163, 167–68

Palestinian (life) normalization, Palestinian normalcy 9, 74, 81, 155, 164-165, 169, 172,

Palestinian question, 42, 146, 150, 160

Palestinian refugee camps, 61, 67–68

Palestinian self-determination, 54, 163

Palestinian self-rule, 13, 15–16

Palestinian state, 6, 8–9, 18, 21, 23–25, 34–35, 42–43, 45–46, 49, 51, 155, 157–58, 160, 162–65, 173–74

Palestinian terrorist groups, 147, 159

Pan-Arabism, Pan-Arab, 53–56, 69, 87-88, 90, 94, 99, 102, 103 107, 116

Pandith, Fara, 103, 171

Pan-Shiite, 110

Pan-Syrianism, 54

Party of Justice and Development (PJD), 127

Patai, Raphael, 91

Patriation, 169–71

Patriotic Union of Kurdistan (PUK), 129

patronage, 135, 157

Peace see Arab Peace Initiative; Israeli-Palestinian peace process; Jordanian-Israeli peace agreement; Oslo peace process; Sadat's peace initiative; Trump peace plan;

Pearlman, Wendy, 32

Peled, Matti, 30

Peres: Shimon, 85, 95; Shimon , 163

permanent revolution, 11, 70, 76, 166

Perthes, Volker, 104, 106

Pew Research survey, 80

Pickard, Duncan, 126

Pipes, Daniel, 167, 173

Pisgat Zeev, 47

Political Solutions, 7, 156, 158

Popular Front for the Liberation of Palestine (PFLP), 31, 59

Pressman, Jeremy, 31

problem, 8, 13, 16, 49, 51, 56–57, 65, 87–88, 141, 144, 147, 168, 170–71, 173

proxy war, 109, 120

Pryce Jones, David, 60, 90

public discourse, 138, 143–44

public morality, 123

public opinion, 53, 100, 121, 124, 137, 142, 144, 153

public sphere, 12, 136–37, 139, 153

Q
Al-Qaeda, 67–68, 80, 103, 113, 128
Qassam Brigades, 114
Qatar, 44, 96, 116–17, 128, 137, 144,
    159
Quds Force, 147, 165
Quran, 143, 149, 152 (*see also* Koran)

R
Rabid, Uzi , 171
Rabil, Robert, 67
Rabin, Yitzhak, x, 16, 21, 23–24, 36,
    106
Rabinovich, Itamar, 106
Radical Islam, xii, 62–63, 113, 129–
    30
Rahim, Gamal Abdel, 123
Ramallah, x, 36, 45
Ramat Shlomo, 47–48
reconciliation, 36, 40, 77, 81, 113,
    117, 119, 149, 152–53, 155, 160,
    172, 177–78
redeployments, 16, 19–20
Referendum, 38, 123–24, 133, 136
refugee camps, 170
right of return, 175
Roadmap to a Two-State Solution,
    35–36, 39, 47, 118
Robert Melson, 79
Rosen, David, 69
Ross, Dennis, 97, 106, 175
Roy, Oliver, 130
Rubenstein, Amnon, 87
rule of law, 41, 125–26, 131
Rumley, Grant, 45, 49
Rwanda, 79

S
Sabra and Shatila, 61
Sachar, Howard, 67, 170
Sadat, 6, 91–92, 97, 121
Sadat's peace initiative, 22

Sadr, Muktada, 129
Said, Edward, 30, 71
Salafist, 98, 126, 128, 150, 168
Salah Jadid, 89
Salama, Abdel Nasser, 123
Saudi Arabia, 131, 174–75
Saudis, 2, 42, 102–3, 109, 111, 145,
    176
Sawalha, Abdullah , 100
Schahak, Amnon Lipkin, 33–34
Schiff, Zeev, 14
Schwartz, Adi, 4
Second Intifada, 174
sectarian divisions, 135
sects, 148
security barrier, 158 (*see also* fence)
security fence, 34 (*see also* barrier)
Selah, Avraham, 57
self-determination, 5, 54, 57, 65, 163
settlement blocs, 18, 23, 39, 47–49
settlements, 2, 6–7, 15, 18–19, 21, 25,
    35, 38–39, 47–50, 159, 163
shame, 90, 101, 116 (*see also* "hon-
    or")
Shamir, Yitzhak, 20
Sharon, Ariel, 27, 34, 36–39, 46–47,
    161
Shehadi, Nadim, 146, 148
Shiites, 110, 128–29, 149
Shuafat, 158
Shukairy, Ahmad, 56
Shura Council, 124
Simon, Steve , 49
Sinai, 6, 22, 89, 115–16, 159, 167, 172
Sisi (see El Sisi)
Sistani, Ali, 110, 129
Six-Day War, 4, 43, 90–91, 107
social forces, 126
social media, 137, 139–40
socialization, 75, 105
soft power, 94–95
Soleimani, Qassim, 147

Sorel, Georges, 59
Southern Lebanon, 61, 67
sovereign state, 5, 170
sovereignty, 8, 25, 61, 96, 116; claim Israel's, 161
Soviet Union, 56, 106
Speckhard, Anne, 74
state apparatus, 123, 137
State of the Law Party, 128
state of war, 22, 103, 105–7, 116
Stein, Kenneth, 7, 99
student unions, 97–98
Sudan, 55, 119, 159–60
suicide bombings, 31, 69, 71, 73–75, 80, 107
Sunni Arab states, xi, 12, 176
Sunni Arab world, 84
Sunnis, 128–30
Supreme Council of the Armed Forces (SCAF), 115, 123
Susser, Asher, 3–4, 166
Syria: government, society, regime, 27–28, 54–55, 58, 68, 84, 88–89, 91, 95, 103–7, 109–11, 119–20, 124, 127–29, 146, 168; society, 106
Syrians, 54, 61, 95, 105, 107, 145–46

T
Tadros, Samuel, 131
Taliban, 102, 125
Talmon, Jacob , 170
Tamimi, Ahed, 146
Tantawi, Hussein, 122
Tanzim, 25, 31–32
Tarel, 123
Tel Al Zaatar, 168
Temple Mount, 22–26, 28, 51
terror, 3–8, 16–20, 32–37, 39–40, 59–60, 62, 68–69, 73, 75, 80, 99–103, 110–12, 114, 116–17, 144–45, 174–75

terrorism, 4, 17–18, 35, 37, 40, 100, 103, 111–12, 121, 144, 154
terrorist attacks, 3, 17, 20, 25, 32, 34, 62, 68
terrorist organizations, 6, 75, 102–3, 111, 114
Tibon, Amir, 45, 49
Tocqueville, Alexis, 136
totalitarian, 59–60, 69, 78, 162
tourism, 73, 92–93
Toynbee, Arnold, 170
transparency, 41, 141, 157
Trump, Donald, 117; peace plan, 155, 157, 159–61, 167, 175
Tunis, 8, 31
Tunisia, 11, 14, 56, 62, 96, 117, 119–20, 122, 125–27, 144, 150
Tunisian government, 126, 150
Tunisian state, 125
Turkey, 74, 114
Turki: Al Faisal, Prince, 111–12; Fawaz, 71
Tutsis, 79
Two-State Solution, 4, 30, 35, 38, 47, 49, 76, 78, 83, 155, 160–61, 172, 174

U
Umma, 67, 113, 164
UNEF (United Nations Emergency Force), 89–90
unemployment, 74, 126, 141, 156
UNESCO (United Nations Educational, Scientific and Cultural Organization), 46, 51
United Arab Command (UAC), 88
United Arab Emirates (UAE), xi, 96, 116–18, 144, 159–60, 172
United Nations, 140, 173
United Nations Educational, Scientific and Cultural Organization (UNESCO), 46, 51

United Nations Emergency Force (UNEF), 89–90

United Nations General Assembly (UNGA), 62

United Nations Relief and Works Agency for Palestine (UNRWA), 170

United Nations Resolution, 46

United Nations Security Council Resolution 242, 3

United States, 174; Britain, 90; Saudi Arabia, 111; Western countries, 171

uprisings, 14, 119, 124, 137

Usbar al-Ansar, 67

V

Vance, Cyrus , 13

Voigtlander, Nico, 78

Voth, Hans Joachim, 78

W

Wagner, Kevin, 138

Wahhabism, 102–3, 143

Wa'il, Abd al Salam, 147

Waqf, 65

war crimes, 108, 174

War of Attrition, 91

war of propaganda, 10, 173

water rights, 16

Weber, Max, 23

Webman, Esther, 143

Weiner, Reid , 70

Weitzman, Bruce-Maddy, 108; Weitzman Ezer, 22

West Bank, 2–4, 7, 15–16, 18–19, 23–25, 34–35, 38–42, 45, 47–50, 58, 68–70, 72, 158, 160–67

West Bank and Gaza, 5, 14–16, 34, 37, 43, 60, 63, 78, 156–58, 161

Western Wall, 2, 25–26, 51

Wilf, Einat, 4

Wistrich, Robert, 99

women's rights, 40, 125, 133, 141

World Islamic Congress, 85

World War I, 54, 63, 80

World War II, 80

Wright, Robin, 130

Wye River Agreement, 19–20, 72, 77

Y

Yaari, Ehud , 14

Yakobson, Alexander , 87

Yemen, 55–56, 84, 88, 109–11, 115, 119, 144–45

Yom Kippur War, 91–92, 105, 174

Yusef Idris, 92

Yussuf, Naser, 33–34

Z

Zionism, 4, 56, 62, 67, 69, 85–87, 143–44, 148, 150

Zionist, 30, 53, 56–57, 59, 73, 76–77, 81, 85, 148, 150, 153–54, 161

Al-Zomor, Tarel, 123

CPSIA information can be obtained
at www.ICGtesting.com
Printed in the USA
BVHW032136230221
600973BV00001B/6